# THE IMPOSSIBLE

*Anomalies, irregularities, deviation from the common rule . . . That is all I will ever care for.*

—Richie Jackson

# THE IMPOSSIBLE

## RODNEY MULLEN, RYAN SHECKLER,
## AND THE FANTASTIC HISTORY OF SKATEBOARDING

## COLE LOUISON

LYONS PRESS
Guilford, Connecticut

*An imprint of Globe Pequot Press*

*to Tanya Sandler*

To buy books in quantity for corporate use
or incentives, call **(800) 962–0973**
or e-mail **premiums@GlobePequot.com.**

Lyons Press is an imprint of Globe Pequot Press.

Text design: Sheryl Kober
Project editor: Kristen Mellitt
Page layout: Melissa Evarts

Library of Congress Cataloging-in-Publication Data is available on file.


ISBN 978-0-7627-7026-7

Printed in the United States of America

10 9 8 7 6 5 4 3 2 1

# CONTENTS

# CONTENTS

# THERE'S THIS KID . . .

## July 30, 2010

OJAI, CALIFORNIA. A little before midnight. A big bald moon shines down through hulking conifer trees made lush by the mountain air and the California sun. One hundred miles north-east of Los Angeles, in his home in the valley of the Topatopa Mountains, Rodney Mullen is watching a rerun of the X-Games finals broadcast earlier in the day. Drinking agave-sweetened tea, as per his wake-up routine, John Rodney Mullen, forty-three, remains the greatest skateboarder in the world, the godfather of all modern skateboarding tricks, and, before he quit competing, the longest-reigning "world champion" of a sport that's a little older than he is, which began as a bad-surf-day activity and today is practiced in America by 8 million people.

Mullen doesn't typically follow contests, but has tuned in to watch the finals on ESPN, where Ryan Sheckler is about to take first place in the street skateboarding competition. Mullen's been watching Sheckler since around 2000, when friend and pro Chet Thomas called. "It was: 'There's this kid, there's this kid—and you should watch him,' " Mullen recalls. "I remember Chet saying that, and Chet never says it like that."

At this moment on the TV, Sheckler's at the edge of the street course in downtown LA, where the Games have been held for the last three years and today are broadcast to 382 million homes across the world. One of Sheckler's weirder abilities is that he can drop his skateboard and be standing on it almost simultaneously. He can also do this with a little step, and then be standing facing you while he moves forward like Dracula, with one sneaker centered on the board and the other a millimeter off the ground. He does this now, moving along the perimeter of the course toward his starting point.

In person, Sheckler looks like a pro athlete and a supermodel. He has a chiseled, tanned body, gold-green eyes, soft hair you want to touch, and a face that glistens into the air around him. But he doesn't look like that now. Now he's at the lip of the course's low roll-in, with the look of removed engagement he's watched clocks and start-lights and sponsor-laden scoreboards with ever since he started beating pros at age ten—a look an elder skater once described as neither caring nor uncaring, and his mentor describes as "Get to the matter."

Ryan is in his sponsors' clothes with his signature shoe's right toe on his board's tail. His left, more intact, more tattooed arm is bent to his waist, and his right, more deformed arm is hanging by his side. Save for one, all pros, parents, and members of the press watch the contest from the dark shade of the white tents at the course's edge. Closest to Sheckler is Nyjah Huston, leaning in the shade of the high camera tower that's hung with dark netting and screened with the Games' big X logo. Rail-thin in huge clothes, antenna'd, with dreads down his back and a heavy necklace down his chest, Huston, fifteen, is the one guy currently ahead of Sheckler, and the guy who at age eleven bumped him from the record books as the youngest pro skateboarder in the world.

Sheckler's facing the slight incline leading down to a handrail spanning seven elongated concrete stairs, then another incline down to three freestanding, odd-angled blue walls that resemble a bowled corner of a skatepark that's been picked up and shattered. He's just changed shirts but is otherwise soaked. His backwards hat is saturated down the brim and his face is shining.

There are long, fat-headed trails of sweat coming from his side-burns and moving down the skin's slick surface, wetting the huge diamonds in his ears, making their incessant flash warped and colorful.

Ryan Allen Sheckler. Sheckler. Ryan. Young Ryan. SHECKS, as the big white letters read across the smeared bottom of his waxed skateboard. An indisputably accomplished athlete in terms of contests and medals and sponsorship. A child prodigy, reality MTV star, guest on *Kimmel* and *Leno,* a producer, busi-nessman, and here, now, a decade-long veteran of professional competing-for-money contests and the most divisive figure in skateboarding, whose historic roster Ryan joined when he was thirteen. A list with names like Davey Hilton and Pat McGee. Alan Gelfand and Stacy Peralta and Tony Alva. Jay Adams. Rod-ney. Tony. Christian. Cab and Tommy. Natas and Gonz. Danny. Mike V and Mike T and Frankie and Jason. Burnquist. Bucky. Ron Allen. Ronnie and Koston. Daewon Song. P-Rod and P. J. Melch and Richie. Nyjah Huston and Dennis Busenitz. Chris Haslam. Antwuan Dixon. Josiah Gatlyn. Chris Cole. Lizard King. Willow.

When the light turns he pushes once off the platform and then bends and kicks out his right leg and lunges forward, eyes on the red waxed rail ahead. Small, muscled, and "made to skate," according to his mentor, Sheckler stays bent as he turns his shoulders 90 degrees and puts his back foot on the board and bends into a Z shape as he lowly roars toward the stairs. Three seconds have passed by the time he clicks down on the board's tail and leaves the ground. An ollie.

A regular-footed skater, he points his toes to the top of the board's right side, toward the rail now just in front of him. Here, though, he's slid his front foot to the board's left to set up for a kickflip. The kickflip—invented by Mullen twenty-five years ago and perfected by Sheckler when he was six—is a staple of modern street skating, and occurs when riders use a toe to flick the board's heel side, spinning it once to then catch it with their feet.

Sheckler's long been able to flip as high as he can ollie, which is high, and before he's halfway up the rail the board is upside down under his new sneakers, with his head and shoulder and forward-facing left knee aligned over the angled spinning deck— his back leg kicked out of the way, one arm extended over the rest of the rail, and one arm sideways, trying to balance his body as it turns 90 degrees as he looks over his shoulder, since he's going to land backwards on the rail. Land backwards with all his moving weight on the concave board on a long metal waxed cylinder a little bit bigger around than a walnut, then slide and fall to the ground. He's bent in the air, with his fingers splayed and his etched arms raised like a soaring ape, and when he lands on the board, he lands centered and slides down the rail for a quarter-second before they both dismount and turn in midair to land rolling forward.

There's the thick squelching sound of all four urethane wheels landing at once, and by the time the crowd erupts, Sheckler's turned and begun pumping toward the waved blue walls ahead. He pumps his foot down and back twice, hard, and on the second kick, turns and tucks and leans back and rolls up the six-foot wall to take flight.

Like a lot of skaters of his generation, Ryan has an ability to stick to the board the way older pros can't—and he's many feet above the wall's jagged lip and turned halfway toward the packed two-mezzanine grandstand when he grabs between his feet and brings the board around. He's now between this wall and another, both curved and odd-angled, moving 10 feet over the concrete, one arm up, his folded shadow stretched down the wall below.

He turns frontside—meaning, the direction opposite the way his toes are pointing. Originally a surf word, *frontside* is still the term riders use when carving away from the wave they face, a backwards or blind carve. So Ryan turns frontside with his head down, back until the top of the differently angled wall enters his periphery and he can stomp down and land and ride away clean. Which he does.

Eight seconds have passed. Tony Hawk is announcing the event from a well-hidden booth. People in 175 countries are watching on ABC and ESPN and ESPN2, and 30,000 are watching from the stands.

Like all big contests, the X Games are somewhat disdained in the general skateboard community, in part because of the point system used to rank skate runs. Similar to the Dr. J. Evans Pritchard method used in *Dead Poets Society*, the rating system ranks an overall run by assigning value to each trick, with more points for more complex or difficult maneuvers. Hence, a frontside boardslide gives Ryan a certain trick value from the judges. A backside or regular forward slide gives him few points because it's deemed easier. Despite the vague notion of point systems— Sheckler once told me most pros don't fully understand them— he needs to do something big and hard to score at least a 91.34 if he wants to beat Huston.

He does this. After a few tricks on the transfer ramps and a grind over an arched rail that sounds like a sword being drawn down a water stone, Sheckler pushes back to the starting platform, pops his board into his hand, waits a breath, and starts again.

This time he comes from the other side, so the rail up ahead is to his left. Canadian pro Ryan Decenzo; Sierra Fellers of Whitefish, Montana; and a fifteen-year-old Illini named Chaz Ortiz have come out from the tent to watch Ryan.

Sheckler tucks into his blastoff stance a little differently this time, because he's actually going backwards. He's choked way up on the board's tail—the end closest to the approaching rail—and his back's straight with his arms wound around his torso. Backwards in skateboarding is called "fakie." Whatever he does on the rail, he's going to start fakie.

He snaps and fakie ollies up over the rail, and spins 90 degrees so he's facing the stairs, like before. Except that's not what he's going to do, and when he's facing down the seven concrete points the rail's not even under him, which is the plan, because he keeps turning and rotates another 180 degrees for a 270, or "full cab," to pin the board and land backwards on the rail before sliding off and falling 3 feet to the ground.

He lands and literally bends over backwards and puts his hand back down so he won't slam his head. His right palm drags him around 180 degrees and then he flings both his arms up with his ass just over the concrete.

"That's gonna count," Hawk says automatically.

Before he's even up, Sheckler's pushing again toward the blue walls and the crowd's roar is still full when he rides up the thin concrete wave and vertically plants his back truck (the wheels' axle) over its thick uneven lip. Then, instead of popping the board off the wall and rolling down, Sheckler, perhaps inspired by the sensed blood of victory, executes one of his trademark blunt-force-trauma moves. With a back wheel locked over each edge of the wall, Sheckler spins like a bestial unicycler and wings his left arm out and windmills his right deformed arm behind him to rip himself off the wall frontside, or blind, over his shoulder, 180 degrees, and roll back down.

"*Oh!*" says Hawk. "Didn't! Even! Pop! Out!"

He softly flips off a thin low ramp leading to the roll-in area and steps off his board to bend down and let it roll back into his palm. Then he puts his left hand back on his hip and puts the board's nose to the course floor, leaning hard and facing the screen.

Hawk says he thinks Ryan has it. The other announcer pretends to disagree.

The lights change. The crowd erupts. Ryan's wet head drops as his right arm bends, his face in a smile, his hand in a fist.

RODNEY MULLEN was watching that night because the 2010 Games were Ryan's first competition since he'd been badly hurt the year before. The top-ranked favorite in 2009, with two previous gold medals, Sheckler had advanced directly to the finals where he flew off a stair set much like the one he dominated at the 2010 course. There he flipped the board, spun his body, and landed with all of his weight—plus the drop's thrust—channeling down his right leg, where he generates his power. When this happened his foot exploded. He was helped from the course, and soon after surgeons screwed his foot back together so it could hopefully start to heal. Throughout his career he's suffered constant injuries, usually hurt ankles and broken elbows, but this was the worst. Ryan was off his board for a full seven months, the longest he'd been away from skating since he'd started at the age of two.

While a common criticism of Sheckler is that he's overexposed, a common complaint about Mullen is that he's so hard to see. His low profile is no accident, but as a result, any recent scrap of his skate footage is immediately uploaded to YouTube—which has become skating's Widener Library—where it's copied, slowed down, looped, or scored by fans who add comments like "Rodney Mullen AAAAAAAAAAAAAAAA" or "?!?!?!?!?!?!?!?" This is partly because of Mullen's ultra-ability, but it's also because since 2003 he's shared a minuscule amount of information for a top pro. He's given two taped interviews, released three five-second clips, a few photo sequences, and in 2007, a video with ninety seconds of new skate footage. The video ended with something called a switch one-foot nose, which Mullen, in a fifteen-minute interview with Hawk, said took longer to perfect than anything done in his thirty years of professional skateboarding.

"Switch one-foot nose" means a switch-stance kickflip into a one-footed nose wheelie. And while most everything Rodney does is unique to his ability, this maneuver is especially, unimaginably impossible. The part was shot in black-and-white with a high-res mounted camera at a warehouse near where Mullen lives today.

It's hard to know what you're looking at when the camera fades from black and the glares expand into the lines of the warehouse's interior. The light is dim and the floor, walls, ceiling, and long platform directly ahead are all black. All the stuff set up for effect might be corny if it weren't for Mullen's part. The music is slow, nearly acoustic techno. They've muted the whooshing hiss of urethane wheels on painted concrete, so we don't hear anything as Mullen rolls into the right of the frame.

He's in a drugstore wolf T-shirt and big jeans and heavy torn sneakers. And while his stance has been regular for the three decades he's dominated professional skateboarding, here he appears goofy-footed with his toes pointing to the board's left. This is the "switch" part of the switch one-foot nose.

By the time he enters the screen, Mullen's already flying out of the familiar X he makes with his arms to give them the most room to build the momentum he'll use to send energy down his body and into the board. He's in the air with the board angled at eleven o'clock before the tail even touches down, and the first sound we hear is the familiar slap of six-layer plywood on concrete.

The board is nearly vertical and a foot from the platform when Rodney flicks its top-right corner with his torn shoe. He's in a position like the board is a stepladder he's trying to climb, though his back foot is an inch over the tail. His wet arms are bent up and out and he's looking at where the board will land instead of at the board. Two seconds have passed.

Before the tail's noise has even carried itself out, Mullen has the board halfway over the platform, a foot from its surface and upside down. He's moved up so his head, knee, and front foot are all directly over the nose. His arms are out like he's trying to hug something huge and he's bent his back leg to keep it out of the way. He's not going to need it here. We're three seconds in.

And before we hit four seconds Rodney brings his front sneaker down fast and traps the nose at the angle he wants, with just enough pressure to keep the back wheels off the ground and give them wiggle room. His body's already in place. He's facing forward with his arms and back leg out for leverage, like a tightrope walker or a flying squirrel. He's still moving forward through the air, and then there's a striking sound when the wheels land on the hollow platform. It's half the usual sound since he's on two wheels, and the sound's got a weird unevenness, because the board's trying to shoot out behind him.

His side leg swings forward up to his front leg as the free tail trembles, and then he swings the free leg back like he's pushing a scooter. The board moves fore and aft under his body, but the whole time Mullen has his shoulders squared and head centered over the front truck, directly over which his sneaker is planted. It's almost like he's roller-skating on a two-wheeled skate with a very wide axle.

And he's got it. The tail does two big nods, and on the second one he has to stick the back leg way out, almost in an arabesque, to correct the balance. But he stays on top of the board, and when he brings the back leg in, his board's at the end of the platform. He gives a little relaxed lift with his knee so the front wheels just pass over the edge as his back foot finds the tail again, and for

the first time, we hear the hard solid *clock* of all four wheels landing at once, because Rodney *al*ways lands everything on all four
wheels. In skating it's called landing "bolts."

It's one of four maneuvers in ninety seconds of skating,
unique to a man who skates every night, alone, and has reinvented the sport since he took it over at age fourteen. The footage is now four years old and, of course, just footage. I hadn't
seen him skate yet. I had only viewed the greatest skater in the
world on a 5-by-3-inch screen inside of a Safari window on an old
PowerBook, worlds away from Mullen's nocturnal, devout life in
California, where he'd fled at age twenty-one, and where skateboarding began around the time he was born.

# 2

# AN EASY HISTORY OF
# SKATEBOARDING, THEN
# ANOTHER ONE

THE ROLLER DERBY SKATEBOARD debuted in 1959 and cost $1.99. It had a short, narrow wooden deck with trucks and wheels made of steel. The toy model and others after it were popular enough for companies to successfully produce a higher-quality and more-expensive product. In 1962, when the Val Surf shop opened in North Hollywood, owner Bill Richards sold skateboards shaped by his two teenage sons and mounted with truck assemblies from the Chicago Roller Skate Company, who at the shop's request had cut their regular four-wheel units in two before shipping. These were arguably the first skateboard trucks, and Val was probably the first skateboard shop.

Val produced ten boards a week and was always sold out and backordered. Within two years Richards was approached by Hobie Alter, who was by then already a famous quality surfboard maker. The two partnered and designed a line of skateboards. In June 1963, another company called Makaha Skateboards released two zeppelin-shaped boards: a shorter one called the Malibu (18 inches), and a longer one called the Standard (29 inches). In two years, Makaha sold 300,000 at $12.95 each. Makaha was owned by Larry Stevenson, a man of many talents, the publisher of *Surf Guide*, and the widely acknowledged grand-father of skateboarding.

The first skateboarding competition was held in the fall of 1963 at Pier Avenue Junior High in Hermosa Beach, California, and included high jump, timed headstands, flatground slaloms, and kickturn races, where riders turned their boards end over end. Nothing was done on any kind of incline yet.

Wanting to expand, Alter shrewdly partnered with Vita-Pakt, a juice company that had just purchased a profitable roller-skate manufacturer. In 1964 they released the first line of Hobie skateboards and organized a promotional team, poaching virtually all of Makaha's riders with temptations like all-expense-paid demo trips to Hawaii. Vita-Pakt was owned by one William Barron Hilton, owner of the San Diego Chargers, grandfather of Paris Hilton, and father of eight, including Davey Hilton, a top-level skater who got the cover for the 1965 premier issue of *The Quarterly Skateboarder*, priced at 50 cents.

During a three-year period in the 1960s, a reported 50 million skateboards were made in America. Skating was the subject of an *Endless Summer*-y feature film called *Skater Dater*, which was nominated for an Oscar. A Marilyn Monroe–esque nineteen-year-old named Pat McGee won the first intercollegiate skateboarding championship at Wesleyan University in Middletown, Connecticut. She was featured in *Newsweek,* and appeared on the cover of *Life* doing a handstand in pedal pushers and a red sweater. Portland, Oregon, became the first and only city to reserve a street for skateboarding. Clay wheels replaced steel wheels, making skating smoother and faster. Hobie introduced the first fiberglass board and a primitive skateboarding truck that didn't catch on. Makaha introduced a deck made of a Nazi-invented plastic called melamine, and netted $250,000 in a single day.

The First Annual National Skateboarding Championships were held May 22 and 23, 1965, at La Palma Stadium in Anaheim, California. They were judged by Alter, covered by three networks, and featured on ABC's *Wide World of Sports*. Teams came from Mexico and Japan to get beat by the Hobie skaters and a team called Gordon & Smith Fibreflex. The prize for first place in downhill, slalom, and freestyle was either a $1,000 check or a $500 scholarship, depending on what source you read from the time. That same year the Week 12 San Diego Chargers game against the Buffalo Bills featured a halftime show by the Hobie Super Surfer Skateboard team.

Nineteen sixty five was also the year skateboarding was declared "a new medical menace" by the California Medical Association. Articles about skating from this time really love to use the word *menace*. Pat McGee's *Life* cover was great, but the headline was THE CRAZE AND THE MENACE OF SKATEBOARDS. A car insurance pamphlet from the time included a section on skateboarding and urged drivers to "keep an especially sharp alert for this new traffic menace." In the August issue of *Good Housekeeping*, orthopedic surgeon John Wilson of the American Medical Association stated: "I have had occasion to observe . . . fractures about the elbow of a magnitude previously not seen in growing bone." Los Angeles emergency rooms were seeing fifteen skaters a month with broken bones. New Rochelle, New York—a longtime host of national figure-skating championships and the home of some of the country's largest roller rinks—reported fifty hospitalizations a month. One death was reported, a head-on between a skater and an automobile.

By August of 1965 skateboarding was banned in a total of twenty cities. Portland not only took their streets back, but also decided to ban skating on fucking Sundays. One police report detailed a chase between an officer and a dog—yes, a dog—named Tiger who skated down an unsanctioned road. Throughout the United States, police confiscated boards and discouraged store owners from selling them.

Larry Stevenson remembers back to November of that year, "the week, if not the day" everything stopped. He got daily cancellations of up to 75,000 orders, just in time for Christmas. *The Quarterly Skateboarder* published three more issues and shut down.

All authorities declared skateboarding dead by 1966, the year Rodney Mullen was born.

## Another One

THE MOST frustrating thing about researching a detailed skateboard history is that everyone who was there gives a different account of people, places, and dates, and then acknowledges that it all depends on who you ask. Thus, as with responsible music writing, skate history often takes the form of first-person narrative, with facts presented in quotation marks so reporters won't have to make a statement they can't prove.

Here's an example from the *New Yorker's* pretty good 1999 profile on Tony Hawk:

> *I called Michael Brooke, who is the author of* The Concrete Wave, *a recently published [really good] scrapbook history of skateboarding, and he gave me an account of the sport's origins . . . Skateboarding's roots, he said, "go back to the early nineteen hundreds, when kids banged roller-skate wheels onto two-by-fours. Sometimes kids attached orange crates with handles to the two-by-fours, for steering. Sometimes kids broke the T-bar handles off of scooters.*

The point is that no one really knows for sure, since there's no one date when a scooter was first stripped down into a skateboard, or when someone took apart the first metal, over-your-shoe skate and fit it over the ends of a 2-by-4 board. But it happened. Sometimes a crate was nailed atop these new contraptions, with a horizontal stick or board for balance, but sometimes not. The scooter was patented in 1921, long after it had become a makeshift kids' vehicle fashioned from roller skates. Records and interviews indicate that a core group around Glendale in Los Angeles was riding sometimes crateless scooters in the 1930s and '40s, but my eighty-three-year-old neighbor, Hugo Picciani—who grew up in Brooklyn—said they did the same thing.

In 1957 Jim Fitzpatrick* of San Diego was making twenty skateboards at a time for friends out of his garage in the La Jolla community. He says he got the idea from the guy who gave him his first board, George "Buster" Wilson, who says he'd been making skateboards since the 1930s. A popular 1970s treatise on skating says the "earliest use anyone has claimed for them is the summer of 1904," but I mean, come on.

So reporting-wise, solid information is really hard to find. And while it can be, as I believe I've previously stated, frustrating, it also is helpful to talk to a lot of people, some of whom were actually there. "Yeah, no one knows for sure," said Dale Smith, who I was able to talk to, once, with the help of the International Association of Skateboard Companies. "You could say that."

Dale Smith lives within skateboarding's 100-mile cradle of life in Oceanside, California. He was a professional skateboarder in the 1970s, a coach of prodigies like Steve Caballero in the '80s, and today runs a small company called Skate Designs that sells

---

* Another true champion of the sport, Fitzpatrick went on to organize the International Association of Skateboard Companies, which finally got skating classified as a hazardous activity in 1997, amending California's Health and Safety code, and thus barring participants from suing if they got hurt. As a result, municipalities all over the state, and soon, the country green-lighted the first public skateparks. Ryan Sheckler grew up skating one of these parks in San Clemente, California, an hour north of Fitzpatrick.

quality boards and wheels online. He is the guy both history and industry people point to if you want hard facts about skating's elusive past. Dale's holdings include 700 unused vintage boards (decks, trucks, wheels, and hardware), U.S. patents, law statements, probably the best collection of early skateboarding photography, and archival paperwork that he's gathered since he started skating.

A number of Dale's patents are for "cold cases"—inventions that never caught on, then died out, and exist singularly in the patent office in Washington, D.C. They are the sport's mud puppies and Pogo Balls and toaster omelets, and are to skateboards today what that bouncing car with the rooftop propeller was to the Wright Brothers' flying machine.

And since skateboarding began as an off-season/fringe/break-one-toy-to-make-another activity, there are a lot of cold-case patents. There is Skeeter Skate, which first retailed around 1945, an aluminum thing on four pedal car-style wheels, with removable handlebars and early steering axles (or trucks). The Scooter Skate was sold throughout the 1930s; its three-wheel, blimp-shaped metal deck also featured removable handlebars, but no steering mechanism. A skate relic even exists from the 1920s, but it's more a ski/scooter hybrid: two tri-wheeled 3-by-10-inch metal sheets that clipped to your feet and came with a pair of poles.

An early and specific history of skateboarding has a lot more loose ends. That the first skateboard simply appeared around 1960 seems unlikely considering how far back we find roller skates (about 200 years) and surfboards (about 3,000). Roller-skating and surfing are inarguably the most direct influences on skateboarding, but we'll see what others come into play, the off-shoots skating itself has spawned, and why the very first skate camp was in Rättvik, Sweden.

▲

ROLLER-SKATING's famous public debut was at the ballet *Der Maler oder die WintervergnUgungen* in Berlin in 1818, although the invention of the in-line skate is usually credited to a very interesting guy named John Joseph Merlin, a high-society Belgian inventor who designed mathematical instruments, then clocks and watches, and then perpetual-motion machines and violins. Among other things, he holds the patent on the compound harpsichord.*

Roller-skating grew in popularity throughout the 1800s, and for a time maintained an identity as a graceful physical art often performed to orchestral music for higher-paying audiences. It was more like ballet than dance or theater, and so it makes sense that the leotard-wearing clichés that came to be associated with this branch of history were the same ones associated with what was called "freestyle skateboarding," young Rodney's forte.

Roller-skating saw periods of growth, shrinkage, and mutation, and in 1863 an American inventor named James Plimpton patented the four-wheel design still used today. Unlike skateboards, roller skates began as high-end recreational purchases like roller skis, or those weird recumbent bicycles that old physicians ride around on, and though expensive, they'd spread throughout the United States by the 1880s. This was during a very cool time when there were bike races in wooden velodromes and different models of big-wheeled penny-farthing bikes, and gentlemen's riding clubs where everyone wore spats and looked like Daniel Day-Lewis or Jason Lee—a time when technology seemed fun and artistic.

---

* It's a famous true story: In 1770 Berlin introduced his in-line invention at a party he hosted in his home, rolling into the crowded hall in a pair of black, wooden-braced, forty-pound wheeled boots that allowed him to move over the hardwood floor as if it were ice. Then, because he couldn't stop, he crashed into a huge mirror, nearly lost his arm, and foreshadowed skating's hazardous reputation.

Roller skates weren't mass-produced until the turn of the century, when technological advances in bearings made them something of a national phenomenon. We'll see this with our sport in the 1970s.

▲

ICE-SKATING is the reason that Sweden and not Southern California hosted the first skateboarding camp* during the boom of the 1980s. Sweden's native provinces have the oldest and deepest connections to skating, and today there remains a competitive and consumer skating culture. Top '80s pros Tony Magnusson (vert, i.e., big-ramp) and Per Welinder (freestyle, and the one person to ever beat Rodney) were both from Sweden.

We'll get to the '80s, but the main reason I want to bring this up is it helps to explain the physical build of skateboarders, probably the biggest reason they as individuals are not considered athletes. More than anything else, the skateboarder's build resembles that of an ice-skater. Athletically the sports are similar. Both skaters' movements are balanced and lithely powerful in a way that's easy to miss. Their bodies end up being thinly muscled in a lean, ropey way that often looks adolescent or scrawny. Skaters' bodies aren't hot. Their builds are non-builds. Look at the small, hard, thin bodies of Scott Hamilton, Brian Boitano, and Nancy Kerrigan and then see, for instance, Rodney, Hawk, Mike Mo, or lean and mean Patrick Melcher (albeit not Christian Hosoi, Daewon Song, Chris Cole, Tonya Harding, and especially

---

* The camp, by the way, is legendary. It hosted top pros like Lance Mountain, Mike McGill, good old oddball Neil Blender, Rodney, and an already way-ahead sixteen-year-old named Tony Hawk. All were teenagers with money, away from home for pretty much the first long period of unscheduled time. Skating was young, with virtually no governing bodies, so the camp was all but unsupervised and by all accounts was like a skateboarding version of the island where the bad kids go in *Pinocchio*.

not Mike Vallely, now forty-one and still on tour, built like a Parris Island graduate who's just come home to instruct).

In 2008, archaeologists exploring Russia and South Finland released a study detailing their discovery of several pairs of ancient ice skates and carbon-dated them back to 3000 BC. The oldest of their kind, they were made of sharpened bone with bored holes for straps and led the team to conclude that ice-skating is the "oldest human means of transport," a statement agreed on as much as archaeologists put in a room with anthropologists can agree on something. They pointed out that South Finland, where the best specimens were found, had upwards of twenty-hour Nordic nights and more lakes in a 40-mile radius than anywhere else in the world—hence, a lot of ice, and a lot of ice-skating.

Drawings and writings (although no artifacts) from the same cultures have led scientists to conclude that skiing is about as old as ice-skating. Longer, wider objects worked best on snow, and shorter, sharper objects worked best on ice. Bones worked best for skates and durable slats of wood worked best for skis and snowshoes. They also share a common ancestor. University of Oxford physiologist Federico Formenti, who served as the 2008 study's sort-of foreman, said: "The origins of ski and skates as passive tools enhancing human-powered locomotion share common roots, probably small wooden plates."

A note on skateboarding diction: People who ride skateboards never call what they do "boarding." As with speed and figure skaters, it's always "skating," as in, "You skating, newsboy?" or "I'm going skating at the warehouse, if you want to come." The word *skate* is probably Dutch/Norwegian, and 300 years before it meant the sharp thing on your foot, it meant fish. *Schat, Scate, Skete, Skait, Skeat,* then, first printed in 1634—*Skate.* Large and flat, still but ever-moving over the deep sandy surface on big black wings. See also *skite,* an offensive person (1874) or *Scat,* and *Skeet.* Excrement.

The term *board* has about thirty definitions, but is traditionally a maritime word meaning the side of a ship; it also means to come up alongside, or go against, or enter in a hostile manner. It also means food.

> Keanu: *You're not gonna start chanting, are you?*
> Patrick: *I might.*
>
> *—Point Break*

All of the above information about ice- and roller-skating touches on skateboarding's roots in art and movement, but doesn't explain the colorful, devoted, and deeply inward culture of skateboarding. For this we need to look at surfing.

SURFING is not from Hawaii. It probably originated in what's now French Polynesia, where it's been practiced for at least 3,000 years. An island nation of seagoing and other-island-visiting people, French Polynesians are believed to have first brought surfing to Hawaii. The earliest written records are from the 1700s, when Europeans first traveled to Tahiti and detailed an activity called *he'enalu,* or wave-sliding. By itself, *enalu* means "wave." *He'e* means "to change from a solid to a liquid." Sometimes thought to have originated hundreds of years earlier by fishermen catching waves back to shore, by the sixteenth century it was a firmly established and developed sport, culture, and spiritual activity. This was clear even to colonizing white guys like Captain James Cook, who watched a lone surfer and then famously wrote in 1778 that he "could not help concluding that this man felt the most supreme pleasure while he was driven on so fast and so smoothly by the sea."

Four kinds of boards were used by the Hawaiians, in different sizes or woods. The "olo" boards were up to 25 feet long and reserved for royalty. Like a knight's sword, a Viking's ax, or a player's guitar, surfboards were important cultural artifacts, created by master shapers who used a combination of hardwoods from trees only they were allowed to cut down. Each board had a ceremony to mark its completion. Surfing had its own chants and prayers, and a symbol that essentially was and still is the sport's crucifix: The posed surf warrior image was carved on cave walls and into the arms of athletes. Priests called *kahunas* were in charge of praying to the sea on behalf of the surfers. Whole villages emptied when the waves were good.

Because it was recreational, spiritual, uplifting, and energizing, the God-loving missionaries from England who arrived in 1820 took special interest in eradicating surfing among the natives. But they eventually started doing it themselves. The history here is a bit elusive and similar to skateboarding history. As surfing was oppressed, it shrank to a strong diehard core of practitioners until around 1900 in Hawaii. And yet a local named George Freeth, who grew up riding waves during this time, is the person most often credited with bringing the sport to California in 1907. A lifeguard and championship surfer, he was invited and paid a lot of money by tycoon Henry Huntington to do a demo that coincided with the Pacific Electric Railroad's opening of its new route from Los Angeles to Redondo Beach, where Rodney's company Almost Skateboards is located today.

HAWAII can also boast of creating something I'd never heard of and still can't really believe exists: *he'e holua,* or mountain surfing—surfing on land. Less known but awesomely still around, *he'e holua* dates back to about the year zero, and, like surfing, was both a sport and a spiritual act. The sled is longboard length and skateboard width, like a stretched cane bobsled or a mini skull on runners. It looks like a long thin ladder, and was ridden sitting, reclined, or standing up down rock washes or trails cut into the sides of mountains. Its runners were lubed with nut oils and the desired paths were packed with dirt and laid with grass.

Though sparsely practiced today, as of this writing there are two sled-surfing runs on the Big Island, hacked into mountainsides and ridden at speeds of up to 50 miles per hour by Tom Stone, a cultural-studies professor who remains the sport's champion—maybe because he's basically its only participant. But what's important is that we're roughly 2,000 years before the invention of roller skates and we're surfing on land, with no handlebars or reins or poles. It's also important that the people doing it are willing to not only risk but assuredly collect injuries you just don't get in the water. Professor Stone's injuries include a hip-to-knee gash and a broken neck, and at fifty-three, he's still at it.

Applicable quote that Sheckler suddenly just said one time when we were talking:

*I think to be a skateboarder, you have to like pain. Or maybe just learn to live with pain.*

*—Ryan Sheckler*

AND IF you're wondering if there was ever a horn-helmeted Nordic king who stood up on a long plank and surfed the snow, the answer is . . . maybe. Few and far-between sources say the Turks were cruising the snow upright on toboggans with gondolierish paddles as far back as 1600, with the first modified standing sled, or "bunker," patented in 1939 by Gunnar Burgeson, a Swedish transplant living in Oak Park, Illinois. No sort of trend picked up for thirty more years, until snowboarding had a skate-like blip in the 1960s. The too-weird-to-ever-be-popular mono-ski was patented in 1964, and the following year a Michigan engineer named Sherman Poppen cross-braced two K-mart skis together and patented the "snurfboard" (snow + surf). Rickety agreement is that somewhere between a half-million and a million units were sold until popularity dropped off, not returning until the 1980s.

WHILE WE'RE AT IT: Sandboarding also had a rise in the '60s. The activity's pretty much indescribable culture (unless you remember the Diegueños Indians in *Blood Meridian*) boasts 20,000 members, with its own online publication and product lines, and is all but invisible to popular culture except for the occasional skate-magazine blurb and a single fantastic episode of *Jackass*.

# 3

# RODNEY MULLEN'S GENIUS ROOTS AND FEMORAL ANTEVERSION

JOHN RODNEY MULLEN was born in Gainesville, Florida, on December 30, 1966. His older sisters, Sara and Vicki, were six and four. His mother, Ann P. Mullen, was a child prodigy and concert pianist who entered college at the age of fifteen and was later crowned Miss U Florida. His father, John Mullen, had a pharmaceutical degree before he joined the navy, was a nuclear bombardier throughout the Korean War, and after his tour of duty became a dentist, then a dental-clinic owner and multimillionaire.

Early on, the kids were chauffeured in air-conditioned Cadillacs to horseback riding lessons at the barn or tennis lessons at the club. They had their own wing in a house custom-built to resemble a Southern plantation. Attached to the residence was a long doghouse for their purebred German shepherds and Samoyeds, big imported-looking dogs of Siberian descent with layers of pure white fur and black eyes. There was also a weight room, a basketball court, a billiard house, sprawling rose gardens, and a sunroom that faced a tall rock waterfall flowing into the pool, 12 feet deep and cleaned with a self-propelled robot Mr. Mullen designed himself.

But it was a house of strict privilege. Starting at age five, the kids had chores. His sisters worked inside, though the family had maids to do the shopping and cleaning, and at age eight Rod was put in charge of the estate's lawn care. He used a push mower for edging and a tractor mower for acreage. He started every Saturday morning at seven, and when the job was done the vehicle was to be washed, rust-filed, and painted. There were a lot of rules and you had better not break any of them.

Mr. Mullen was also a real estate developer and a boxer, closing deals after work at the clinic and taking zero days off from his regimen of running and lifting weights. His eyes changed color when he got angry, which happened frequently and sometimes without warning. He took certain words or incorrect pronunciation of certain words as disrespect, along with laughing, a poorly edged lawn, or any general task left undone. The dogs were afraid of him, and his kids all called him "Sir." No meant no.

"You get one no. After that, watch out," Rod recalls, putting up his fists.

Mrs. Mullen had genius roots. Her dad had one of the highest IQs of anyone to graduate from Columbia, and her brother, like her, was a young prodigy, finishing medical school at the age when most finish undergrad. She aced college as a physics major, and before she met Mr. Mullen, she taught high school while still in her teens. She began working in nuclear research at the university laboratory, but after getting married, she left her career to raise the family. Once the kids were in school she ran the local rose garden chapter, played beautiful sad stuff on their grand piano, and at the club swam laps and dominated the other lean, tan ladies on the tennis court with a loose, laughy carefreeness that Rod never saw her exhibit anywhere else.

Rodney was born with what today what would be called *femoral anteversion*—crooked feet. He was so pigeon-toed that he tripped over himself, and by age two had to sleep in corrective braces for his feet—hard, heavy, flexless leather boots that went up his calves and connected at the ankle, making his feet stick out in a V.

Rodney was surrounded by teachers his mom knew, and sometimes spent weekends with his mom's parents, who were also in education. He could read before he entered kindergarten a year early at a university-run progressive school that his dad was suspicious of. Soon after school started he began reading a children's version of the Bible, which he still does today (the Bible, not the children's version), each morning and night. When he was five, his mom showed him an electromagnet, which he points to as the thing that sparked his lifelong interest in science. There are more examples to come, but from the time he started school, Rodney was one of those calculator watch–wearing kids with a four-point-something GPA, because of the extra credit. He just chewed up and spit out anything his teachers could throw at him along the lines of advanced classes, skipping grades, or extra-extra credit. One teacher gave him a recorder to play up in a tree when he was done with his extra work. Another accused him of plagiarism because he wrote so well. Another later taught him general number theory on his lunch hour because Rod was tiresomely acing the guy's AP math class. You get the idea.

Mr. Mullen had other plans. He was excited to complete his family with a son, and shall we say, started forging his namesake's path early on. He took Rod along to job sites so he could watch his dad work and negotiate and never once lose an argument. On weekends the Mullens traveled to their other and even more rural house in the country, where they had a barn and horses. On one family ride, Rodney fell off his horse and broke his shoulder. His father made him finish the ride, after which Rodney wouldn't go near the creatures again. Mr. Mullen also took him hunting. Soon after Rod sparked an interest in the piano, he was enrolled in karate lessons twice a week. An hour before each class he got a stomachache.

He was seven years old at this point, and his hobbies were rescuing bugs from the pool for a calculator watch–timed sixty minutes each day and wandering construction sites at night, collecting things. His room was burned and stained from miniature construction projects, and there were nails and metal pieces and pimped jars of dry mortar on the floor. Hung from the ceiling were spiked cement spheres that Rod could swing at intruders (though no one ever came into his room) because he was "obsessed with self-defense." He sometimes sneaked off to the very back of the doghouse or the equipment closet of the pool house to relax or sleep. He calls these spaces his "panic rooms."

Factoid: For years, when traveling on the pro circuit, Rod would jerry-rig an alarm in hotel rooms by tying a length of dental floss from the doorknob to his board.

Rod paced when he was nervous, and by the end of elementary school was regularly visiting the nurse's office for anxiety. Rodney had no friends at school, and recalls, "I didn't break this pattern until college," when he met a chemistry grad student who liked punk rock. Rod *did* ride bikes with some older neighbors, and with practice became one of those kids you see maintaining a wheelie down the entire street. One friend was a tall teenager with size-fifteen shoes that everyone called The Wizard and was even weirder than him. Wizard spray-painted 20-meter increments on the sidewalk to measure his wheelies and could beat everyone in the neighborhood, until he was dethroned by Rodney, who was then eight years old.

Also just down the road was a fourteen-year-old named Jack Iverson. Jack was another eccentric kid, a very regular and generous pot smoker who was reportedly the son of a neurosurgeon dad and a mom who only spoke Elizabethan English, and who at dinner once asked Rodney: "Wouldst thou enjoy a feast of swine?" They hung out almost every day.

Among other things, Jack owned a purple Banzai skateboard.

# 4

# TONY HAWK DOESN'T KNOW WHEN HE STARTED SKATING

Tony Hawk's memory of his first time on a skateboard is odd. History's greatest vert skater doesn't really remember when he started skating. The official version is that he was nine, but Hawk has also said his first time on a skateboard was during his brother's visit home after his family moved, when he was six. Steve Hawk, who went on to edit *Surfer* magazine, had a blue fiberglass Bahne that retailed for around $30. He let Tony try it. Steve taught him to carve and kickturn, then let him keep the board, which Hawk still has today. Tony would take it out now and then for a half-hour, but, "to me it was just another play object," he remembers. "Like a Nerf football."

He didn't start skating regularly for about six more months, around age ten, and that was because some friends of his started skating; even then, it didn't become a daily thing until the following year when he first visited Oasis Skatepark in San Diego. Asked to relive his first time on a board, Hawk's answer is this: "I don't know. It was fun."

His story sharply contrasts with that of most legendary skaters, who vividly recall when and where they started, how it felt, and how it was all they wanted to do.

"My life began the day I started skateboarding," said street legend Mike Vallely.

"As soon as I got on a board," said Christian Hosoi, a glandularly monsterous vert expressionist, and Hawk's great rival, "all I wanted to be was a pro skateboarder."

"Skateboarding saved my life," said Ryan Sheckler, who was eighteen months old when his mom noticed him kneeing along on his dad's old Powell board, and soon not wanting to do anything else.

These "and the rest was history" stories are all very similar, and usually told in such a way that you can tell the skaters mean it. Rodney's story is one of them.

It was 1976, and Rodney was in Jack's driveway. Jack asked the question and then toe-pushed the board over to Rodney. The Banzai had bright clear wheels sticking out from underneath a metal deck. He stepped on the board and it all just came together. No rules. No coach. No clock. Nothing timed. No right or wrong way, and pretty much no forwards or backwards or front or back, since the deck was a doubletail and he had no stance, yet. Looking back at the moment, he thinks of his mom on the tennis court.

"I felt then the unlimited possibilities," he says. "Nothing in my life up until then had allowed such total creativity. . . . It was the first thing that removed me from the anxiety I felt surrounded by." In 2005 he was invited to speak at UCLA. (His one other time there had been to skate and security escorted him off the campus.) "I found what I loved," he said of that moment. "If there's one thing I can say, it's that I found in life what I loved."

Later, Rod stared at the pictures on his friend's wall with such transfixion that Jack gave him a copy of a new magazine called *SkateBoarder*. It was a *Surfer* publication, with the same editor and contributors as the previous decade's *Skateboarding Quarterly*. Rodney's copy had a guy named Greg Weaver on the cover, completely horizontal on the white wall of an empty swimming pool, barefoot on a tiny, flat, wood board, a long frogman shadow stretching down and across the pavement toward the drain. Rodney would read the magazine every night, cover to cover, then read the three-point-font subscription card and its wax-paper envelope, then start at the front again. The cover had a teaser for a new craze in the sport called "Freestyle."

▲

AT HOME, the Mullen kids could have pretty much whatever they wanted. His sisters each had their own horse and Rodney had, among other things, a miniature 20-gauge shotgun, customized just for him. All he and his sisters needed to do was maintain perfect grades and never question Mr. Mullen's word. To do so meant disownment. Rodney's maternal grandmother, who taught him to read, had made that mistake about two years before, and he hadn't seen or heard from her since.

Hence, the night he asked the question, Rodney was very careful. The family was sitting at the dinner table, having spaghetti. Mr. Mulllen's answer was "*Hell* no!" words Rodney says his dad "boomed." "Not just 'no, Rod,' but '*Hell* no!'" Enumerating on huge, hard fingers, Mr. Mullen's reasons were—one— "they're bums"—two—he had just operated on a skater who knocked his teeth out, which ended up being the first thing Rod did when he finally got a board. Dad concluded: "That's not going to happen."

But at this point Rodney had the bug. He rode over to Jack's house almost every day (sometimes in one long wheelie) just to cruise around on Jack's board. He went from obsessively reading *SkateBoarder* to copying it, then memorizing it, and soon, he was regularly visiting the nearby Inland Surf Shop to "study" the decks on the walls and the wheels, trucks, risers, hardware, bushings, bearings, and stickers in the glass case at the counter.

He remembers: "I couldn't let it go."

So Rod wanted a skateboard, and his absolute-law-making dad said he couldn't have one. Yet there was hope, because Mr.

Mullen was so extraordinarily decisive and loud and hard and unmoving that the whole house had developed communication networks to circumvent him. Rodney's sisters were teenagers these days and rarely home. Rodney's mom's main vice at this point had become shopping for things like mink coats (plural) until certain accounts were empty, and then at the last minute switching funds around so you-know-who wouldn't find out. She left the really expensive stuff at her banished mother's house. Such purchases included a bed that had possibly belonged to the king of Spain, which sat unused in her mother's attic for years, and to the best of Rod's knowledge, could still be there.

Mrs. Mullen, to whom Rodney dedicated his 2004 autobiography, *The Mutt*, could see how much skating meant to him, and together they planned to take what now seems like the extraordinarily bold risk of asking Mr. Mullen a second time for a board.

They waited four months, with Rodney rehearsing his lines and his mom commenting to her husband about how much their son seemed to like skateboarding—how it was a good physical activity with minimal risk, as long as he wore full pads—which he would—meaning not just knee and elbow pads, but a helmet, wrist guards, and the leather gloves he wore doing yardwork.

NEW YEAR'S EVE 1976. Friday night. There's a party at the Mullen estate. Mr. Mullen is in high spirits. He's had a few. There are toasts. Rod and Mom are waiting and when Mr. Mullen proclaims "I love my family!" they move. Rod starts in, and his delivery is gorgeous. He asks his dad does he think, if he's careful, "the most careful I've ever been . . . doyouthinkIcouldhaveaskateboard?" and Mrs. Mullen is right there to reiterate that she's sure it'll be safe if he's careful, which she's sure he will be, right Rodney?

There's a long pause. Sara and Vicki can't believe what's happening. No one has ever asked their dad anything twice. Rodney remembers feeling "really afraid." He also remembers watching his father's eyes to see if they were turning from blue to green, in which case—run. Mr. Mullen doesn't say anything at first. Rod starts to twitch, then hyperventilate. His Mom is standing there with a practiced smile of violent peace.

Mr. Mullen answers. Rod falls to the floor.

# 5

# WHAT'RE YA CRYIN' ABOUT

THE NEXT MORNING, Mr. Mullen and Rodney took the Cadillac to Inland Surf Shop, where older sister Sara bought her surfing equipment. Rodney had been visiting the store for two months already, taking inventory and mentally building his board. He could already list every deck on the wall, left to right, top to bottom. Rod chose a 6-by-24-inch black Banzai, metal, with a doubletail.* His wheels were Jell-O-like translucent orange generics, and his trucks were ACS 500s, long-extinct and poured in Pittsburgh.

Rodney came home, padded up, and skated until it was time for bed seven hours later. Sunday, since his chores were done the morning before, he skated from "about nine to maybe seven." The next day after school he skated until they made him come in for dinner at six, though it had been dark by five. By Friday he could do a clean 720 on flat ground and carve like a surfer, as he'd seen skaters do in the pages of *SkateBoarder*.

He hadn't told Jack or anyone else that he had a skateboard. He was secretive partly because he thought he looked like a gay storm trooper when he skated. Even circling in the flat, shadeless driveway, he had to wear knee and elbow pads, wrist guards, leather gloves, and taut, striped socks tucked up under the pads' elastic. Specific skateboard protective gear didn't exist quite yet, so like a lot of skaters, Rodney wore a hockey helmet. His was a

---

* Now somewhat popular, the doubletail had vanished by the end of the '70s, and didn't reappear for another twenty years, with the famous Mike Vallely farm board by World Industries, cofounded by Rodney.

Cooper brand with a silk-screened rainbow. Wearing all of the armor was half of the agreement he'd made with Mr. Mullen; the other half was that he couldn't get hurt. Breach of either stipulation meant he quit forever.

But the real reason he kept things quiet was because from day one, skating's been a deeply personal medium of expression for Rodney, who still skates alone, every night, alone. The night I watched him skate in late 2010, he said I was the fourth person in five years to do so.

That same January the new *SkateBoarder* arrived with an inside photo of a rider doing a handstand on a rolling board. Rod padded up, hit the asphalt, and nailed the trick in four hours. This was also when he began what for the next twenty years would be a habit of wrapping his shredded hands with layers of hockey tape, using up to one full roll a day. (He also wrapped his sneakers and smeared the most-worn areas with a skate-catalog adhesive called Shoo Goo). Despite all of his precautions, cuts and scabs and bruises began to appear all over his body to the extent that his teacher asked if everything was okay at home.

BOTH Tony Hawk and Mike Vallely tell similar shocked-doctor stories from their own childhoods, and this is as good a time as any to talk a little more about injuries in skateboarding. At its essence, skating is about feats of balance accomplished on wheels, over a hard surface. The surface can be a driveway, sidewalk, parking lot, stair set, street course, bigger park course, empty pool, or a halfpipe, but inevitably—as with ice-skating or skiing or surfing or snurfing—participants lose their balance and fall. The difference is, skaters fall on concrete or a ramp with about as much give as a hardwood floor.

All pro skaters have suffered serious injury. As of this writing, Sheckler has broken his elbow ten times. The last break required a surgery in which doctors removed a ligament from his wrist and grafted it into his arm. Previous breaks had left the arm too deformed to heal on its own. Hawk has capped teeth as a result of an early spill in a pool, as do pros Mike Taylor, Bob Burnquist, and Rodney Mullen. Rod's injury was due to a fall he took on a mini-ramp shortly after he'd started skating, when he landed on his face, split his lips, and cracked his two front teeth. As Ryan bled and wept, Mr. Mullen marched over. Rodney remembers the exchange:

"What're ya cryin' about."

"I just don't want you to make me quit."

His son's response took Mr. Mullen aback, and Rod was allowed to go on. Mr. Mullen remained impressed with Rodney's dedication and drive as he watched his son skate, and later, as he watched him win in competitions. One morning after chores he informed Rod that they were building a ramp. It would be one of Rod's rare happy memories with his dad. They worked all weekend and make a 7-foot quarterpipe for the end of the driveway. Mr. Mullen even built a starter ramp, a short, steep roll-in that gave riders quick speed, like the gates of a ski run.

Soon Sara's surfing buddies were coming by to ride the ramp. Rod was ten and Sara, fourteen, although most of her friends were older and had more skate experience. They could do slow carves and fast turns up the ramp, surflike maneuvers where you ride up the vert and turn or balance your back wheels on the coping and come back down 7 feet of vert into the flat pavement. Really good skaters can do it on one wheel. All participants signed liability release forms typed up by Mr. Mullen's secretary. Once and only once did a neighbor come onto the property to complain about the racket.

Within three weeks Rod could do everything the teenagers could, and it was his dad who first noted, "You're better than all of those older guys."

And he was. Because now Rodney was ten but in seventh grade, and his other interests were quickly disappearing. He liked sugar, homework, the Bible, *Star Wars*, and skateboarding. At night in his room he laid his board on the bedspread and tried out different patterns of stickers from the display case he stared into at Inland. He shaped a tiny board from a sanded piece of surfboard glass, Shoo Gooed with hardware from a Hot Wheels car, and made a cardboard ramp with coat-hanger coping, which he kept on his desk. After lights out he sat up under his blanket with a flashlight, fingerskating.*

Monday nights in the fall, Rod brought the little ramp to his parents' room, where he was required to sit in bed with his father and watch football. It was a ritual Mr. Mullen thought up. There was no sign on the door that said NO GIRLS ALLOWED, but no girls were allowed. During play Rod fingerskated the ramp, trying out different turns and pressures and sequences. During commercial breaks he had to put the ramp down to "GO FOR THE LONG BOMB," sprinting to the other end of the room to catch a winged pillow for a touchdown.

Meanwhile, Rod kept up with his studies—maybe because of parental pressure, but also because he'd always had that collie dog's wiring of needing constant engagement. Thus, maybe it made sense that he was a pothead among the older BMX kids

---

* This is hard to believe, even if you skate, but fingerdecks, aka Tech Decks, are now a $120 million industry. Pretty much any skate shop sells not only fingerdecks with hardware, but sometimes little fingerskateable stairs and ramps and rails (and most recently a mega-ramp). Some videos—this is true—are nothing but fingerskating. And while they were once about as wrongly proportional as Hot Wheels cars, fingerdecks today have concave, spinning wheels and flexible trucks, and starting in the '90s, are all to scale, thanks in part to the person you're reading about now.

at age ten, but he also kept reading the Bible, even though his mom rarely went to church, and his dad was basically an atheist. Skating now ruled his life the way it did for so many of the top pros when they were starting out. Tony Hawk, for instance, had no other interests besides records and the violin, and he never attended so much as a school dance.

What makes Rod exceptional for his time is he graduated high school. Mike Vallely, Valley, Mark "Gator" Rozowski, Christian Hosoi, and later, Danny Way and Bam Margera, never did, and it rings true when they all say "Skating was my life." One pro who could tell you all about this is Jamie Thomas, who ran away from Dothan, Alabama, at seventeen and is today a respected industry magnate, but back then panhandled in the Embarcadero to stay alive so he could keep skating.

TODAY Mullen talks about his creative process as a series of flat lines and big spikes. He still works obsessively—skating every night and sometimes doubling up his schedule—without feeling much progress. Then a wave hits. When he finally gets a few tricks, he explains, "the rest cascade."

He remembers his first big spike, four months after he'd started skating. It was at home in Florida, two hours from the nearest skatepark, where a thirteen-year-old skater named Alan Gelfand was practicing an odd thrusting turn maneuver on the lip of an empty pool. Skating continued to grow as an independent sport, but remained very connected to the surf culture. At Rod's local shop, the skate stuff was off to one side, the way it was during the late '80s wave at places like Champs Sports, next to rock-climbing gear and expensive pogo sticks.

Rodney was already a pretty obsessive loner, but he also loved the skate culture, and went at least weekly to Inland, just to hang around. People skated out front the way they always do at a shop, and eventually he joined in. One week in April he went from being able to do five consecutive 360s to twenty, which pros were doing in contests at the time.

He remembers this as a huge break, the first time he realized the key was "finding my center." Pros like Antwuan Dixon will tell you that he's told them similar things. Rod remembers being angry with himself for losing so much time, trying to just do a maneuver rather than trying to see the parts that made it whole. From then on he decided to focus on the mechanics of each trick. "Every motion would be taken apart and cycled over and over in my mind, whether I was on my board or lying in bed, from foot plant and weight distribution to where I held my shoulders and eyes."

In two more months this eleven-year-old could do what then was called a kickflip, and now might be called a goatflip or underflip, though it's a whole different thing today. At the time, a kickflip was done standing ankle to ankle, centered and facing forward with a still board on flat ground. Skaters hooked a toe under the bottom of the flat deck, jumped, flipped the board, and landed how they started. Rodney got it in a day, the same amount of time it would take two young '80s street skaters named Natas and Gonz to learn a Mullen signature move called the magic, or kickflip.* The difference is they would land it while rolling.

The owner of Inland—and perhaps the most indirectly important person in all of skateboarding, a guy named Bill Murray—let Rod hang out all day, and sensing his obsessive ability,

---

* Today, Rod, at age forty-four, can approach a curb in a rolling handstand, ollie, and flip the board up the curb with his hands, landing on his feet in a nose wheelie.

gave him a discount on merchandise. He started calling Rod "Mutt," short for "little skate mutt," a cognomen first given to Rod by an older guy and sex addict who didn't skate or surf, but hung around the shop all the time telling really dirty stories to the kids who did.

Rod's next board was a 30-percent-off Stacy Peralta Warptail by Gordon & Smith (G&S), with Road Rider wheels and is important to our story in all kinds of ways. Peralta, for one, ended up becoming Rodney's mentor, and is the whole reason Rod first came out to LA, which, as things got worse at home, became a kind of light at the end of a long, really fucked-up and casualty-heavy tunnel, with walls like that toothy hole monster where they throw people in *The Empire Strikes Back*.

Peralta also emerged as a Hawk-level figure in the '70s, a top skater with that special gleam that brought him outside of the sport and into mainstream magazines and TV shows. In 1978, he was a top rider for G&S, the company he joined after leaving the Zephyr skate team, now better known as the Dogtown Z-Boys. (If you've heard of them, it's due to a movie Peralta wrote, produced, and directed.) He would soon leave G&S to partner with a surfer named George Powell and start the top skate company of the raging 1980s, and manage the best, most famous team in the sport's history.

Around this time, Rodney attended his first contest at the long-bulldozed and little-known Kissimmee Skate Park, two hours away. It was the first time he'd seen a skatepark, with wave-like banks of concrete that snaked their way down to open bowls. There was also a freestyle area, or piece of pavement, which is to a skatepark what a putting area is to a golf course.

Freestyle skateboarding is a 100 percent technical form of skating done on flat ground. Riders mostly stay still while the board flips and turns and rolls around their feet. It's never been anywhere near as popular as vert or street, but was a constant of skating in the '70s and '80s. Mullen was skating everything at this time, but says he tended toward freestyle, since he could do it anywhere and do it more often. It also speaks to his nature: technical and obsessive, and not as loud and huge and scary as vert skating. Freestyle boards didn't exist yet, though freestyle events were prevalent at contests (and would be throughout the '80s) because no space or park or ramps are needed.

Anyways, Rodney never took his run at Kissimmee. It had all been a setup by Bill Murray. Not having a great read on Rod's nerves, Bill thought a sudden surprise performance would be just the thing to bring him out of his shell and suggested they go check out the park. As they watched the freestyle contest that happened to be going on that day, Bill proverbially whistled with his hands in pockets, retracting into the crowd. Then the loud-speaker called Rodney's name. Rod literally ran and hid. Fortunately, Kissimmee regularly held freestyle contests, and when Bill finally located Rod, he agreed to come back and compete the next weekend. He practiced his freestyle routine during the week, and ended up taking first for his age group, with a flawless forty-five-second run.

The prize was a silver pendant in the shape of a board, and his victory encouraged Rod to come back and keep competing. But more importantly, that day Rodney encountered another competitor named Tim Scroggs, an early top freestyler from the '70s who became a member of the first Powell team and an early mentor to Rod.

Scroggs competed that day, and since there was no Internet or VHS, and skateboarding was rarely televised, this was the first time Rod had seen someone skate on a pro level. The guy also happened to be a freestyler, so while everyone still carved on concrete banks or rode up and down concrete bowls, Scroggs was all tech: He could flip the board with his feet, catch it, and do a quick 180 before hitting the ground. His showstopper was to pull into a centered tuck and lowly whistle while spinning fifty rotations so a warping pulsar siren sound emitted from his blurred core. Rodney was too scared to approach Scroggs, so he quietly shadowed him until it was time to go home.

# 6

# ROLLING INTO STACY PERALTA, AND THE STRANGEST DAY OF MY LIFE

ONE MONTH after winning his first competition, Mullen was practicing a handstand at Jacksonville's new Kona Skatepark when he rolled into Stacy Peralta. At the time Peralta was a very bright star in skateboarding, visiting Kona for the pro event of a big East Coast contest. Peralta had shoulder-length blond hair and at that point was the most successful split from the Dogtown crew, even appearing on *Charlie's Angels* two years prior in one of those caddy-like '70s skate-team uniforms people also wear for televised cricket.

Fedora'd pro Dennis Martinez was there, and sponsored amateurs from all over the country. The events were slalom, barrel jumping, and freestyle, won by Martinez. Rodney placed third in amateurs and was approached by Bruce Walker, of Walker Skateboards, the biggest skate company in Florida, which at that time had the second-biggest skate culture in the country. Walker put Rod on the team, which meant free gear, from Walker, but also meant he couldn't stay sponsored by Inland.*

Rod had been going to Inland most weekends, but now traveled every few months to Walker's house in Melbourne to train with the

---

* Today Mullen would be called a "flow rider," meaning he doesn't have his own board and doesn't get paid, but is on a team and gets an influx of free gear. It's a mid-step between Am and Pro. Sheckler was a flow rider for his local IWS Boardshop. He was seven.

43

team and perfect his freestyle routines. In the '70s, teams still had coaches who not only took care of riders but actually worked with them on their skating. Think dance, gymnastics, or figure-skating. Like warm-up outfits, this trend was forever gone by the '80s.

Rodney Mullen has had a pretty exceptional career in what is a very exceptional sport, and the next step follows suit. He became the only skater with not one but two coaches, the other guy being Barry Zaritsky, a mustachioed, T-shirt-into-beltless-slacks guy who owned a nearby skate shop and had his own skateboard safety road show, a 1970s mountebank dedicated to teaching kids about skating safely. It was through his two coaches that Rod traveled all over Florida, competing with Walker and visiting schools with Zaritsky, where he padded up and let normal kids his age bounce eggs off him to better understand the importance of wearing pads. Mullen also started doing demos at malls, sporting-goods stores, and parades, where he once tried a rolling handstand behind a long line of Clydesdales on a hot Florida day.

Both Walker and Zaritsky were serious mentors, carting Rodney all over Florida, making sure he had all the gear he needed, and successfully enduring long interviews over what Mrs. Mullen said would just be dinner. It was Barry, who ended up working at a new nearby park called Sensation Basin, who first told Rod, "You're going to be the best." And, like it or not, Barry was going to help him get there. Even in the context of this odd era, Barry was pretty fucking weird—forever telling Rodney to "use the force" and lecturing him on the virtues of the number 3—but he's the guy Rodney points to when asked about his early success.

FYI again: Another notable thing about Mullen is that while being his sport's Aristotle, he's also totally selfless. In that rarest egoless mega-genius category, Rodney's *always* hedging his achievements by pointing to other people, saying he just copied them and just added to what they were doing, though he's so far ahead that most of his stuff is additions or mutations to his own earlier work. The one other person I've talked to like this was not an athlete. It was Ken Vandermark, a reed player who won the MacArthur at thirty-four, and sitting with him you'd think he played the triangle or was a PR person for everyone in the jazz world except for himself and Ken Burns, who if you decided to bring up during an otherwise relaxed and positive-feeling interview, stand back.

BARRY not only made Rodney stop eating four candy bars a day, but he also cut off his peanut butter intake and put him on an exercise regimen. He also wouldn't let him look down to skate or tie his shoes, and set up a wall of mirrors outside of Sensation Basin so Rod could practice while watching himself.

And if you're thinking dance or figure-skating here, you're right on the money. Freestyle skateboarding at this point was dance on wheels. Each skater had a rehearsed "routine," and routines were "scored" with music. They'd roll or tumble or cartwheel off their boards, and some wore leotards. Some contests had rules requiring each pro to demonstrate a minimum of two "upside-down tricks." Dennis Martinez had a whole routine where he would roll his hat up and down his arms. Mullen remembers one guy doing a whole disco dance not on but next to his board, then rolling away at the end. All skating was number-scored by judges at folding tables with big cards, just like dance, gymnastics, figure skating, and freestyle skiing.*

---

* Personally I see this style in the skating of Richie Jackson, twenty-three, and a pro on London's Death Skateboards. The young Aussie can launch off a set of stairs, pop the board into his hand, and sprint sideways down a wall for about three seconds too long before he throws it down, falls back to our plane, and rolls away. It's very *Matrix*-looking, except he's wearing emerald bellbottoms with a ruffled shirt patterned with nitrous-spring flowers and a symmetrically curved mustache.

Freestylers are to the world of skateboarding roughly what NYU Tisch kids are to the world of performing arts. Along these lines, you could think of street and vert skaters as people in rock bands, who tend to share tricks and encourage one another and delve into other forms of the sport (at the 1983 national championships at Del Mar Skate Ranch, Hawk took seventh in the freestyle). Freestylers are the theater kids. They're both insular and cliquey but also communally nasty while being cannibalistic and individually secretive, hiding tricks from one another while constantly talking trash—a community without mutual support (or financially invested parents), and you can bet no one was real happy to have his ass kicked by an eleven-year-old, who'd begun to look like he was riding on a hoverboard out there on the concrete.

Rodney was regularly competing now, and while he'd later say he hated competing, he also admits to having his dad's thing when it came to winning. He wanted to beat everyone and trained specifically and obsessively to do so, timing his various practice routines, running laps, and grading himself in a notebook. The character we see in early TV interviews is still tiny and squeaky and blond, and he won't talk into the microphone or look at the guy asking questions. More than anything he looks like he's trying to disappear into his knees. But during competition, we start seeing a different person—a personality his skating seems to wear. There's an empty, massive confidence in a smile that's almost sly, like he knows something we don't. Footage is out there. Watch. He's still a small child, but he doesn't look small when he's annihilating everyone, and maybe now, for the first time, knowing it, or feeling it. Under a big black helmet, his expression is almost foxlike when he stops and tucks and goes into an excessively long spin, the small crowd's noise changing from excitement to awe to something else. When he's done he doesn't stare at the ground anymore. He steps off his board, sucks air into his chest, smiles wryly, and puts his arm in the air, his hand curled into a one.

A LOT happened in 1978 and 1979. Rod won three major contests against other sponsored riders and took third place at a professional contest at the famed Clearwater Skatepark. People from all the major teams were there, including Tony Alva, skating's brightest star, world champion, and successful businessman with his new company, Alva Skates. Rod noticed that Tony's board had weird, upturned sides to enable carving. Rod was twelve, and the only ones who beat him were Jim McCall and Tim Scroggs, who had just started riding for a new company called Powell-Peralta, a merger between Stacy Peralta and a guy named George Powell.

The Mullens had also moved. New neighbors sprang up on their rural road, pressures mounted, and they had to tear the ramp down. Mr. Mullen destroyed it and shortly thereafter bought fifty acres in the country, on which to build an even bigger house with even more expensive things in it. Even the light switches and doorknobs were ornate. They were now located twenty minutes outside of Gainesville, with cow pastures on both sides of their property. Their closest neighbor was an elderly farmer 2 miles down the road whom Rod never even met. It now took him seven hours to shovel shit, mow the lawn, file and hose and paint the mower, then pound fence posts with a ranch hand named Tank, a happy, squeally-laughing guy who was Mullen's only friend, since there were no other kids around to play with.

Home movies from the time show a smiling cherubic kid now controlling his board with eased totality, walking and spinning and shoving and turning it, moving over what looks like a dream's white runway spanning in every direction, with the viney Florida woods in the background and sinkholes left here and there for decorative trees. He's still in full space gear, a helmet and pads and jacked socks coming out of high-top Vans, octopussily knotted with the little bit of loop stuffed back under the laces.

"It's hard to emphasize that growing up, I wasn't really around people," is how Rod sometimes begins interviews. "There was me and there was cows."

He was more and more interested in freestyle skating, technical tricks on flat ground without moving. The flattest, cleanest space was the garage, a soaring poured-floor space big enough for three Cadillacs, with big hanging lights and a workbench and one of those huge ghetto blasters. Freestyle boards hadn't been invented yet, so Mullen was still using a Ray Bones Powell deck with the sides shaved down to the basic freestyle measurements of the boards that would premiere in the '80s.

In 1979 Rodney won the National Amateur Freestyle Championship in front of ten thousand people. The victory didn't help things at home. Mr. Mullen had never been a huge fan of skating in the first place, and as Rod got more obsessive and started turning nocturnal, things began to go downhill. Rod was getting screamed at, and we don't mean figuratively, for not doing the chores he wasn't told to do or because the lawn was edged improperly. A new task appeared on his chore list every week. One involved removing and cleaning individual parts of the lawn tractor. Mr. Mullen had been suggesting that Rod should use his talent "for something worthwhile, like golf," because "that's a sport where athletes really compete." His dad frequently and audibly wondered whether Rod might function better in military school. Rod knew what was coming. Before leaving home, his sister Sara had been a longtime dancer who spent her summers doing ballet in New York; she'd had the lead in the local company's production of *The Nutcracker*. Soon after she turned sixteen, Mr. Mullen announced that she was quitting, and that was that.

He laid it down one night at dinner: Rod could keep skating through the spring and summer, but when school started and he turned fourteen, it was over. "You're growing up, and you need to start thinking about your future," is what he said.

Rod knew this was coming, but the timing was horrendous. That coming fall, the Oasis Skate Park in Del Mar would host the world freestyle championships. Thirteen-year-old Rodney had no way to get there, no place to stay, no wealthy sponsor to pay for him. The one time he'd flown to a contest was for the National Amateur Freestyle Championship, but he'd traveled with his sister Sara, who had graciously and beautifully chosen a trip to California for her graduation present the same week of the contest.

Things looked dim. Rod sadly daydreamed while Bill devised a completely foolproof plan to get him to Worlds. He would sell his furniture to raise the money, and then lie to Mr. Mullen's face about an in-state contest he and Rodney would attend that weekend. He would then pick up the not-having-an-anxiety-attack Rodney, and instead take him to the airport.

But then Stacy Peralta called. It had been two years since their run-in, and Peralta had stopped skating competitively after breaking both wrists. His new company, Powell-Peralta, was doing well, and Scroggs, their first freestyler, still knew Rodney from the local circuit. Scroggs had been passing down some of his flow gear to Rodney during the past few months, convincing him that he was on a kind of Powell B team. It was mostly bullshit—like, if you were sponsored by Nike and gave your extra gear to your Uncle Floyd, would that mean that he was sponsored by Nike? So it's shaky, but it's also how Rod would end up competing at Worlds—not as an Am, but as a Pro. Scroggs had also been talking Rodney up to Peralta.

It was a huge fork in skateboarding's road. Had Peralta not called, Rod wouldn't have gone, and wouldn't have won. And no one really knows if he could have kept skating. It's not just obscure, but wrong and almost evil to think of skateboarding without Rodney Mullen, had he stopped there. Without Peralta, Rod would have had no choice but to quit, and he would have stayed in Florida, where the scene was beginning to die.

It was now 1980, and while new insurance costs were closing parks across the country, skating also suffered from the same abrupt loss of interest seen in the '60s. Sensation Basin was open but barely alive, trying to make money by hosting Roller Boogie on Friday and Saturday nights. Disco people came in fascinating platform roller skates and circled around the course with lights strung through the hanging moss while a weird blond kid ran backwards around the alligator pond. A few prominent Florida competitors relocated in Southern California.

RODNEY REMEMBERS the day as being "one of the strangest of my life." He wakes up and there is just a shine in the air. He mows the acreage before breakfast, then dissects, cleans, files, and paints the tractor before hosing down the courtyards and helping Tank pound fencing. Then he skates for two hours. His mom answers the phone and calls him to say it's Stacy Peralta. He wants Rodney to come and compete at Oasis, and he wants to pay for everything.

Mrs. Mullen suggests this could be a good last fling. Mr. Mullen shrugs.

# 7

# GUNITE, SNAKE RUNS, AND THE LATE GREAT '70S SKATEPARKS

THE PARKS Rodney visited during the first years in his career were the brightest highlights of '70s skateboarding, a period when technological advancements and a mysterious new popularity produced a reported 40 million skateboards. This is a lot, considering the sport's utter disappearance after its magazine-cover-getting eighteen-month spike the decade before.

This said, skating's never died. It's followed the same steep rise-and-fall pattern for three decades, starting in the mid-'60s and ending June 5, 1995: There's a spike in popularity about every nine years, massive outside investment just before its peak, and a bottleneck effect after each fall, where the core group that holds on ends up changing everything. For the '70s wave this included Stacy Peralta, Alan Gelfand, and Tony Alva. No less important is a guy who called himself Lowboy, a writer, photographer, and businessman who proved to be the sport's first marketing genius.

Skating was not popular in the late '60s. Sweating investors tried various tactics to revive the sport, including a last-gasp $40,000 investment by Larry Stevenson in 1969, who'd lost $250,000 in 1966, "the year skating died." Things were so bleak that the sport's sole media outlet shut down for the only time in its history.

But it was also not the end. A tiny core crowd in the San Fernando Valley surfed either Malibu or Santa Monica in the mornings and skated in the afternoons. Pros like Steve Tanner, Ty

Page, and Brad Logan continued to demo around Hermosa Beach. As early as 1968, two years after our sport's official tombstone was resurrected, pros like Torger Johnson and Davey Hilton were skating the long, smooth irrigation ditches at Paul Revere and Bellagio middle schools in Santa Monica.

Pools and parks were important to the '70s because they fostered a new culture of skating that found its way from streets and hills to smooth irrigation-ditch grades, to swimming pool walls (sometimes extended with plywood), and eventually up into the air. Bowl skating in parks was a precursor to the vert explosion of the next decade, but it by no means replaced '60s slalom and downhill and freestyle racing, which supposedly vanished due to legal problems and bad product. It was probably sudden lack of interest more than anything else. Pools and parks were a new face of skateboarding that appeared when the old trend reappeared around 1973 (the year the urethane wheel hit the market), and a very cool union existed between all branches of the sport. Be it the fast, destructive gorgeousness of pool riding or the calculated grace of freestyle, one informed the other, and it's this informational exchange that yielded the next decades' best skaters—namely, Mullen and Hawk.

> *If your city doesn't have a good skatepark, then your city is the skatepark.*
>
> —*Bumper sticker*

SKATEPARKS came along for a few short and great years in the 1970s, and were as fantastic as anything a bored kid ever drew on the back of a worksheet. Some were drawn up by investors and so weird they never come to fruition, like the Pentagon

Bowl in Anaheim, California, but those that were built looked like water turned to stone. Ever-changing cores of shape with bulbous tentacles of encompassingly rounded space, rolling and innovatively surreal, extravagant in the special way something made during a short, prosperous time is extravagant. Parks were poured rivers of white concrete, rising and sinking and snaking into themselves, everything curved and smooth and connected so that each ramp and bowl and run and pipe were manifestations of the same big thing.

From Alaska to one in Nebraska, hundreds of privately owned parks were built from 1976 to 1979. Zoning boards quickly approved parks because they helped remove skaters from the public spaces they'd occupied over the last decade, and investors jumped at the opportunity to profit from the resurgence of a sport where participants were spending a reported $400 million a year. (Again, we don't have definite figures; no one started keeping track until the '90s.)

Contrary to a popular 2001 film about this time—which we'll talk about later—1970s skating was done much more often in concrete parks than in pools or drainage ditches. Besides stand-still freestyle skating, almost no one rode in the streets for any reason other than going to a park or hill or pool. Tony Alva remembers not skating to the spillways where he'd skate, but riding his bike to spots with his board over the handlebars. It's still all about carving across that incline.

Parks usually had a snake run (a curvy, banked path) and a swimming pool–size bowl with vertical walls. Early ones had a long wooden starter ramp that looked like the big slide at a carnival. Later ones had full concrete pipes, a response to another strange and beautiful riding trend of the time.

A popular booklet from this period talks about a bulb-binging moment in 1975 when an upholsterer named Joseph Gee nearly collided with a skateboarder on a sidewalk near Pomona College. Walking on, he thought about how nice it would be to have a place for this sudden influx of skaters to go, as well as the monetary potential in owning such a place—or places. He soon formed a skatepark firm called Sidewalk Surfin' USA with partners Glenn John and William Russell, then a TV screenwriter. They began to draw up ridiculous blueprints.

The model they came up with was called Skateboard Heaven. It would be a chain of parks all over the country, each one 200 feet by 200 feet, at a cost of $180,000. Each park would comfortably accommodate 300 skaters at a time, each of whom would pay a roller-rink fee of $3 for a four-hour session, after which the park would be cleared and swept. The next group would enter and skate till dark, at which time the lights would come on, the park would be drained and scrubbed yet again, and a final group would be let in to skate till close.

All surfaces of the park would be made of gunite, or spray-on concrete, that was broom-painted with urethane. Each would have a ramp 14 feet high and 150 feet long for racing and slalom, a bowl, a mogul area, banked turns, winding "grapevine" paths, a freestyle area, and a "vortex," which would send riders around a wide 360-degree turn that would drop them 9 feet into a tunnel of Plexiglas, hosed from the outside to create a surfing effect. Park employees would direct all skate traffic, and shrubbery would outline pathways and keep riders on course. Sponsored contests would be held, judged by visiting Skateboard Racing Association members. The entrance to the tube, the top of the vortex, and all sharp turns would be reinforced with plastic air bags. Each park would house a store, refreshment stand, and a booth renting pads, boards, and sneakers.

Two Skateboard Heavens were built, but neither one by Sidewalk Surfin' USA, which might well have never existed because there is no trace of the firm or its members anywhere in skate history, LexisNexis, or even on Google.

The first skatepark opened in Port Orange, Florida, in 1976. Skateboard City had a wooden take-off ramp and snake run, a long, thin, squiggly ditch dug with a bulldozer, reinforced with rebar, and poured with concrete. (All parks in the '70s were concrete, though Ocean Bowl in Maryland was asphalt.)

Carlsbad Skatepark* opened a week later and got the cover of *SkateBoarder*. Often called "the world's first skate park," it was bigger and, unlike most, designed by skaters. John O'Malley grew up in New York skating the asphalt walking paths that wove through Salisbury Park in Nassau County, and at age eighteen moved to Carlsbad, next door to Jack Graham, business associate of Larry Grismer. Grismer owned Carlsbad Raceway, which was already zoned as a commercial property, which was key.

The 88,000-square-foot park included a low, scrunched snake run, a mogul field, and a shallow tri-level pool so riders could carve up to different stages of vert. The park cost $250,000 to build, but was such a success that the investors formed Skatepark Constructors, an engineering firm responsible for the majority of the decade's big parks.

---

* The famous Carlsbad Skatepark was bulldozed in 1979 and left until vert pro Mike McGill built a short-lived ramp park on the property in the late '80s. When the vert wave collapsed, ramps were dismantled and dumped into the park's original basin. For twenty-five years, ramp lumber rotted on what looked like an old gray parking lot, and the surrounding lawns were permeated with the concrete tips of the plowed mogul field. In 2003 a group organized to revamp and expand the park and build a skate museum on the property. Spearheading the project was architect Louise Balma, daughter of Larry Balma, a very important person who appears in the next chapter. For a year they met with the town, submitted plans, and talked with local media. The problem was that the once-rural 165-acre parcel was by then surrounded by industrial properties, and in 2005 the land was sold for $6 million. Carlsbad was unearthed and destroyed, the site was graded, and today, an office park sits in its place.

Parks made money from admittance, concessions, and shops that rented sour, crispy pads for 50 cents. They hosted contests to get exposure and boost attendance. Contests were the same as the last decade, with slalom, downhill, freestyle, and barrel jump, though the new community also had an interest in bowl skating, where riders rolled up and down the vertical concrete walls, turning at the top. The Pro Bowl Series premiered in March 1978, and was skateboarding's first vert contest.

Other parks sprang up in Sweden, Australia, Japan, North Carolina, and Fort Lauderdale, Florida, and ran at a boil for about two years. It was the '60s pattern. In 1977, Solid Surf Skate Park in Fort Lauderdale welcomed 3,200 customers in four days. Wilmington, North Carolina's Wizard Skateboard Park had a capacity of seventy, but grossed just under $8,000 in its first week, with lines from open till close.

In the fall of 1976, Skatepark Constructors announce a freeze on all contracts because they're so backed up. And once again it lasts about two years. Parks are too big, and there's too much to worry about. There is much more spectator and town-meeting talk than actual participant injury, but it doesn't matter. In September 1978, good old *SkateBoarder* runs a story on the fragile state of parks (i.e., the state of skateboarding at the time), interviewing the prominent developers and operators, who are usually one and the same. Florida park owner Robert Spence said: "The sport is at a critical point at this time, and unless some insurance carrier can be found to write liability insurance for the owners at an affordable price, we could see the demise of this industry."

By 1980, virtually every skatepark had closed for the reasons the owners said they would: higher numbers of participants that led to impossible insurance costs. And just an FYI: Very few lawsuits were ever filed; it was simply the rising cost of insurance that grows with admittance, exacerbated by outside parties complaining.

Skating was already in trouble. Like the decade before, a sudden celebritic popularity was followed by massive investments and public opinion that went from having just read an interesting article about a wealthy teenage Stacy Peralta in *Newsweek*, or seeing Tony Alva alongside Leif Garrett in the movie, *Skateboard*, to uninterest, to interest in eradicating the places skaters congregated. (The thinking here, I guess, was that such actions would evaporate skateboarding instead of dissipate it—this, the complete antithesis of what led to so many parks being built in the first place.)

Concrete's not easy or cheap to dispose of, so most of the parks were bulldozed. As previously footnoted, two decades would pass before these laws changed and communities instead of businesses would build the first public skateparks. The 1990s parks nursed a new generation, kids raised not on private office-park steps or curbs or ramps but on moonscaped worlds of perfect public concrete. "I didn't even know what street *was*," recalled one young pro after winning his first X Games gold.

POOL SKATING, by the way, was by no means "discovered" in the '70s. A decade before the first pool-riding Dogtown article ran, the premier issue of *SkateBoarder* featured a pool story and listed other pool spots, one of which had been utilized since 1963. How much the famed great drought of 1975 opened up pool skating is a little dubious, too. It seems like sneaking into someone's yard would be about as easy as it would be today, though Alva—now fifty—still does it. But like every decade in the sport's history, skater's ventured away from the previous one's accomplishments, doing stuff no one imangined before while finding new terrain in and over and on which to do it. Contests in the '70s remained the same, and skating was no less banned than it had been in the '60s (it was more so). Although the number of parks was growing, kids still needed places to skate.

LA County does have over 2,000 miles of concrete tunnels, and 150 erosion basins and canals, and in the past 60 years has been paved and detreed, which is why every summer, amid floods and fire, people lose their homes to landslides and bring about the demand for more concrete. These tunnels and erosion basins were all utilized, albeit mostly just in California.

From what I can tell, Don Autry—whom everyone called Wally or Waldo—was the first real pioneer of wallrides. He might even be wall-e's namesake (a "wall-e" is an up-and-over wallride trick). Autry also pioneered another type of skating that was rarely covered or discussed much because it was so crazy and illegal. Pipeline skating was an activity that, according to him, began with big-wave surfers who sought out huge tunnels to traverse since drainage ditches and skateparks didn't offer enough of a rush.

These tunnels were buried or about-to-be-buried lengths of pipe that a tractor trailer could drive through and were laid in with that type of alien machinery they make documentaries about—factory-size machines that roll on treads and have ladders up to a cockpit manned by several technicians. Autry snuck into construction projects at night or hiked to the Mount Baldy Pipeline in the LA National Forest to skate these things. Autry and his friends were known as "the tunnel team."

Autry's off pipes these days, but pictures from the time are still astounding. A green-socked guy riding up past the vertical point of a concrete wave, turning at about ten o'clock to fly and fall for a second on a board a little bigger than his shoe. In an interview two decades later, the forty-one-year-old said he'd recently been turned on to luge skating because he loved the thrill of standing up going 50 miles an hour. "Imagine what it's like," he said. "Who would have figured?"

Pipelining still goes on and today attracts enough extremists that it has its own magazine, *Juice: Pools, Pipes & Punk Rock*, to which Dogtown cofounder Jeff Ho is a frequent contributor. *Juice* not long ago interviewed a master of the genre named Matt Hensley, a street wizard from the early '90s whose video part was scored with Operation Ivy and who favored the very edge of the pipe so he could pop up and vertically railslide the concrete edge for a second, then somehow find his way back into the pipe so he could ride up the other side and do it again. This is stuff I've only seen in the last three years from the very, very best people, like Chris Haslam and Patrick Melcher, who cites Hensley as an early hero.

Also worth checking out is early footage of Sheckler skating lengths of pipe somewhere in a desert grove. The lengths are short and maybe ten feet high, with wide gaps between them. Sheckler not only moves up past the vert like a pro, but he also passes over the gaps one after the other, first just cleanly sailing over them, then flipping his board in the air while he goes from one sideways-arched metal surface to another. You don't even know it's him until the end, though the footage gives you the same "Who is that?" feeling as his other stuff. When they finally zoom in, our little shredder is standing in the curved bottom of one of the pipes. The proportions are similar to a nut in a jar. He's tiny and fat-cheeked and looks a lot like his youngest brother Kane does now. Yet again, who you're looking at doesn't quite match what you've just seen.

# 8

# TECHNICAL REINVENTION OF THE 1970S, OR HOW MITCH HEDBERG DID NOT GIVE URETHANE WHEELS TO EMIL HERSH IN HEATH LEDGER'S SKATE SHOP

SKATEBOARDING starts with the skateboard, and the leaps made in wheel, deck, bearing, and truck technologies in the '70s are so important to skating's history that we have to leave Rodney and spend a whole goddamned chapter talking about them. This is the decade where boards changed from roller-skate-wheeled planks into smooth-riding, responsive machines much like the ones ridden today. It's a time when skaters first designed their own equipment, founded companies, and when the early skateboard empires began to take root. It's also a time when pretty much everything was made out of chemicals.

THE URETHANE in urethane wheels is actually polyurethane, a versatile polymer used in resins, elastics, insulation, and—beginning around 1950—in surfboard foams. *Polymer* basically means "big molecule," from the Greek word *poly,* meaning "many," and *menos,* meaning "parts." Its structure allows it to house smaller molecules with various characteristics you wouldn't always naturally find together—in this case, strength and flexibility.

Though a popular Hollywood film would suggest otherwise, sadly, Mitch Hedberg did not walk into Heath Ledger's surf shop with a sack of these golden wheels and magically give skaters the power to ride on walls. But, this said, the urethane wheel is the most-referenced thing in the '70s resurgence for good reason. It's a huge evolutionary step in skateboarding, and it came along just before the other technologies that helped resuscitate and change the sport forever.

A few spare urethane wheels reportedly sat untouched in a few shops during the 1960s, but everyone will tell you that it was a longboarding nerd who really brought them to skateboarding. His name is Frank Nasworthy, and he grew up in coastal Virginia. He surfed and owned an early clay-wheeled Hobie skateboard that mostly sat in the garage. He was high school friends with a guy named Bill Harward, whose father ran a backyard shop called Creative Urethanes. One of his customers was a roller-rink chain called Roller Sports, which commissioned Mr. Harward to make small quantities of a more-durable wheel they could use for their rental skates. The wheels were translucent and gummy and smooth, made for painted Masonite floors but not meant for concrete, because they'd be too slow, so they thought. Frank was visiting one day and saw a fifty-five-gallon drum of the wheels, designated for the trash.

What happened next is what happened ten and twenty and fifty years ago: A surfer put roller-skate wheels on a board. The wheels happened to fit perfectly on Nasworthy's trucks, and he and Bill rode all over D.C., astounded by the difference. The ride was smooth and solid, like water skis on water. They let others try their boards, and got the same response. It was 1969.

Nasworthy attended Virginia Tech for a year, and then in 1971, moved to California with Bill to surf. Bill moved to LA and Frank ended up settling in Encinitas, California, a kind of Tree of Souls in what's now skating's valley of life. He surfed the morning breaks and worked at a restaurant in town. He knew the wheels still had potential, especially on the smooth, seasonless ocean of urbanized Southern California. Bill's dad couldn't sell him another customer's roller-skate wheel, so Frank decided to design, cast, and oven-bake his own prototype. He then ordered 250 sets from Bill's dad, invested $700 in his new venture, and he and Bill took out an ad in *Surfer* (*SkateBoarder* is still buried). Next, they drove around to surf shops and the few remaining skateboard retailers, including Bahne, who was still producing decks and trucks.

They called their wheels "Cadillac," which, according to them, is a name they took not from the luxurious, smooth-riding, positive-association-having car, but from a dog food commercial. The wheels came in a package that was meant to hang on a rack, a red, yellow, and white wave patterned card with a hole at the top and a plastic dome casing the wheels. They were advertised as "the best skateboard wheels in the West."

They retailed for $8, nearly half the cost of a full board, and what would be roughly $60 today. Skating was then at the lowest point of a low tide, and no one knew what to think of these extremely expensive but really good wheels. Bill and Frank ended up giving most of them away the first year, but then sales picked up. The next year they got orders for two thousand, followed by orders for four thousand. In two years Frank quit his job and partnered with the Bahne brothers, because single orders were topping $50,000. It was 1974, and both skating and skate technology were on the upswing, and the businesses were booming. Roller Sports (Bill's dad's client) finally bought out Creative Urethanes so they could make skateboard wheels. New wheel companies surfaced, including Kryptonic, Sims, and soon-to-be market-ruling Road Rider Wheels.

Wheels started small and roller-skate-size, then got big. Cadillac's "Stoker" looked like a modern-day roller-ski wheel, and stuck out from under the slim '70s boards like a clown's shoe. This was the peak of the '70s skate boom in which these new wheels played a huge part, so everyone wanted to make the newest, best wheel. The Bahne brothers eventually left the market, but remained businessmen and advertising geniuses, organizing a road show to promote their boards, trucks, and wheels. Though it was the pool era, Bill Bahne designed massive wooden ramps, including skating's first mega-ramp, a 15-by-30-by-150-foot behemoth ridden for the famous Del Mar Championship in 1975, which Rod read all about in recently resuscitated *SkateBoarder*.

THE DECK Rodney picked out with his dad that fateful New Year's Day in 1977 was historically important. He chose a Stacy Peralta Warptail by Gordon & Smith (G&S), the surfboard maker founded in 1962 by a surfer and chemistry student named Larry Gordon and a lesser-known guy named Floyd Smith. Larry's dad and uncles ran Gordon Plastics in Pacific Beach in LA, and this is where they shaped and poured their first surfboards. Two years later skateboarding was everywhere, riding its first popular peak, and they decided to make a deck. Operating out of Floyd's garage, Larry shaped a maple core and around it poured a fiberglass-reinforced epoxy called Bo-Tuff. Bo-Tuff is a patented polymer that's still used in bows (as in bows and arrows), and for a while, a bow made with this material held the world record for shooting an arrow more than a mile.

The board was extremely weird. Where all others in 1964 were flat boards, this deck was laminated and plastic-looking, with an arched back. But it was also extremely responsive at a time when everyone was riding flat wooden pellets with clay wheels affixed by roller-skate trucks. They made a thousand decks with a hand-turned press, then sponsored a slalom team of top-placing people you've never heard of, who dominated the first Annual Skateboard Contest in Anaheim in 1965, the year demand fell off a cliff.

They were a decade ahead of their time, and when the '70s craze came around, Larry was ready. He got a new partner (Jim Hovde), and in 1974, using the same press, they produced the Fibreflex skateboard by Gordon & Smith. They began making 25 a day, but within a year, moved into Larry's dad's factory and started pressing 500 a day. They were backordered for six months and released different versions throughout the '70s chemical period: a freestyle deck with a kind of an early concave sunken middle and stiff-coiled spring-feeling model, called the Bowl-rider; and the more middle-ground Teamrider, used by both vert and freestyle skaters.

Since everything in the skateboarding '70s was made of chemicals, Peralta's wooden deck was something of an oddball. Yet it sold so well they made a Warptail II, and again were a decade ahead because they built the deck with layers of veneered maple* instead of one piece, meaning they used less wood and made the deck lighter, but almost as strong. Even in the chemical age, the Warptail became a sort of Ford Mustang of '70s skating, with 110,000 selling for $25 each between 1976 and 1978. It was the plywood design that took over the '80s, and they gave pro

---

* Layered maple still makes the best boards in the world. Because most of it comes from the Great Lakes region of southern Canada, it's maybe not a coincidence that the guy who introduced maple to the industry was Willi Winkels, of Brampton, Ontario. The son of a door maker, his new maple laminates ended up being the buzz of the whole thriving Canadian scene. Winkels was eventually recruited by Sims to make decks. Most decks today are assembled in China, with one exception being New York City's Shut Skates, who keep it all local.

models to some more people you've never heard of, except for Dennis Martinez, the freestyle guy in the fedora.

▲

PRECISION BEARINGS are almost as responsible as urethane wheels for '70s skating's new smooth ride. As with trucks, skate companies began developing their own technologies instead of depending on those of the roller-skate industry.

At first, '70s skaters were using roller-skate bearings from the last decade, which were not developed for skating's new speeds and terrain. What happened a lot was this: You were going really fast or really hard, like, say, up a 12-foot pool or down a steep hill, and the bearing's outer casing fell out and sixty-four tiny steel spheres exploded from the wheel socket. The wheel jigged out and you lost control of the board, and fell. Wheel makers monkeyed around with different techniques to makes rides smoother. Some added washers or sold lubricating oils—one of which, according to New York City legend Rodney Smith, turned the urethane from solid to liquid.

Precision bearings placed eight (and recently six) balls between two tracks, called races. Think of each race as an edge of the path Indiana Jones is running down as the boulder's rolling after him. The balls rolled in their races around the axle with the skateboard's wheel—the same idea, improved. But now the balls were sealed into the bearing on both sides with what looked like little washers, called shields. The ride was a *lot* smoother than the ball bearings used throughout the '60s, wherein a band of steel gripped the wheel from the outside and tiny steel spheres rolled around the axle from the inside. If you ever have a chance to ride an old skateboard, you'll feel the difference—it's akin to running in sneakers versus running in gravel-filled loafers—and you'll see why, as with the new wheels, everyone quickly abandoned one for the other.

The aforementioned Road Rider wheels were the first on the market with precision bearings, and they promptly took over. The wheels were made by a new and very important company called NHS, founded (and named for) three friends who worked together at Santa Cruz Surfboards, Richard **N**ovak, Doug **H**aut, and Jay **S**huirman. In 1973 they shaped a fiberglass skateboard deck, and then decided to start their own business selling decks and wheels. A year later, Shuirman knocked over a cast of 100,000 ball bearings and decided to find an alternative, eventually buying sealed precision bearings from a Rhode Island company called Quality Products. Road Rider wheels were born.

NHS was also the first company to apply silk-screen technologies to skateboards, which is why Santa Cruz's early graphics still look so much cooler. That's the '70s. In the '80s, their new head of development—a former freestyler named Tim Piumarta—developed a number of new concave designs and arguably the first board with an elongated, upturned nose. He also developed stackable riser pads that fit between the deck and the truck, and in 1989 discovered a thermoplastic called Everslick, a hard coating on the bottom of the board that makes everything slide-able. In the '90s Tim, with Novak, invented the NuWood, a plastic-injected board that's basically indestructible, and after that created a griptape printed with sharp full-color images. Still going strong, the innovation of NHS seems to know no limits.

Improvements on Road Rider wheels were hardly attempted until the next decade, when Powell-Peralta introduced Bones Bearings, $20 a set, made in Switzerland, and still found in the case of any good skate shop. Few have challenged them since, though a recent attempt *was* made to crack the market by Shake Junt, a tentacle company of Blitz Distribution, owned by former pro Per Welinder, that one guy to ever beat Rodney in a contest. Shake Junt was founded in 2008 and seems lax about taking financial risks, like releasing a deck in the shape of a prison shank, or a pro model with a cartoon graphic of a most certainly unlicensed Tasmanian Devil roaring atop a pile of dead pigs in police uniforms.

Shake Junt put together a home-style infomercial starring arthritically fluid pro Mike Plum, aka, Lizard King, sitting on his patio in a lawn chair, smoking while he keys the bearings onto his trucks. Next to him on the picnic table is Shake Junt's patented black box that says GETCHA ROLL ON, framed in lights. The bearings are the color of Slimer and match Lizard's board and griptape. He's got a black knit sailor's cap and a blond mustache the size of a rolled-up newspaper.

There's a cut and now we watch as Lizard skates not over but down a long flight of stairs, through a bed of gravel, then along several paths in the woods. Somewhere in here the sky turns purple with this effect that was old and cheesy when the Beastie Boys used it around 1990. At the end of the forest scene, Lizard hits a bank and manages a three-foot ollie before riding away in a cloud of dirt.

"So we just rolled through as much shit as possible, so let's see if it rolls."

Now we're back at his house. He's under a beach umbrella. He spins the wheel up to the camera with a sharp shushing sound. "Thars a lotta pas-sion right there, bayy-bies," he says in a bad imitation of a Hispanic accent. "These Shake Junt bearings *work*."

TRUCKS were also reinvented in the '70s, changing from the upside-down T at the bottom of a roller skate to pretty much what you see today. Trucks are made of a baseplate that's bolted to the deck, an axle that holds the wheels on, and a kingpin that connects the two. Most of what you see—the thick, wide-metal triangle—is protective casing. When the first skate companies started engineering trucks in the '70s, the challenge was to make trucks flexible enough to turn and carve but stable enough so the board wouldn't wobble.*

How much you want to know about truck development I'm not sure, though one company—Independent—became the sport's Viacom and changed skating forever. Throughout the '60s and early '70s, the Chicago Roller Skate Company basically had an unintentional monopoly on skate trucks. Then in 1974 Tracker Trucks was formed when a carpenter named Dave Dominy worked with rising kingpin Larry Balma to modify preexisting product, making a truck that was higher, wider, stronger, and more stable. Their first version was called the Fultrack and sold well enough to find a distributor, skate powerhouse Gordon & Smith.

Bennett trucks came along with the now-industry-standard idea of moving the kingpin up closer to the board so it wouldn't drag (pool skaters have now begun to grind the coping). The inventor is Ron Bennett, an OC architect and engineer who introduced the Hijacker in 1975. Freestylers favored it because it was small, and because one of the top freestylers at the time, John Hudson, rode for Bennett. They offered to replace their

---

* Speed wobbling, by the way, is part of riding fast, and is scary as shit the first time it happens because it's usually on a hill, moving fast enough where you can't run out of a fall if you step off the board, which, when I was ten years old, felt less like it was wobbling and more like it was trying to buck me. Ever incorporative, skaters like Dennis Busenitz take speed wobbling to a high art, riding straight down those San Francisco streets you don't even want to drive on. Seriously—check him out. He just ollies over a low wall and is gone like a skier down a chute, a flapping silhouette rapidly shrinking down the wet pavement, little quivers of speed moving up his legs. The whole trick is that he's simply still on the board.

baseplates free because they frequently broke, and then invented a baseplate out of something called Magalum. As competition picked up, they released other synthetic and really '70s-looking boards like the Lightbeam and Spacedeck. Bennett didn't last.

Mike Williams was a shipbuilder and pro downhill and slalom skateboarder who decided he wanted a better ride. He ended up approaching HPG IV, an aerospace tooling company, and developed a ⋀-shaped split-axle truck that had both adjustable tension and turning radius. He called it the Gullwing, and moved 800 units in January of 1976 and 13,000 in February of 1976. He became a power player in the '80s, along with Thunder Trucks, who would sponsor Reese Simpson, a rare Ty Cobb figure in the sport's history. Simpson was forever getting kicked out of parks and contests and generating sizable debate in the close-knit skate community. Although he's never done anything that the bad SportsCenter suits celebrate each night, he's worth mentioning, as he still skates, and someone with the same name is a competitive bass fisherman.

INDEPENDENT TRUCK COMPANY is huge within their own market, the industry as a whole, and the history of skating. They debuted two models in 1978, and within six months had half the market share. There was a whole other company and truck that came before Independent (to be called "Indy," hereon), which started in the mid-'70s with two San Franciscans named Fausto Vitello and Eric Swenson. They wanted a truck with more independent suspension, and thus formed Ermico Enterprises. They made a truck—literally made it in their shop on Yosemite Avenue, buying welders, lathes, and drill presses—called the "Stroker." It had springs and sprockets and bushings and looked like a cross between a Marker ski binding and something from Doc Brown's Olde West laboratory in *Back to the Future III*. In 1975, a single one cost as much as a full board—$26.95—although a pair sold online recently for $1,300.

The Stroker was a hit among downhillers and enthusiasts of a now thankfully extinct activity called streetcar racing. Ermico also produced a two-kingpin truck similar to Gullwing, called the Rebound. Rebound eventually was distributed by NHS, who sold the truck with their Road Rider wheels and Santa Cruz skateboards. For thirty years NHS has been the innovative and entrepreneurial godhead of skateboarding.

Turn to 1978. Vert was increasingly popular, with Alva as the poster boy. Fausto was still trying to perfect a versatile truck that turned tightly like Bennett and cruised like Tracker. While this was happening, fellow NorCals and skate pros John Hutson (vert) and Rick Blackhart (slal) were working with NHS to find an alternative to Tracker and Bennett. That was how they met Fausto. Rick says they wanted "a truck that turns more and hangs up less."

They did either four or five prototypes before "The Independent" was born. It was a hit the way the new wheels and bearings were a hit. Within six months, Indy had half the market share. They were everywhere. Everyone had to have Indys the way everyone had to have Air Jordans. At the Hester contest in Newark, vert pro Bobby Valdez replaced his Trackers with Indys partway through, and won. By 1979 NHS had significant shares of the board and wheel markets and over half the truck market. Life was good.

Indy's success rocked the industry. Everyone tried unsuccessfully to win back clientele. Tracker, for just one instance, came out with "magnesium" trucks and something called a coper (pronounced cope-er), which is a piece of plastic that snaps over trucks to protect them, and in the '80s was the equivalent of head-gear, a thousand times worse than the tail-protecting skidplate. The coper sold so well that Indy copied it and started selling its own "Grindmaster Device." This is '70s skating, remember, and skaters couldn't buy new, plastic, gimmicky things fast enough. And you'll never guess who rode with not one but two spotless white copers, even though he did freestyle and didn't learn to grind till he was thirty. Rodney also ended up creating, engineering, and patenting a whole new kind of truck called Tensor, a top seller for the last decade.

# 9

# DOGTOWN, STECYK, AND THE BUSINESS OF SKATE MEDIA

YOU MIGHT HAVE seen a movie about '70s skateboarding called *Dogtown and Z-Boys*. Released to acclaim in 2001, it follows a group of young Santa Monican surfers and explains how they brought skateboarding from the street to pools and eventually into the air. The "Z" in Z-Boys stands for Zephyr, a surfboard manufacturing company founded by Jeff Ho, Skip Engblom, and the very important Craig Stecyk. They rented a place on Grandville Avenue in Santa Monica for $300 and made recognizable high-quality surfboards that Stecyk painted using a lot of the techniques he used on hot rods. Zephyr formed a promotional junior surf team, and then a twelve-person skate team with the same riders, three of whom became top-placing skate stars throughout the '70s: Stacy Peralta, Tony Alva, and Jay Adams.

It was Adams and Alva who introduced the team to urethane in 1973, so they were slightly ahead of everyone, though not by much. It was in the spring of 1974 that the team attended the Bahne-Cadillac Ocean Festival (BCOF) and made its mark. The movie got this right, though not the year or the name of the contest.

The BCOF was the first big contest of skating's reemergence, sponsored by the leading manufacturers of boards and wheels. In skate lore the contest is famous. Engblom showed up in a white fedora and long-sleeved Hawaiian shirt the color of Windex. He carried an empty briefcase, cut ahead of everyone, and told the guy at the sign-in table: "We're here to win."

They were as good as the best pros, but didn't quite kick everyone's ass the way young Rodney and Ryan did. It's more that they did stuff no one had ever seen. Freestyle was still very dance-oriented, remember, with practiced routines that included handstands and long-held poses, which you better believe were mocked by the Zephyr team. The freestyle area was basically a big stage raised on one side and surrounded by bales of hay.

The Zephyr team essentially introduced the world to an early form of street skating, a hard grace they demonstrated in pools and irrigation ditches, with an approach no one else would use until the next decade. They rode low, planting their hands and kicking their legs out for these big sweeping 360s that in footage look a lot like the turn on a wave. This all gets brow-beaten into us in the film, but it's very cool to watch. Thirteen-year-old Adams did what was really an early pre-ollie '80s move, launching himself off the end of the platform and landing on his board. Alva and Adams took third and fourth in men's freestyle, and the skate press was there and remembered them well: "They were more like a street gang than a skateboard team."

*SkateBoarder* ran a feature on Zephyr the following year called "Aspects of the Downhill Slide." It would be the first in a series of articles and other media about the team, and today you can see why those images got attention within the community and had resonance and box office success thirty years later. It was happening all over Southern California, but the photos show a tiny group of beautiful kids doing completely new things in an alien landscape. They're in drainage ditches surrounded by sand and fence, holding surf postures on flat wooden boards barely bigger than their feet, gliding across long rolling concrete planes with no one around except other kids who look like them.

That's how the photos look. How they feel is different. Few had seen these movements or landscape before, but there's a new empty, prohibited air to where they are, a vibe somewhere between trespassing sneakiness and territorial discovery, like coming across treasure in a junkyard. What they're doing is gorgeous and fluid. Where they're doing it is basically a big sewer. Yet the long graded planes are uniquely spooky and beautiful, much like the riders.

The kids in this new territory wore almost what they wore in the water, and were yellow-haired and brownly naked but for iridescently faded jeans, moving across waves of cracked concrete in new fluid postures, ten tanned bare toes hanging over the chipped nose of the board. It was a subculture's subculture—remember, almost everyone skated in parks—but it's also a bright period of wild innovation that was communicated in the photos and film of the time. The people in them are explorers, and we as readers got to see them exploring. The hunger of their skating is happy, ingenious, and dedicated without knowing what that really means because they love it, and it's much more through pleasure than pain that they reach these new heights.

Riders knew of Jay Adams, but hadn't really seen him. (Remember, there were no videos yet.) Adams was the sport's first natural, whose skating still looks like a combination of amber and mercury and whose body looked like an ocean road at dusk. Like Lindbergh or Jordan, he could not take a bad picture. He was smoothly weathered, beautiful and sun-kissed, and his hair was all but white and his teeth were crooked and he smiled in photos like he was singing. He was lean and muscley and almost gaseous on a skateboard. And he was the youngest and the best on the team, and rode with a blend of fluid balance and wild creativity, where he would megaspin on the board just as it ran out of energy

at the top of a ditch, or finish an incredibly fast tight slalom barefoot and then tuck and disappear into a sewer pipe, or just cruise,
arched gymnastically backwards with his hands behind his head,
moving barefoot over a steep, cracked bank.

The Dogtown stories hit. Other reporters came to shoot and
write the exact same stories. Skate-beat journalists said they had
not seen anything like it, because they had not seen anything
like it. The team proved to have the talent to work with photographers, and like dancers or models, all pros have photogs they
prefer. (Mullen's photographers are the only people who see him
skate regularly.) After word got out, and Peralta, Alva, and Adams
began to regularly place, other photographers were dispatched.
By then the guys were skating regularly in dried-up swimming
pools, and it was photographer Glen E. Friedman who captured
the even greater, strangely surreal beauty of skating's latest territory, including the conceptual moments when skaters pull over
the wall's edge and take to the air.

It lasted about two years. Zephyr's fame looks to be the
thing that proverbially tore it apart. Coverage led to popularity
and demand and business growth, which inevitably led to money
issues between Jeff Ho and Kent Sherwood, stepdad of Jay
Adams and owner of the fiberglass shop that manufactured all
of Zephyr's skateboards. He left to start Z-Flex and took Jay and
Alva and Jim Muir with him. Peralta, Wentzle Ruml, and Shogo
Kubo stayed on at Zephyr and ended up facing off against their
old teammates at a contest at LA's Cow Palace. They spread out
soon after that, and then Zephyr folded. Stecyk went on to partner with a guy named George Powell. Englbom formed a company called Santa Monica Airlines, whose first skater was a weird
Lithuanian surfer named Natas. Peralta went to G&S. Alva soon
left Z-Flex for the short-lived Logan Earth Ski, before parting to
start Alva Skates.

Remembers Adams: "We weren't having as much fun."

ONE OF THE BEST Z-Boys, by the way, was a girl. Peggy Oki took first in women's freestyle at the famed contest, and was a biology major at Santa Monica City College when she became Zephyr's only female rider. Like young Rodney, she just kicked everyone's ass, dominating the woman's circuit for as long as she was on the team. A group of disappointed female contenders approached a judge at Del Mar after she took first, and the judge told them that Oki was not only better than them, but she was also better than most of the guys. As of this writing, Oki's a watercolorist in Santa Barbara and looks pretty much the way she did back then.

THE FAMED DOGTOWN articles that appeared in *SkateBoarder* were authored by someone who usually called himself Lowboy. His writing is said to be like the guys from the neighborhood—raw and wild and in your face. Jake Phelps, editor of the skate magazine *Thrasher* (and the last person to interview Rodney on camera) once described the articles like this: "It's like Hunter Thompson. We're fuckin' with you. We like to fuck with you. And, you know what—we're good at it. How's that?"

The articles, to me at least, feel more like they're written by Eli Cash than Hunter Thompson. The narrative's tone is collegiate and masturbatory, and the stories have a made-for-TV adventure-screenplay feel in which the main character is usually the author. They're also jammed with statements of great pointed finality, like "In any given situation new approaches invariably precede the new technology," and "the entity you don't want to look at but have the urge to see." Long questioned for their accuracy by other skaters, reporting-wise the articles are so low on facts that the author himself finally starts including Oprah-ish bullshit about essential truth in his stories, and how we're not supposed to care. "Most people probably won't understand some of this," writes Mr. Boy. "But that doesn't really matter since the intrinsic elements are meant for those who really skate."

What these articles did for the first time was truly embrace the menacing identity skating had fought against since 1965. The articles were as subjective as the ones in *Good Housekeeping* and *Consumer Reports*—they just took the skaters' side, and much more than before sold the 1-percenter idea of not caring about money or success or what anyone else thought. It was a hugely successful marketing tool and it changed the way skating identified itself. The new identity was not just exclusive but aggressively so, an identity skating has stuck with and that we'd see sold again and again in companies like 1980s Pushead or 1990s Fuct, 2000s Bitch Skateboards, or 2010s Dirty Ghetto Kids and Deathwish.

The box-office smash *Dogtown and Z-Boys* did the same thing. It was written by Peralta and Stecyk, and while I personally got sick of hearing the same group of old fat guys saying things like "We didn't care about anything—we just wanted to skate," and "Tony was Mick Jagger," and "We were the heavy-metal, punk-rock Dogtown," I know skaters who liked the movie. Peralta's company, by the way, would distribute manuals to riders in the '80s detailing everything from what they could wear to what they could say, which ended up being attacked in a lesser-known documentary called *The Man Who Souled The World*, all about the *next* generation of skateboard badasses, who in another decade would celebrate their independence and not-caringness once they were old and safe (Rodney Mullen excluded, of course).

The one person in *Dogtown* who comes across as not just repeating Sean Penn's lines is Jay Adams. Today Adams is a skatepark manager in Costa Mesa, and his face is a mask formed by decades of not just drug use but intravenous drug use, with old tattoos and deep scars, a blown-out nostril, and kind eyes behind a been-*way*-down-*that*-road looking face that bears no resemblance to the singing blond kid of the '70s.

Of course I don't know, but in the film Adams seems to shy away when Peralta prods him about all the stuff he's done, and looks uncomfortable when they tell him to look into the camera and rub his head while they play "Old Man" by Neil Young. Adams still skates, and actually, the last time he was out of jail (drugs), he was met by a camera crew and now-sober pastor Christian Hosoi, former vert master and Tony Hawk's aforementioned rival in the '80s.

NONE OF THE Dogtown stuff would bother me the way it does if it didn't turn out to be a big commercial, which is why Craig Stecyk is so important. "Lowboy" is one of Stecyk's pseudonyms, and I'm pretty sure is there next to his real photo credit to hide the fact that he's a partner in Zephyr, writing appraising articles about the Zephyr team. He wasn't the first person to do shrewd stuff like this (see Hobie in the '60s), although he was the first to do it to this extent.

Whether right or wrong, this PR is another '70s happening that sets the standard for what's to come—in this case, the standard for the strangely unconflicted skate media. It's a media that will form in the next decade, and will be run by those who control most of the skate companies.

Fausto Vitello, who we just met as a founder of Independent Truck Company, soon got involved in both board and wheel sales, and then started *Thrasher* magazine in 1981. *Thrasher* was the top-selling skate magazine throughout the '90s, using 35 percent of each issue for Vitello-affiliated ads. That's ads. The magazine also ran more sober-sounding stories and profiles that praised riders on Fausto's payroll, stories that we came at with our guard down, which even if the stories were good and legitimate and heartfelt, were still hard to read once we learned all of this, since it's like reading a book review by the author's editor.

Tracker Trucks founder Larry Balma did the same thing, starting TransWorld Skateboarding (now TransWorld Media) the year after *Thrasher*, and while he covered skating pretty honestly, he still used it as a flagship for his various companies (Tracker, etc.), and didn't run any ads for Fausto affiliates. We will see the same thing in the next decade, when former pro Steve Rocco founds *Big Brother*, later owned by Larry Flynt.

These three men would go on to control not just nearly 100 percent of the skate media, but also 70 percent of all industry sales. And, like all ever-dealing ad guys, they knew that the hard truth of their corporate image didn't sell anywhere near as well as one of artistic independence and hate of The Man, the sell-outs, the masses, the money, and the corporations. They also knew that kids who were more-independent outsiders, artistic, and less group- or team-oriented were especially prone to this message. They literally bought the idea of the rebel. Balma actually told a reporter: "There's a consumer out there who in his early teens really wants to identify with [a product.] . . . If it's part of one corporation, then maybe that's not so neat."

# 10

# OLLIEBURGERS, A WORLD CHAMPIONSHIP, AND THE SKINNIEST PERSON I HAVE EVER SEEN

RODNEY FLEW ALONE to LAX on August 15, 1980, with Peralta's support and one parent's blessing. Stacy met him at the airport and they rode in his Volvo back to his parents' house in Santa Monica, passing through the Dogtown neighborhood Rod had read about in *SkateBoarder*. Stacy's parents both hugged Rodney when he arrived and put him in a guest bedroom with star stickers on the ceiling. Rod unpacked, padded up, and showed Stacy what he'd been working on.

They were in the Peraltas' driveway with the garage door open. Rodney started out with a helipop, a very '80s-sounding thing that's basically an early nollie 360, where he kicks down on the nose but does a split motion with his legs to throw the board into a full rotation, picking up his feet to get out of the way, then coming down on the board. Next he did a maneuver called a 50-50 casper, where he flopped the board over and swung it upright so he was balancing vertically on the board like a pogo stick, with one foot on the back truck and the other wrapped around to the griptape side.

Rodney was still skating vert and snake runs, but at this point was pretty much a freestyler, using a Ray Bones deck that he'd shaved down, with a skidplate, trucks as tight as they'd go, and white copers affixed with metal washers. (Freestyle boards aren't invented yet.) Minus the copers, it was a regular freestyle setup, and 30 percent heavier than the boards used today—a stat that speaks loudly to the power and agility of pros at the time.

After a few more moves, Rod did one he'd been saving. He kept the board still, as always, then squatted and stepped hard on the tail, the way you would if you wanted to pop it, vertical, into your hand. When the board was at 45 degrees, with the tail touching the ground and all four wheels in the air, Rod jumped forward, sliding his front foot up and nudging the nose so the board leveled out in the air. The whole thing was off the ground before coming down flat. An aerial, except he didn't use his hands.

It was an ollie—a flatground ollie.

Rod had invented the ollie one day in his garage upon returning from the skatepark, where he'd watched a vert pro named Alan Gelfand pull a no-hand aerial in a pool. It was Gelfand's signature move (and his nickname),* where he'd ride up a wall with a bit too much speed and scoop his tail and turn 180 degrees. For the second before the front truck found the coping, the board was airborne. A precursor to the trick, Gelfand told me, was the "disaster," where the front truck rolls over a ledge or curb but the back truck doesn't. In 1976 Gelfand learned to do a sort of half-jump when his back truck hit a ledge. Without his full weight, the impact lifted the board a bit, and soon he was popping up off the front steps of his middle school. The following year he adapted

----

* All skate literature and the OED reports that "Ollie" was Alan's nickname, but none ever indicate why he was called this. It turns out he was called Ollie because he ate a lot of Ollieburgers, a signature dish at Lum's restaurant chain in Florida. The burger is named after Oliver "Ollie" Gleichenhaus, originator of the still-secret recipe he sold to the chain for $1 million. Lum's is long gone, but Flashback Diner and Coffeehouse sits in the old location once frequented by Gelfand and still has the Ollieburger.

the trick to vert, perfecting it in the bowl at Skateboard USA in Hollywood, Florida.

After watching Gelfand consistently pull off these no-handed aerials, Rod went home and fiddled around in his garage until he figured out the kick-jump motion. Within an hour, he had a foot and there in Stacy's garage was popping even higher, clean and huge and hard every time.

So Rodney Mullen invented the flatground ollie, which if street skating was the planet Earth would be like inventing water. There's a whole cascade of quotes from famous skaters about what this means. A very good one comes from Mike Vallely: "The flatground ollie is the beginning of everything," he said. "The birth of modern street skating starts with Rodney Mullen."

Here's another one from Jamie Thomas: "Street skateboarding exists as it does now because of Rodney Mullen."

Or Tony Hawk: "Every time you ollie, you should get down on your knees and thank Rodney or take him out to eat if you see him skating around Los Angeles."

Although maybe an articulate young blogger said it best: "Everything you do—Rodney invented."

Mullen was not going to use this maneuver at the Oasis contest. Like a great conjurer, he often practices new tricks for up to two years before he debuts them. But this time, and this visit, was the beginning of his competitive decade, where basically no one could even badly copy most of what he did. This is when he started not just finding but inventing new plateaus, and then reinventing them. Over the next ten years he would place first in thirty-four out of thirty-five championships in a row. And it pretty much started right there in Stacy Peralta's driveway.

Peralta stood there laughing. He'd been getting reports from Scroggs, but hadn't seen Rodney since their roll-in two years earlier, when Peralta had shoulder-length silken hair and the clean, youthful image of the pre-disgraced Tiger Woods, all while basically being skateboard champion of the world.

Things had changed. Peralta had retired from competition. He'd left G&S and partnered with George Powell and Craig Stecyk to form a new company called Powell-Peralta. His hair was shorter and tousled, and he met Rod in jeans and a Hawaiian shirt. He was a partner, a team manager, and a really talented scout. He was also, as they established on this trip, Rodney's new boss and mentor.

The garage was not only full of gear, but full of Powell gear. Piles of decks and wheels, boxes of shirts, kilo-sized plastic bags of stickers. Powell-Peralta was still in embryo, but had already grabbed the community's attention with its pro talent and cutting-edge designs. Skaters knew Powell stuff when they saw it, and when skating exploded again for a bigger, crazier, messier, brighter third time, Powell and Powell's riders would be ahead of everyone else. The images on the stuff in Stacy's garage became timeless, and still appear on shirts and boards today.

At its peak the team had nearly every top rider, but a big part of their lasting exposure is due to Peralta's graphic artist, V. C. Johnson. Johnson created most of the well-known images in '80s skateboarding, images so famous they would be parodied in the sport's next strange wave, and images you might recognize even if you never skated. They include: Hawk's skull over a Celtic cross; McGill's spooky skull wrapped in a snake, whose corneas are sideways; and the regal skeleton-with-sword Ray Bones board that Rod liked so much. Sheckler, by the way, has a Johnson-looking tattoo on his right shoulder: a gleaming skull in a tilted crown. On the topside of Powell decks is another famous Johnson image of a skeleton peeking out of the metal pair of wings that bomber pilots wear.

The bomber at the time was Powell's trademark, and kind of fit with the whole death-and-skeleton motif. Riders for Powell were called the Bones Brigade. The Bones Brigade became the single most important team in terms of accomplishment and publicity for skating's huge breakthrough in the '80s. And in 1980, being on the Bones Brigade for skating was like playing with the Ramones at CBGB. They led an outside culture that respected them for being independently cool and cutting-edge, and soon they'd be big-budget-movie popular, recognizable outside of the community, which continues to respect them.

Peralta was and still is a natural industry guy. As a teenager he was practically the only pro smart enough to save money and present himself in a way that got him into magazines and on TV, and at this point in the story, in addition to spotting and selling physical and artistic talent, he had wised up to the marketing aspect. He had designed a cool and (he'd made sure) coveted T-shirt, which Rod already knew all about. It was yellow with the Powell wings logo and two bombs on the left sleeve. Ask around: Every skater knows about this shirt. It was before this reporter's time, and I knew all about it and knew you had to be on the team to get one. And that night, in Stacy's garage, Rod got one. He was officially a pro on the most prestigious skate team in the world.

Oasis Skatepark opened in either 1976 or '77 (sources disagree). It was underneath Route 805, fifteen minutes from downtown San Diego. The park required all skaters—most of whom were teenagers partaking in a desert climate sweat sport—to wear pads, which Oasis rented. One pro from the area said he never once saw a can of disinfectant or a bottle of soap in the little rental closet of the shop.

Even so, this place was heavenly. Oasis had huge, deep, womblike white pools, a snake run full of hips and banks, a concrete "halfpipe" (with no flat between the transitions), and the good old freestyle area. There was a big octopus of highway ramps over the park, and skaters were frequently bombarded with garbage and sometimes bottles, if you ask anyone who skated there.

After check-in, Rod went off by himself to warm up, feeling good until he saw Steve Rocco. Rocco was then a pro for Sims, and the number-one freestyler in the world. Rodney knew all about him, and though their world was small, he was Rodney's opposite. Rocco skated in fast,* smooth, curving lines, slamming successional technical tricks, carving all the while so he didn't slow down. His routine was one hard chain. Aside from his top technical skill, his speed let him fit more tricks into his routines, giving the judges more to watch—a big reason he was number one.

The contest was between him and Rodney, partly because they were each at their own ridiculous levels, and partly because everyone else kind of sucked. Skating—especially their never-popular form of skating—had been in decline. No one seemed to have kept up with freestyle, yet they'd decided to compete in a world championship. Footage of the contest looks odd. There are maybe a hundred people watching, most of them non-freestyle pros between events, standing around what looks like a drained kiddie pool bisected by 805's dark shadow. There's a guy in a pants leotard with those Y-shaped suspenders. There's a guy who kneels on the board and rows with his arms. And there's another balding yet big-haired, headbanded guy who rolls forward in a bent, rickety handstand for two seconds before falling into the board.

Rod wore his high yellow-striped socks and his shirt tucked into Daisy Dukes, and was the only freestyler with pads, or a

---

* I'm not sure he'd be considered Rocco's contemporary, but Tom Knox was a '90s street skater who had regular pro technical ability, but did everything at absolute top speed and is a guy we just can't leave out here. Even standing on a board at top speed is scary, let alone hitting rails or flipping the board away from you and then trying to catch it with your feet and land, fast. If this shot-from-a-cannon style is down your alley, your guy today is Dennis Busenitz, though Danny Way holds skating's current land-speed record, at 74.5 miles per hour.

helmet. Rocco wore shorts and a Sims T-shirt, and whizzed around pulling tricks two and three times as fast as anyone else. Each skater got two forty-five-second runs to their choice of music and was scored out of 100 points. Judges took the best score.

Footage of the contest shows a small blond boy skating with the same total focus he skates with today. When "Psycho Killer" comes on, Rodney rolls out and starts up. Once he begins he won't move more than 3 feet from his starting point. He's sometimes a wreck at contests, but he's not here. He hasn't even switched into his usual autopilot mode. Rod remembers it as not quite being there. He'd been practicing sometimes nine hours a night in his garage and training at an empty park, where Barry yelled at him about the number 3 while he ran backwards around the alligator pond. In the footage, it looks much more like the game is playing him. He's all but still, with what looks like an enchanted Jacob's ladder folding around his feet. He puts his arms out if he needs to catch his balance at the end of something really hard, but other than that, looks to be standing there, levitating 3 inches above the ground.

Rod does a helipop and lands and rolls the board onto its side, so he's balanced on the wheels. It's a setup trick, but he falls, costing him points and putting him behind Rocco.

He gets one more run, but so does Rocco, who goes first. Rocco nails everything as he loops the course in fast, hard ovals. He consistently lands pre-ollie 360 shoves, and backwards M-80s, where he centers himself on the board with his ankles together, then 180 flips it as he turns the other way, catching it all with his feet and turning another 180. It's all hard and clean and fast. Rocco's board is big and tapered at the ends with a wide space between the griptape. He's still ahead.

Rod's got one more. He feels calm. He says a prayer as Talking Heads come on again and he rolls out and the music goes away and everything unfolds and flows and it's all perfect, down to the trick he's saved to stop the show: a 540 shove-it, unheard of then and pretty much unheard of now. He picks out a judge, locks his eyes, kicks it, and lands, blind.

ROD walked off the course, looking at the concrete, Stacy shook his shoulders and told him what he knew: He had a 95.33 and a 95.0. Rocco had a 94.33 and 94.00. Rodney Mullen was fourteen and the new freestyle skateboarding champion of the world. Steve Rocco was twenty-four and the old one.

"I was really surprised. Shocked. Say I was shocked," is how Rocco put it in a later interview. "It's hard to get mad at something like that," he said in another. "He was going to take it to a level I couldn't take it to."

Rocco reportedly sprinted around in circles, not yelling but screaming, "HE DIDN'T WIN! RODNEY DIDN'T WIN!" Then he walked around, explaining to people that Rodney hadn't moved around at the bottom of the bowl, and he had. One observer described him as "rabid."

Rod remembers Stacy "bursting with excitement," while he himself felt "serene." At first. He was making peace, saying goodbye to skating, accepting it because he didn't know what was going to happen when he tried to stop. They handed him one of those giant plastic trophies with a volleyball-padded skater on top. For the last year he'd focused with his dad's special drive on winning this contest. Now he'd won it.

ROD HAD THAT after-qualifying-exam or leaving-your-retirement-party feeling. He walked down to the other end of the park to watch the skaters ride the bowls. Among them was a ragged blond kid who Rod remembers as "the skinniest person I have ever seen. The kid lived fifteen minutes away and skated to school at 8 a.m. so he could skate for half an hour before school started, then skate home so his dad could drive him to the skatepark. When a homework assignment asked him to describe a fantasy invention, his response was 'a gun that would turn ocean waves into concrete so I could skate them.'"

The kid's wearing elbow pads on his knees and tape around his shoes and weighs so little he can't build the momentum needed to roll off the ramp's lip and get airborne. Instead, he jumps his board off the coping, catching it in the air, which gives him greater height and longer hangtime than anyone's getting right now, since no one's ollie-ing into air. Rodney locks into his skating because their approach is the same. Every move is a seeable step into another one, and the parts make a whole fluid sequence. Rod can appraise that each trick's been dissected and each part studied and tweaked and put back and tried again and again and again, until it gets that strange absent feel that looks slow and easy, although it's impossible.

Sore-losing kids have actually given both skaters the same nickname: Robot. Rodney was so stoked that he got up his courage to introduce himself. The kid's name was Tony. You could think of Tony Hawk as a ramp-skating version of Rodney with a really supportive dad. Tony was twelve that day at Oasis, and unknown. It would be another year or two before he would really start to win, and then another year before he joined the Bones Brigade with Caballero and Christian Hosoi, shortly before turning unbeatable. Tony's trajectory was not the same as Rodney's, whose trajectory, while amazing, looks like a baking-soda rocket next to that of Sheckler, who grew up an hour away. It's not just a PR thing that Rod and Tony were and still are friends. It makes sense. They are both technically minded obsessives who only want to skate, and as a result, they're much, much better than everyone else.

Rod called home that night and flew back the next day. He rode to the airport in the new corduroys and polo that Mrs. Mullen had bought him for the trip, and after Stacy dropped him off he walked back out to the pick-up area's big sidewalk so he could watch him drive away. He didn't skate that morning outside the airport, or down the long tiled hallway at the beginning of *Jackie Brown*, which is too bad, because it's a great place to skate. He'd promised to stop skateboarding after the contest, and it was after the contest.

# 11

# UNABLE TO DO ANYTHING, MAGIC MOUNTAIN, V. C. JOHNSON, AND THE CHESS KING

RODNEY'S MOM met him at the Gainesville airport. It was a two-hour-long, mostly silent ride home, and when they got back, Rodney took his board upstairs and put it in his closet. That night he laid everything from the trip out on his bedspread: an LAX tourist brochure, stickers from Stacy, receipts from every purchase (including the one for his first smoothie), and bundled them all in a paper-bag time capsule, which he kept hidden. Rodney spent the next two days fingerskating and writing a novella-length account of the trip. He was "unable to do anything with the time in which I formerly skated."

At the end of the second day he received two calls from Powell brass, and the next night, a call from a reporter. This one wrote for *Skateboard News*, a vague, now-extinct newsprint publication that also covered roller-skating. They were doing an article on him, and so were some other reporters, including one for *Skate-Boarder*, who teased the Oasis contest on the cover, and whose article featured three photos of Rodney.

Rod hung up fifteen minutes later and was summoned to the family room for an interview about the interview. Mr. Mullen had heard everything:

"Who was that?"

"A skateboard magazine."

"A real magazine?"

"Yes, sir."

"They're doing an article on you? Just you?"

"Yes, sir."

"Who called last night?"

"Stacy Peralta."

"Stacy . . . Is that the guy who took care of you in California? He paid for everything?"

"Yes, sir."

Mr. Mullen chuckled, which was usually a good sign.

"Damn, Rod, I can't believe that all these people are calling you from across the country. I like how you handled yourself in that interview—very mature. I'm proud of you. You know, with all of these people investing money in you, maybe you should keep skating. It wouldn't be right for me to tell you to quit—if they have all this money invested."

Rod shakily grabbed Mr. Mullen's hand and bounded up the stairs, then out toward the garage. The last time he'd skated was at Oasis, and there was still California desert dust all over his board. There was a time of brief celebration and attention and celebrity in the skate world that he lived nowhere near. Rodney had just turned fourteen but looked much younger, with big cheeks and blond hair and militarily engrained old school manners. Stories about this cute child world champion were safe. Editors could take out his quotes about math, which they still do today.

It was a bonsai version of the attention Sheckler received the year he turned pro, at age thirteen, winning the four biggest contests of the year. Mr. Mullen kept saying, "Just know that this is very temporary," but new things seemed to keep happening. Rod could freestyle skate in one place, without a ramp that required hauling and assembly in a packed mall or TV studio. You can still watch footage of morning-show people standing there smiling with wooden-looking haircuts, in outfits that only existed in

1980, talking into pencil mics: "Please welcome skate . . . boarder extraordinaire, Rodney Mullen!"

He would glide onto the set and execute what today would be like a nollie 360 and somehow land it bolts, without rolling away.

Rod also had the best marketing person in maybe the whole history of the sport. Like Tony Hawk, Peralta's athletic talent was revered in the community. Also like Hawk, very soon after leaving competitive skating, Peralta established a name for himself as an industry figurehead. Everyone knows he has a great scouting eye, but Hawk and Rodney also praise his mentorship. Peralta was selective. He chose a small team of versatile riders who dominated different aspects of both the sport as a whole and each individual contest, skaters he could offer up to various sponsors so that no one truck or wheel company would flow the whole team. And he not only saw Rodney's limitless potential, but also the very fragile casing it came in, and the pool of robotic-shark-infested acid in which the case was floating. He worked with the family and answered any and all of Mr. Mullen's questions, calling him "sir." Apart from all this, he was there for Rodney, who remembers: "He let me know that if I ever needed anything, at any time, I should not hesitate to call him."

Peralta pretty much saved Rodney, and it's hard to imagine what's happened to the countless nearly-as-good skaters who didn't have a Peralta in their lives, and today dwell nameless just outside skating's strange history, a history that if you look close or just talk to a few pros you'll see is full of neglected, abused, manic, and un-nurtured people.

BY THE END of the year Stacy had Rodney on another flight to LA, and for reasons this reporter doesn't get and no one will explain to me, arranged for him to stay with Steve Rocco. Rocco was still the second-ranked freestyler in the world. A high school dropout who did accelerated number theory problems in his spare time, Rocco liked to fistfight with his four brothers at their house in Hermosa Beach, which had a balcony where they hung out and threw comp'd wheels at passersby.

The night Rod arrived, he, Stacy, and Rocco went out for a skate. It's the first time Rodney stood on his skateboard without pads. It's also the first time he loosened his trucks at Steve's (shall we say) suggestion and began to move a little instead of staying in one place, which becomes a lot more important later.

Stacy introduced him to Craig Stecyk (Lowboy), and they got on great. They drove to the Coca-Cola factory for his first photo shoot. He also met V. C. Johnson, who, thanks to talent-eyed Peralta, was the new main graphics guy at Powell.

They discussed a pro model, and they all—or Johnson alone—decided on a robotic dog, a mutt, which Mr. Mullen later said looked like a rat. Not only did it not catch on, but the board had such a screwed-up shape that Rod couldn't even ride it, and went back to shaving down Ray Bones decks to freestyle size.

But his next deck is a classic: a shrunken, narrow, rounded freestyle board with a scooped nose and low tail. The graphic is as famous as the Hawk skull: a skeleton locked in a casper on a chessboard, whirling a crown on his bony finger. It was a pro model, which contractually meant Rodney made almost a dollar for every deck sold.

It was 1981, and about two years before skating would pick up again. Historians point to insurance costs that closed the majority of the skateparks, but it's hard to think a supply wouldn't have existed if demand was still high. Regardless, sales plummeted just as makers were completing massive orders from skating's peak the year before. Like the end of the 1960s wave, warehouses were left full of '70s boards and the cylindrical glow-in-the-dark wheels—the other reason it's easy to find a '70s board today. *SkateBoarder* had turned to an extreme sports/BMX magazine called *Action Now* to stay alive. Oasis closed weeks after Rod had won there, leaving almost no parks open apart from the famed Del Mar Skate Ranch, Hawk's stomping ground inside skating's cradle of civilization. One local described Sensation Basin being as "crowded as the moon," and the park now had only one employee: Barry.

There are all kinds of reported statistical illustrations to offer you, but the important thing is that sales were way, way down. The royalty checks Rodney earned for his board were often under $10. Peralta assured him it was okay, and it was.

Rodney was also in a new place, feeling supported but also having entered a cascade period where his obsessive work started paying off. In late '81 he easily won his second pro contest, retaining his world champion title and fourteen-year-old communal celebrity status.

After the contest, which was held at Six Flags Magic Mountain in Los Angeles, Rod and Rocco rode the Colossus. It was there, in the front row, where the second-best freestyler in the world told him: "No one's going to beat you anymore."

12

# THE GOLDEN AGE OF
# SKATEBOARDING, OR TONY HAWK
# WAS SIXTEEN IN 1984

SKATEBOARDING'S GOLDEN AGE followed the '70s crash. The 1980s saw the rise of vert skating, the birth of street skating, the death of vert skating, Tony Hawk in a *Police Academy* movie, the apparel industry explosion, and the birth of our other main character. It was a busy time, and it's not going to fit into one chapter.

In 1981, Powell-Peralta was making 500 decks a month and released a sixteen-minute video that went nowhere. Stacy Peralta briefly took up acting and managed the team part-time.

*Action Now* folded after six issues, with final stories on mud-pit swimming and the extreme equestrian culture. Oasis skatepark closed. So did Skateboard City and both Skateboard Heavens. Thirteen parks shut down in two years around Los Angeles, the skatepark capital of the world. Rodney's stomping ground, Sensation Basin, was also history.

The numbers had dropped off again, but this time there was a strong core of skaters with a more confident identity, a core that revealed itself before the sport even fully bottomed out, and a core the industry guys knew was not just there, but hungry. Indy Truck Company's Fausto Vitello published the first *Thrasher* magazine in January of 1981. It cost $1 and was a thirty-page sheaf of newsprint. A far cry from the glossy pages of *Skate-Boarder*, *Thrasher* identified and marketed the culture's idea of embraced rawness and the loud voice of the outsider, just like

95

Stecyk's articles had. Skaters wrote the Trick Tips section, and readers were invited to send in their own photos for the Photo-graffiti page. *Thrasher* had a motto that showed up on stickers and T-shirts: Shut up and skate. Articles included "Secret Spots," and were almost as much about trespassing into public water facilities and industrial parks as they were about skating them. A lot of the vert riders in photos weren't wearing pads. An Indy ad pictured Rick Blackhart using his board to smash someone's window. The same guy also had a column called "Ask Dr. Blackhart." *Thrasher* covered and endorsed underground music, especially the local SF punk scene. The book's dimensions match those of *Rolling Stone* a few blocks away.

*Thrasher*'s premier issue also included instructions on how to build a wooden skate ramp alongside a call to arms: "Ramps provide the same vertical rush that can be so commonly found in a park or pool type situation," read issue number one. "It's free and it's legal. The only rules are your own."

It was true. As the last parks closed, more and more wooden ramps appeared at skaters' and skaters' parents' homes. The sport moved onto private property, removing the operating costs, especially for insurance, that had wiped out the last gener-ation's places to skate. Throughout the '80s, the vast majority of not just vert skating but vert contests were held in people's back-yards. They were named and known the way parks were in the '70s: Joe Lope's Ramp in East Bay, Raging Waters Ramp in San Jose, Clown Ramp in Dallas (with its blue and yellow stripes), and the Barn Ramp in Rochester, New York.

It's hard to apply these home-front scenarios to most other sports, but if you think of them as venues for concerts, it makes a lot more sense. It also explains why images of '80s contests look more like those of performances than sporting events, makeshift and often outside, with uneven crowds fit into the free spaces around the show. Besides the ramp's edge, there's never much of a barrier. The lawn around the ramp is unevenly packed, and the Pros are always on the platform with the Ams, photographers, and fans—especially female fans. At big events, sometimes you see people on the roof or up in a tree.

Ramps weren't bowls, or even really "halfpipes." They were built of 2-by-4s covered with plywood; the riding surfaces were often layered with Masonite. They were shaped like a U with an elongated flat bottom that met a wall in a quick transition. A really quick transition. So quick you couldn't believe it. So quick that your first time you'd likely ride not up the ramp but into it, hitting the vert like a wall. (I hit the vert like a wall.) Then a few turns later, if you pumped hard and stayed low, you might get up a few feet but might also lack the g-forces to stick, which meant you'd flop over as if trying to stand in a spinning funhouse tunnel.

At the top of the 10-foot wall is a right angle where the vertical wall and the horizontal platform come together. They don't quite come together, though. Usually there's a 2- or 3-inch gap between the wall and the platform, and placed here is a length of steel pipe, called the coping.* Coping protects the ramp's wooden lip and mimics the edge of a pool.

First an obstacle, coping was incorporated by pool skaters who executed the first grinds, slides, and one-wheeled turns before rolling up into the air. Once adapted to ramps, coping became a straight length of steel instead of a chipped curve of concrete. This opened up a new plane of sliding and grinding that hugely informed the beginnings of street skating, a curious sideways development birthed from the vertical culture.

---

\* *Coping* is a masonry term from the Latin *cappa,* meaning "cap." It also means to cover, as in a cope, or priest's vestment. *Cope* also has a second definition: "to cut."

Because of the coping, an aerial off a vert ramp wasn't a clean launch from the wall into the air, like a ski jump. It just looks that way. Watch some footage: Riders pick up their wheels or roll over the coping before they're airborne. And different ramps have different coping. SoCal's Upland Pipeline ramp had a far-protruding lip that one pro said "ripped my board out from under me." This gradually improved, and today a good craftsman will sometimes fit the coping *inside* the ramp, so the steel lip just slightly protrudes from the gap between the wall and platform.

As in pools, airs started out small, like an energized turn or disaster; the board went up over the lip and landed with the coping between the trucks. But riders were soon executing more of a bank or hill move you didn't see much of in pools: handplants, wherein the rider did a quick one-handed stand on the coping, gripping the board with the other hand, then either turning around or going down backwards, a little like a cartwheel or gymnast's vault over a horse. There are also footplants, wherein the rider keeps one foot on the board and pushes off or turns on the coping with the other.

Both plants developed endless variations (sadplant, beanplant, eggplant), and pros like Neil Blender and Eddie Elguera emerged as pioneering experts of lip tricks. Eventually skaters held poses like these as they launched, pulling tricks like the Madonna Air, gripping the board's nose with the front leg kicked out behind and the back foot on the tail. They also left both feet on and held with one hand, bending their knees (backside air), or they kept their front leg straight (melon), or back leg straight (bone). Tricks could be done in reverse or with toeside or heelside grabs, or no-handed, or without turning around (aka, "to fakie"), or higher or faster or just bigger. It was a whole catalog of moves, taking place first on the ramp, and then above it.

Ramps quickly got bigger and better, with skate shops and companies chipping in, or building them inside their warehouses. They varied width- and lengthwise, but within a sport that's rooted in variation, full-sized halfpipes were and still are almost always 10 or 12 feet high. It's the height that matters. Skating was growing. Soon there were many more ramps than there had ever been parks, and many more contests than at the peak of the '70s.

Winning basically all of these was Tony Hawk: sixteen years old, world champion, a growing 6-foot-1 and 135 pounds of cuts and tape. Footage from the time shows a kid in pads that look like basketballs on his legs and a neck so penciled that his helmet's proportional to one of those giant foam cowboy hats or something. He doesn't look particularly engaged or removed or aggressive or not aggressive. They just call his name and he walks over and clicks onto the coping, then steps on his board and rolls down the wooden wall and stiffly bends as he hits the first transition, then stays bent, flying across the bottom of the ramp and up and off the other side, into the air.

Every other pro grabs the underside of the deck as they're blasting off, but Hawk usually won't even touch the board for the first 4 feet. He's kind of standing with his back and knees a little bent, going higher and higher with the board floating underneath him. He and his board have the same angle and trajectory. His shoes are pink rags a size thirteen. His bangs are white out from under his helmet and his nose is huge and his expression almost passively goofy. He's looking down at the board that's moving out and up from under his feet. It all seems slow and easy, like an end-zone lob, but it's only been three seconds, and the one moving piece has become two moving parts.

The board's nose lands in the web of his lax left hand. He's about 8 feet over the steel cylinder of the ramp's lip, which is 12 more feet above someone's packed lawn. The platform is crowded with older skaters and still-older photographers. Mark Gonzales wears a shirt with Tony's picture and the word TECHNICIAN. There's that moment after he roars off the ramp when all you can hear is the wind through his clothes and the slowing oiled hiss of his wheels. Few people talk when Hawk skates. They just scream when he lands.

Just before he starts to fall, he twirls the board in his fingers. He's already picked up his feet to make room for the roll. His body is slightly bent and tilted to maybe one o'clock and 20 feet above the ground as his sneakers touch the griptape, the deck's tip between his thumb and forefinger. He's in that place between rise and fall, high above, biting his lip in puzzled bemusement because the trick is done and he has all the time in the world.

Hawk called this move "the Mutt Air," an adaptation of the flatground invention Rodney named "the fingerflip." On this particular run, Hawk would turn as he fell, and land with his back wheels all but clipping coping that's out 2 inches from the wall, then ride down 10 vertical feet of chipped plywood across the ramp's flat with four seconds to set up something else. Sometimes if he was in the mood, he'd land backwards and go into the next air to fakie. On this day he'd do a handful of things that he'd invented and that no one else will even try, because the other best people in the world just barely know where to start. They don't have technical wizardry, persistent creativity, or unearthly power of flight, and he does, all at once, in spades.

Hawk was one of those guys who was so good that people forget about the other really good guys, like Blender or Duane Peters or the prodigy, Steve Caballero, who at the peak of his powers could sail 10 feet high and invertedly push his foot off the warehouse ceiling's I-beam. At the first X Games, Hawk privately asked the press to expand their coverage to some other skaters. But they wouldn't, and they wouldn't because there's a reason everyone saw him and forgot about everyone else. In this way he's a lot like Rodney.

⌃

CHRISTIAN HOSOI was Hawk's one close competitor, and if Hawk was a robot, then Hosoi was an angel made of fire. His skating was purely, expressionistically pyrotechnic. His tricks were poses, stretched at top speed, going both incredibly high and far across the ramp, upside down with his back arched and mouth screamingly open and one hand in the air. He did huge backside airs, but did them sideways with his shoulders parallel to the ground. He did 540s, but with a seeming slow motion that no one still understands today. He had that Shaun White thing, where he was just 3 feet higher than everyone else, and that Troy Polamalu thing, where his moving shape is just different and changes the air around him. Hawk will tell you that Hosoi went higher and faster than anyone, and basically every big contest that wasn't won by Hawk was won by Hosoi, with Caballero in third.

Hosoi was also Hawk's opposite off the ramp. The son of the Marina Del Ray skatepark manager of Pacific Island descent, he had untied hair down his back and a rare chiseled build, and either cut his shirts into streamers or wore them on his head or stuck them in his pants so they'd flare out as he flew. He joined and quit most every team, including Powell, before starting his own company, Hosoi Skates. He also had probably the weirdest board of the entire skate-huge '80s, the "Hammerhead," which featured a small curved nose with giraffe knob shapes at the end.

The board was painted an uncommon-for-skateboarding white with a big red sun rising on the back, and was so popular that counterfeit models were sold.

Vert's rise was Hosoi's rise, a time when skating took flight, in large part due to him. There's never been anyone like Hosoi, and to understand this, you kind of had to have seen it, because describing it is like trying to describe war and sex. Caballero was a great expressionist, but also technically sharp, and there's a cancellation factor since you can't see both at once. Hosoi was just a stretched, flaring black shape in the air, so far above the ramp that he seemed nowhere near it, and closer to something else, like the sky. His height and hangtime kept growing, and his airs took him not just above the coping, but seemingly out over the middle of the ramp, his hair down to his waist now as he blasted off, leaving his crouch as he grabbed his board and took to the air, legs straight and together, arms at three and nine o'clock, flying.

Though ever united, at contests some skaters veered toward either a Hawk or a Hosoi camp, though of the two, Hawk had more influence. This is because he was so technical, it allowed skaters to dissect and try to copy what he created. Hosoi, on the other hand, was one of a kind, a huge purple flame, and no one could really get near what he did, whatever that was. His skating was more of a presence you were in. Remembers pro Jason Lee: "He shook the ramp."

Like his skating, Hosoi was larger than life. He rode shirt- and sometimes helmetless, bringing girls up onto the halfpipe that he was about to dominate and had just been smoking pot under. During vert's peak, he bought the old W. C. Fields estate in Echo Park and installed a giant halfpipe on the lawn. He had so many people and parties there that it was more like one huge unceasing party. When Hosoi wasn't in LA he liked to hang out in

Maui, this twenty-year-old, convertibley cruising around with "a million girls" and a posse of yellow-Walkmaned skaters trying to look just like him. There were no parents or coaches or managers or accountants, and he was reportedly making $250,000 a year, and it makes sense that he went down with the '80s.

SKATING WAS GAINING MOMENTUM. Nine months after its premier issue, *Thrasher* had a glossy cover and eighteen more pages. In the spring of 1983 the folks behind Tracker trucks published the first *TransWorld Skateboarding*, a more photo-based magazine printed on better paper, with the motto "Skate and Create." It was $1.75 per issue, more reader-friendly, and quickly found a solid readership. Life was good. Rodney had the top-selling freestyle deck, and while Tony Hawk's first signature model featured a Wildlife Treasure Card–like illustration of a hawk clutching purple lightning bolts in its talons, it was soon replaced with the famed hawk-skull graphic. His monthly royalty checks went up from $4.50 to $1,000.

HOME VIDEOS came to skateboarding in the 1980s, and were so revolutionary that we need to spend four paragraphs talking about them.

In 2010, Tony Hawk referred to a Battle at the Berrics contest, where P-Rod beat PJ Ladd with a nollie front-foot flip. The Berrics is the most-visited skate site on the Internet, with more traffic than all of the skate-media sites. It's updated every day with different videos filmed in an LA warehouse skatepark owned by former pros Steve Berra and prodigy Eric Koston. The site has footage of various pros skating the park, contest battles between different skaters, team visits, and a section where visitors can watch a pro do one trick over and over. (Check out Lizard King's 4-foot kickflip. It's the sickest thing you ever saw.) During runs, certain tricks are slowed down, and when a skater does a longer line, the cameraman will skate alongside. Besides what you see, there's little information about what the skaters do in these runs. The regular viewers know, because they're skaters. That's the site's whole approach and one reason it's the most popular.

Inevitably someone was going to create a popular "skaters-only" video, but Stacy Peralta was the first. In October 1984 Powell released *The Bones Brigade Video Show* on VHS and altered the sport yet again. It wasn't the first skate film, but it was the first skate film made by a former pro who was also a marketing genius. It was organized with filmed parts for each rider, but also by terrain, with segments where the team skates in a pool, half-pipe, the LA River's banks, or famous street spots kids had only read about in magazines. Skaters could sit at home or crowd into shops and watch and re-watch the pros' latest advancements. The really hard stuff is shown again and again, then again in slow motion, just like today.

The video was another Peralta/Stecyk collaboration and thus brilliantly catered to the audience they knew was out there. It begins with Peralta pickaxing a cheesy TV news story on skateboarding, followed by a punk-scored barrage of quick-cut footage, some of it shot from a skateboard. The video doesn't introduce ramp or downhill or freestyle, and each skater is introduced with a he-needs-no-introduction introduction.* Especially the team's young wunderkind, who enters the picture when good old Lance

---

* Rodney's section includes an I'm-pretty-sure-unexpected walk-on of two policemen, wherein his music stops and Peralta plays the *bus-ted* horn riff from *Dragnet*. Police run-ins are a part of every skate video. We'll explain why in Vallely's section.

Mountain sees the hawk-skull deck on a shop's wall, and then there's a cut to the same board, held high on the lip of a concrete wall by a thin bandaged hand. Spacey music is playing. Peralta doesn't tell us who it is. He knows we'll recognize the skater and his board. It was a risk to confusingly not point any of this out, but it was also a very calculated non-risk, because the bond he would form with those watching, those in the know, those whose parents kept asking questions they got to answer with a loud exhale. And those people would stick with Peralta and love his movies in the same way they love *Thrasher* and the Circle Jerks and a new bumper sticker that says SKATEBOARDING IS NOT A CRIME. It's this attitude and sales approach that helped Powell build an empire.

The video cost $15,000 and was a huge success, quickly selling 30,000 copies at $20 each and prompting Powell to invest in a second project the following year. The video, *Future Primitive,* was released in 1985. It opens with a scene simply labeled SF: GUERRERO that follows street-jumping-over pro Tommy Guerrero down the hills of San Francisco. The movie, even more insidery with harder music and shots of some of the skaters in drag, was even more successful. Each member of the Powell team started selling over 7,000 decks a month (with $1 royalty), and Peralta directed four more top-selling videos, now all available on DVD.*

By 1987 skating's colors were flashing. Everything came in color, often in neon or calico, from wheels to trucks to rails and copers. Griptape turned from black to blue and then to pink and lime, and was laid out in hand-cut patterns or decorated with Magic Marker. Decks were now layered wood and stained or painted, but the graphics that used to include just the brand's

---

* In 2005 Peralta rereleased *The Search for Animal Chin,* his most famous and successful Bones Brigade video. The special edition included an extra DVD with the punk rock score, a making-of documentary, and commentary by all the guys.

name on the top became more detailed, like the Bones Brigade logo. New wheels were curved on the inside to prevent hang-ups on coping. Lots of clothes came in that dark turquoise that only existed in the '80s. Skaters started designing pads you see today, like Rector or Pro Designed. A young Hoosier named Axl Rose did a portrait for *Circus* magazine with his McGill board. The Swatch watch company sponsored Rodney.

Skating became so popular that Hollywood came calling a second time. The Bones Brigade is featured in *Police Academy 4* and showed up again in *Gleaming the Cube*, wherein a young heartthrob named Christian Slater plays a lonesome skater trying to solve the mystery of his brother's murder.* Scoring his first speaking role is Hawk, who drives a Pizza Hut delivery truck with a roof like a Pizza Hut. Before the big final chase there's a solitude-before-battle scene in a high empty building site, where Slater takes his shaved-down, skidplated deck for a freestyle session. The scene was shot by Peralta, who was the second unit director on the film, and the skater is actually Rodney, silhouetted in a terrible wig, balletically manipulating his board before the big red setting sun. His scene ends with a megaspin, and when he finally spends the last of his energy, he's on the edge of one wheel, turning in what looks like slow motion.

*Thrashin'* appeared the year before and was for all intents and purposes the same movie but with a teenage Josh Brolin, wearing his wrist guards backwards on the poster. Club MTV set up a mini-ramp in the studio, and after an odd bit of dance-skateboarding, Downtown Julie Brown endured a short, uncomfortable interview with Mark Rogowski, aka Gator. Nickelodeon premiered *Sk8 TV*, a Saturday morning show directed by Peralta

---

* The Cube, if you're wondering, is "the place you skate when you let *go*," explains Slater's friend Yabbo, in the not-even-proofread-for-a-skater script. The talk takes place in Yabbo's very cool subterranean hideout, complete with a pipe for skating.

and hosted by a young full-head-of-haired Matthew Lillard, of *SLC Punk!, Scooby-Doo,* and *House* fame. *Sk8 TV* was shot at the Pink Motel in Sun Valley, with a gorgeously deep whale-shaped pool, and hosted top pros like Alva and Hawk, but also did spotlight segments on newcomers like street wizard Jeremy Klein.

SKATE APPAREL made its first real appearance this decade, and quickly dwarfed all other sales. Kick-starting everything was Vision, who in 1989 reported an $89 million turnover and whose Vision Street Wear line produced shirts, pants, shorts, shoes, big fanny packs, and those weird berets made of T-shirt material, which Peralta wore throughout this time. Board graphics like checkerboards and crossboned skulls and crackles or Gator's cubistic whirl found their way not just onto shorts and shirts but also sneakers. Christian Hosoi got his own Vans shoe with a rising sun logo, an early step in what was going to become a $2 billion market. Soon everyone was following suit, including surf apparel companies like Gotcha and Jimmy-Z.

Everything was growing. Caballero hit 11 feet above the coping at Raging Waters Ramp. Blender, who by the end of the '80s proved to be one of the strangest people in the history of professional sports, invented lip tricks the way Mullen invented freestyle tricks, and filmed a video part in drag with a lampshade on his head. Powell sponsored a young, fearless, and extremely competitive teen named Danny Way.

Powell was at the forefront, with the best image, riders, artists, and a lot of the top-selling T-shirts. Note: Like surf shops, skate shops always sell merch, which like pro sports apparel is really expensive considering what it is—a screened T-shirt for $15 in 1987. Powell bought a 185,000-square-foot facility that housed product and a private skatepark, and a tour rig with a full-size ramp that unfolded hydraulically. Life, still, was good.

Hawk, whose deck royalties had reached $20,000 a month, bought a second kind of country home that one pro described as "a Jonestown for skaters." The house had four acres and a crazy bowl-into-halfpipe mega-ramp Hawk built with his dad, Frank. While at camp in Stockholm, vert technician and Powell rider Mike McGill figured out—over one legendary lunch hour—how to work a forward flip into a 540, called the McTwist. Hawk was there, and while he didn't get McTwists at first, he'd amped his 540s up to 720s, and could get two full rotations every time. It was then that he began to wonder if he could one day get another half-rotation. Could one day get a 900.

# 13

# RODNEY INVENTS AND WINS EVERYTHING, AND HIS DAD MAKES HIM QUIT, AGAIN

APPLICABLY, the 1980s was an important time in the life of history's most progressive skater. He was a prominent member of skating's greatest team during the sport's golden age, but remained in Florida, free to develop with little outside influence, at a distance that would prove safe once the tide began to shift.

From 1982 to 1984, Rod flew three times to world contests but otherwise stayed at home to obsessively work. He was between the ages of sixteen and eighteen, and his practice regimen was two timed hours of hard skating every day. He stopped his Casio if he needed to drink or pee, and didn't start it again until both feet were back on the board. He eventually timed his breaks, and whittled those down.

He had all the free gear he wanted, no parks to skate at, and a lot of room to run. The rural environment offered few distractions (the closest skater was 20 miles away), but it was mostly just that Rodney's drive had reached full bore. He'd become admittedly a lot like his dad, and he pretty much was going to stay this way. Work was hard and he had a strict routine, and nothing could interfere with it. He ran stairs every day and counted his calories and lifted weights, and once a week, he ran a mile faster than the week before. At the end of every skate session (around midnight) he notebooked what went on, what he'd tried and achieved, and outlined a hypothesis for the next night. His grades were award-assembly-winningly perfect even though he was missing school for demos, and two different teachers were tutoring him in number theory and advanced mathematics.

This is also around the time when Rodney began looking less like a tomboy and more like a Ken doll. Obsessive training and diet, mixed with Florida farm work and very good genes, had turned him lean and toned, which complemented his full, parted blond hair and nice tan. He still hiked his shorts up over his hips and tucked shoelace slack back into his sneakers, but overall we're really improving. He'd also started doing math problems on his own, read the Bible three times, and in general, become the person he is today: an obsessive, studious, nocturnal prodigy, possessed by genius and the need to progress.

At sixteen years old, he was circling his garage on a little deck with a skidplate and noseguard. In the next eighteen months, he would introduce the world to modern skateboarding. Rodney finally premiered the ollie in Whittier, California, at the 1982 Rusty Harris Series, a contest named after a late skate photographer. He'd nurtured and perfected it, and before the contest showed Peralta how high he could go. Peralta made him do it over and over again, and after the win they drove up the coast to meet Fausto and set up an arrangement with Independent Trucks. While there, Rodney was also shot by Stecyk for the October cover of *Thrasher*, padded in high, stiff socks at the apex of what looks like a two-foot ollie.

*TransWorld* also covered the Del Mar 1982 Championship for their first issue. "Then came Mutt to give another clinic," was how they put it. One of the judges didn't give Rodney a 100 and someone yelled, "What did he do wrong?!"

By April of 1983, Rod was back out at Del Mar, where he premiered what is still his favorite thing to do on a skateboard: the kickflip, then referred to as the Magic Flip because no one knew what the hell they were looking at. He made it up for the contest, and in seven years, when everyone else caught up, it became a staple of modern skateboarding. Think of the flip, spin, and roll (which we'll get to) as all of the staples of modern skateboarding. Think of the ollie as the stapler. And think of Rodney's brain as the twenty-four-hour Kinkos on the outskirts of town, where kids would come and skate the loading dock late at night.

The kickflip originated from failure. From the countless times he'd tried to turn the board in midair but the weight or thrust was off and it had spun away, out of his control. Rod decided to get it under his control. He started to kick out on purpose, experimenting with pressure and placement and timing. Rod is regular-footed, so his left foot is up by the nose. He developed a front-footed downward flick on the heel side of his board, a motion he practiced until the board flipped the same every time. Now he needed to land it. To do so, he changed his ollie. He kept his rear foot straight across the tail but his front foot angled and hung over to the left. He popped the tail, and before the board was at its peak, he flicked down. He had it in two days. By the following year, when Peralta was shooting his part for an upcoming video, he could do four in the time it takes a fast person to do one today.*

Rodney has described the feat in a lot of different ways. It was a big, big deal to someone to whom skateboarding was so important that his mind and body would shut down if it was taken away. "Suddenly I could control my board after it was airborne," he recalls. "It was as if I'd learned to skate on another plane, one that hovered above the ground." He thinks of Hawk on vert. It's "a totally different feeling."

---

* In the next decade we'd see Mullen pioneer 360 kickflips, which were first askewed as a passing fad (so he'd double them), and then something called a helicopter flip, a 360 flip + 360 body varial, whose greatest champion is Chris Cole.

The new maneuver got a bigger response than anything he's ever done, before or since. It was 1983 and a lot of freestylers still did balletic stuff like handstands (which Rod in a couple more years would combine with a kickflip). And even the ones who weren't saw what Rod could do, and had a guitar-player-who-sees-Hendrix moment. They could not and did not want to emulate him. They wanted to quit. Oddly, it was at Del Mar that Rodney got the most crowd love of his life, and, due to a fall, where he placed second for the only time in his competitive career. He was beat by teammate Per Welinder, who later partnered with Hawk to form Birdhouse Projects. Hawk was also there that day; he took first in vert, and just for fun, competed in freestyle and placed seventh in a pro-level event at an international contest.

"THE IMPOSSIBLE" came about sometime in 1982, when Rod realized he could somewhat vertify the 360 shove-it, where your front foot lightly pins the flat whirling board so it won't flip over during a full rotation. Using good old trial and error, Rod figured out how to whirl the board end over end around his front foot, like a baton around an open hand. He called it "The Impossible," and it pretty much looks the way it sounds, though it makes more sense when you see who's doing it. For all practical purposes, he was the only person in the world who could do this for nearly a decade. Rod officially debuted the Impossible in 1982, at what's still often considered the biggest, most prestigious world championship of all time: Vancouver. He took first place, won $1,000 (Canadian), and scored the only perfect 100 in the history of the sport.

Rod named the maneuver the Impossible because when he first brought up the idea on a car trip, another freestyler said such a thing could not be done. (He won't say who it was, but I bet it was Welinder.) That the board just couldn't be made to roll end over end on the Y axis instead of the flat, off-to-the-side X axis. And while it is clearly possible, the trick is rare today, even among top pros. It's like you need preserved freestyle DNA and nerveless shins, and also, not care if you look like a moron the first 999 times you don't get it.*

Both skate magazines were either profiling or interviewing or having Rod write trick tips nearly every month, and by now his skating and image were as communally famous as Hawk's. He'd filled out, but his look was growing distinctive, skating in kneepads but no helmet, with selected fingers and both wrists wrapped in tape, with the Casio over the tape.

IN PHOTOS and video from this time, Rod was often shirtless because of the heat, and this is as good a time as any to point out that the reason skaters often look disheveled or grubby is because they're sweating hard. The stop-and go nature of trying a trick, stepping off, then trying it again sometimes credits the myth that skating falls on the lax side of athletics, like baseball. But skaters tend to sweat in both a general athletic way along with the way a body sweats when it's engaged with a racing mind. The way a musician or performer sweats. It's also why, regardless of the time of year, skaters rarely wear anything more than a hat, pants, and maybe a long-sleeved shirt under a T-shirt. In Mullen's later video parts, his back is always soaked with a giant dot of sweat. The exception here would have to be good old Lizard

---

* This said, a 2008 video featured Mr. Chris Haslam ending a dizzying line with a no-comply impossible 180, planting his back foot on the ground, turning 180 while his foot spun the board, and hopping back on. Rolling away, he clutched his head. Everyone else moaned.

King, who in early footage skates through Salt Lake City, clearing handrails over icy pavement in a cable-knit sweater. But believe me, skating's a sweaty sport.

▲

THIS PYROTECHNIC PERIOD of Rodney's development comes to a close at the 1983 World Championships, again in Del Mar. He gives the crowd and judges what they'd all been hearing about, debuting three new things no one knows the names of because he hasn't named them yet, and at the end goes into his showstopper. He's nailed everything perfectly, and now he crouches down and starts to spin on his back wheels. It's a 10,800—a thirty-timer—and as he whirls, teardrops whip away from his face.

Rod's dad had made him quit again. His reason: College was starting in the fall and it was time to grow up. But really it's because his dad was weirded out by the insomnia and anorexic training habits Rod had developed during the past two years. His dad laid it down this time, and in such a way that when he stood up from his chair, Rod instinctively took several steps back. He had no choice. Anyone who disobeyed or challenged his father was exiled and not spoken to again—no exceptions.

It was a bigger deal than last time. Rod had a young Mike Tyson's record, and debuted new forms of bewilderingly creative, technically difficult tricks every time he competed.

Most everyone at the 1983 contest knows he is quitting, and that this time, it's for real. People have been asking him about it all day. Fausto, now an industry power, had written Mr. Mullen a pleading letter, to no avail. It's over.

Walking off the course, Larry Balma's wife Corsa runs out and grabs Rod's face. She is crying harder than him. She says it's not the end. He scores a 99-99-99-99 and a 98. He is "incapacitated."

Weeping. A world champion. He stumbles over to the ramps to watch the vert contest. Hawk wins with a routine that includes the Mutt Air.

# 14

# NATAS, GONZ, AND THE BIRTH OF STREET SKATING

ONE GOOD REASON to call the 1980s the golden age of skate-boarding is because it was really two golden ages: vert and street. First called streetstyle, this form of skating took the giant step of leaving ramps and parks and hills, incorporating all things paved into the sport and opening up a whole new world. It's been said that the first big street wave rose from the ashes of vert, but in fact, both were born around the same time, pioneered by a similar small group of geniuses, some of whom were also competitive vert skaters.

Skaters had been incorporating street elements into the sport since at least, say, 1978, when the cover of *SkateBoarder* featured a pro named Paul Hoffman in a hang-ten nosegrind on a curb. But nothing was official until 1983, when the first street contest was held at Golden Gate State Park. Orchestrated by Fausto Vitello, the contest took place without a permit on—literally on—Conservatory Road, with a pyramid ramp made of wood that looked like this ⌒, and bigger wedge ramps that looked like half of that. Tommy Guerrero entered as an Am but won as a Pro, and the same year *Thrasher* ran a cover story called "The New Etiquette for a Street Society" (Stecyk, again).

Early tricks on street resemble early lip tricks on ramp. No one's ollie-ing quite yet, so skaters at the time would pick up the board and whirl it around, then jump on it or throw down on curbs or steps or walls. The quintessential boneless, like a footplant on vert, was a front-leg jump while your back foot stayed on the board. There was the "no-comply," a sort of one-footed push-kick to get over curbs with just your feet. As with vert, numerous foot- and handplants began to appear, often incorporating a wall to throw onto, ride down, or ride up in a weird handstand.

Two young pros who completely trailblazed this new genre were Natas Kaupas and Mark Gonzales. Natas grew up in an artistic household in Santa Monica, in proximity to both Dogtown and Peralta's parents. The Kaupases are Lithuanian, so Natas was and still is very fair, with bright blue eyes and hair that looks like wet white fire. He skated and surfed mostly alone; one day he won a surf contest and was awarded a promotional deck from SMA, or Santa Monica Airlines, founded by Skip Engblom.

Engblom, you'll remember, was the original shaper for Zephyr, and left to start SMA surfboards out of his garage. Prior to that he had worked as a teenager for Makaha Skateboards during skating's first wave. In 1978 he started making SMA skateboard decks, screened with a famous seaplane logo drawn by his girlfriend. The boards were wing-shaped and cutting-edge and sold well until the '70s crash. It was one of these discontinued boards that ended up under the young Lithuanian's feet.

Natas showed up one day at Engblom's shop, where he was still shaping surfboards. Engblom recalls, "One day this little kid comes skating up to the back door of the back room where I'm at, and he goes [in a bratty little kid's voice], 'I'm Natas and I want to be on your skateboard team.' "

Engblom watched him skate for under a minute and made him SMA's skateboard team and sole rider, since SMA didn't make boards anymore. Yet, like Rodney, Natas's accomplishments only fueled his drive, and he quickly started skating all day, every day, also alone. He is a creative genius and talented artist who devours information and tends to just see and think differently. His style was surfish. He took his board on long runs through areas where the driveways and homes and sidewalks of the neighborhoods were all one big angled concrete break, and he rode street lengths like they were one long wave, first just weaving but then going off stairs and drops and those steep little dips where driveways are set into curbs. He didn't skate one-spot, but instead followed a long clean line, passing through a series of points. No one else was doing this.

At fifteen Natas figured out how to hold onto his board while he jumped up on a wall, riding sideways for a second. It's called a wallride, and he was at least the first skater photographed doing it. Shortly thereafter, he began to do it no-handed, where he popped onto a wall and rode up or sideways, cruising along for a second on a whole new plane. Keen Ancell, a graphic artist and local skater at the time, saw an early execution of this. He said: "Mother. Fucking. Little. Bastard."

Natas ended up shooting pictures in Venice with Stecky, who sent them to *Thrasher*. He got the September '84 cover, riding a wall, and to see how far ahead he was, it's best to look far ahead rather than back. Natas had the quintessential heavy '80s hardware with a fishtailed deck, rails, and cylindrical wheels. Yet he did stuff the most unique guys are doing today. See, for instance, Daewon Song, foot ninja and Rodney's teammate, blurrily executing 540 flips not on flat ground like a normal sensei, but off angled banks, or on ramps placed on banks so they're angled at 80 degrees. Natas did nearly as impressive moves twenty years before off the base of a streetlamp post, a flipping 360 motion with a board three pounds heavier, once again finding and expanding a different plane.

Natas still skated to skate spots but also incorporated everything around him—the essence of street skating. He began grinding curbs, then plant banisters, then the bumpers of cars (shot by guess-who). The bumper shot ran in an issue of *Thrasher* that was picked up by another LA skater who preferred street to the craze of ramps. His name was Mark Gonzales.

Like Rodney, Gonzales (Gonz, hereafter) has creatively dominated at a pro level for more than thirty years, but unlike Rod, Gonz is a writer, filmmaker, and visual artist who has been doing such work for just as long. In 2009 he had a show of his sculptures and paintings at Half Gallery in New York City, and recently shot a Super-8 video for Coconut Records, Jason Schwartzman's band. He's collaborated with everyone from Spike Jonze to Harmony Korine (who filmed him in *Gummo*, wrestling a chair), and in 2008, at age forty-three, showed up at the Brooklyn Banks to shred before a generation-spanning crowd of cell-phone-wielding fans.

Gonz grew up in Los Angeles, was sponsored by Alva at fifteen, and the following year got *Thrasher's* November '84 cover, bonelessly launching off a jump ramp. No one was more aggressively creative than him, except maybe for Natas, and it makes sense that they found each other.

They're obviously not street's only pioneers. Powell rider Lance Mountain had a move where he walked his board along the wall, then went into a handplant he'd land on the pavement. Natas credits Zephyr rider Dan McClure with the original idea to skate up a wall. He also points to Eric Dresden, young Julien Stranger, and Jesse Martinez, who early on rode the board *down* walls instead of alongside.

Flatground ollies had mostly been a freestyle thing, but they got them quick, and went higher and higher, especially Natas, who had calves like a running back. Gonz used smaller, harder freestyle wheels to make higher ollies. They also studied Mullen's kickflip in the first Bones Bridge video, then took it outside. In a day they had it, except they were rolling. Soon they were doing it off curbs and higher off of streetlamp bases and paved hips.

They were way out there. The Natas Pro Model was released during this time of heavy metal and skull and general death graphics. His board was white with a black panther reaching his paw down from a triangle enclosed in ferns, and sold so well that Skip couldn't fill the orders. So Natas, then sixteen years old in 1987, brokered a deal with giant Santa Cruz, who agreed to partner with SMA if they could put their logo on the board. (I'll bet anything it was Natas's idea to put it at the center of the back truck holes, so you can't see it.)

Their footage today looks older, yes, but not if you look at what everyone else was doing on the street—or not doing. Companies were just starting to widely release videos that included vert, freestyle, an until recently extinct downhilling part, and "streetstyle" footage of skaters riding somewhere, doing fast 90-degree slides (aka, powerslides), then sliding back into place to keep rolling, sometimes rolling off banks or drops.

It was nothing like what these two and an upcoming inland Jersey punker named Mike Vallely were doing. One day Natas told Mark that he recently slid a handrail and wasn't feeling up to it right then, so maybe he should try it. Gonz made the first attempt, followed by Natas off the side of the stage at an Oceanside contest. He fell but he was close.* And they kept going. Natas did a truck stop on a fence. Skaters looked at gaps or benches or hydrants and said: "Natas could ollie that." They studied Mullen and went higher and higher with this newfound plane. They

---

* Rodney's best contribution to the rail genre is called a "darkslide," which is a railslide except the board is upside down, so the griptape side is sliding. It was Gonz's idea. Rod just figured out how to do it without holding on. And if you're wondering what the handrail situation is today, check out Lizard King's 270 spin into a backwards slide down a two-flight handrail, or Leo Romero, who in 2010 was the first skater filmed sliding *up* a handrail.

nailed handrails, first beautifully captured in 1988 in front of the LA Federal Building, a massive leap at a time when vert was just starting to slip.

One day Natas got a call from a Frenchman named Pierre, who represented a company called Etnies, Sheckler's first big sponsor when he was eight. Natas, already a top pro and manager of the SMA skate team, ended up designing a shoe for Etnies, as well as handling all of the ads and marketing.

In 1989, perhaps the biggest and brightest year in the whole fantastic history of skateboarding, Santa Cruz released *Streets on Fire*. The video has an infamous clip of Natas rolling around a corner and ollie-ing up onto a fire hydrant. On his way up he hooks his hand around a signpost so he can spin like a centrifuge atop the bolt of the hydrant. It's a 540 rotation, and he spins off then weaves back around the corner. He doesn't even land and stop, like, maybe to fall on his knees to pray. It's unprecedentedly technical, powerfully balletic, and skull-thumpingly original. Even within the most creative of physical pursuits during a time of great innovation, it's surreal. H-Street Pro Jeff Kendall, who will blow your mind in *Hocus Pocus* (out the same year), still remembers this: "I don't know," he says with a very serious shake of his head. "I still think it was smoke and mirrors. I don't know."

The next year Santa Cruz released *Strange Notes*,* featuring Natas 180-ing onto rails, 180-ing during long curb grinds, stuff you can look at right now on the Berrics website. Natas and Gonz were way ahead, but they also spearheaded the next, strange movement of the sport, as skating came crashing down and once again returned to the street.

* *Strange Notes* is also the name of another web video series featuring a recent small part with Chris Haslam doing what he called a hectop flip. P-Rod explains it in chapter 18 but it's basically a 180 switch-stance flip into a reverse back foot bigspin (360 boardspin + 180 degree body varial). It's so complicated that it takes multiple paused viewings in slow-motion mode just to see what he's doing, but it's about as easy as it sounds, and the best example I know of how far we've come.

# 15

# THE 1980S END, AND SKATERS DIE AND GO TO JAIL

TONY HAWK made $150,000 in 1989, $75,000 in 1990, and six months into 1991 was making less than his wife, Cindy, a manicurist at the Fallbook mall. She rationed him $5 a day for Taco Bell and ramen. The crash happened that fast, and while some point to the new popularity of Rollerblading to explain skating's demise, the sea change is also right on schedule with the nine-year tide of the sport's rise and sharp fall in pop culture.

The problem this time was that skaters had never been flying so high. The sport would be permanently altered four years later, and this crash would be the last of its kind, but the results were newly catastrophic for skateboarding at the time. They happened during the dormant period following the early '90s crash. In January 1993, H-Street pro Josh Swindell was jailed in Mexico for trafficking firearms. *Thrasher* interviewed him in a Tijuana prison, three months before he was arrested and convicted of the second-degree murder of a gay man outside a nightclub. Teammate Danny Way knocked the man out and testified at the trial, but walked. The same year, 1993, Santa Cruz airman and park owner Jeff Phillips committed suicide on Christmas Day with a .357 magnum. Before vert fell out, Mark "Gator" Rogowski went through a whole glam phase, changing his name to Gator Mark Anthony before losing everything and going to jail for rape and murder.

The best pros still skated, but not much. Steve Caballero played in a band. Lance Mountain raised his son. Hawk borrowed

$8,000 from his parents to buy secondhand video-editing equipment so he could freelance for street-skating companies. He did demos, but sometimes didn't get paid, or got paid and the checks bounced. He once traveled to Paris for $300, but the demo didn't cover expenses. He and his wife soon sold their house and demolished the ramp.

Christian Hosoi reportedly founded four companies that all failed, and then filed for bankruptcy. He started smoking meth, then smoking meth every day, then started smoking crack. He was arrested twice for drugs, and then a warrant was put out for him for skipping his court date. To avoid arrest he went underground, crashing with friends and sometimes non-friends for five more years, agreeing to appear in contests like the Extreme Games and then not showing up. He was finally arrested at Honolulu International Airport with a *Trainspotting*ly huge amount of meth (.68 kg), and sentenced to ten years.

Why did all this happen? It happened because kids were making a lot of money and no one was looking out for them, including the people who were making a lot of money by exploiting their talent. The typical overall figure assigned to the skate industry by the early '90s is $150 million. Naturally, a pyramid-style power system formed around this kind of money in a free-market country, and by the early '90s, three men controlled 70 percent of industry sales.

We mentioned them earlier: Fausto Vitello, Larry Balma, and newly emerged mogul Steve Rocco. We'll get to Rocco, and how this twenty-seven-year-old dropout ass clown would start World Industries, which he sold in 1998 for $20 million. Money like this can't be controlled by only three people without serious amounts of exploitation. By the end of the '80s, top vert riders were making between $100,000 and $200,000 a year. Many were teenage dropouts, and none felt the consequences until it was too late.

Vallely, Hosoi, and Rogowski all left high school to tour after they'd turned pro. Turning pro means you can compete for money. Turning pro is also the last point on a slippery slope of skateboard endorsement, and for the best pros is a step toward endorsement deals outside of the industry, for much bigger companies like SoBe or Nike.

The first step in sponsorship is small. It's getting free stuff from a shop. This can be as basic as the discounted gear Mullen got, a free pair of shoes, or a deck or two or three. A skater might put a shop's sticker on his board, or might not. As previously footnoted, a consistent relationship like this between a shop and a rider is called "flow."

Flow started for Rodney at age eleven. Ryan Sheckler was seven. P-Rod was fourteen. Flow usually starts with a shop, and branches out from there. P-Rod's flow shops were 118 Boardshop and Valley Skate & Surf, then DNA Skateboards who has a relationship with DVS Shoes, his first product sponsor. Naturally, there's never any oversight when it comes to the owner of a tiny skate shop giving kids stickers, and anyone who suggests there should be would face scorn, especially from skaters, since shops are usually skater-owned. But that's the first step, and it's a fairly quick ascent, especially if you're good and get attention. Being made a flow rider can also put you on a shop's team, which means you'd compete in competitions as an amateur, an Am. The next step for an Am is to turn Pro, becoming a paid rider who competes for money and rides a personalized Pro Model, wherein the rider receives a percentage for each deck sold.

Vallely quit school at sixteen and moved to California to skate for Powell, who at that point was the industry's Disney Studios, famous for distributing an instruction manual informing riders what they had to wear and what they could say in interviews, etc.

Vallely signed for Powell and Independent, and was soon making $100,000 a year. He signed his contracts without an agent or a lawyer, as did every other pro skater at the time.

A few were lucky and had deals brokered by people they could trust—Rodney with Peralta, for instance. Part of Hawk's legacy is that he was the first one, in 1998, to get an agent or lawyer, and was given shit in the community for doing so. Once represented, he learned he had been getting one-tenth of what he should have been making as a pro athlete.

At the time young skaters weren't considered actors, whose earnings and work environments were uber-monitored, and whose money would go into a hopefully evil-proof trust fund.* If skaters were treated like actors, working hours would have been restricted to times away from school, or they would have been supplied with private tutors. They would have had to come to work with a parent or designated guardian. Young pro skaters were also not considered amateur athletes, like basketball players. Had this been the case, recruiting would have been monitored on one end by a coach and on the other by the NCAA, which sets strict limits on scouts' contact with athletes.

Skate teams had—and still have—managers, who roughly double as coaches, but don't follow any kind of higher protocol with their athletes, the way a counselor would while working with a young student at a tech school or the business management program at a grocery chain. This is because one communal entity doesn't exist to monitor sponsorship relations in Am or Pro skateboarding. Organizations like CASL (California Amateur

* Applicable example: I went to high school with a guy who went on to play Sir Bedevere in *Spamalot* on Broadway. Once I told him a funny story I'd heard from a friend, who'd just seen the child actor who played Screech do standup in someone's garage. My old chum stopped time with the look he gave me, and said yes, he knew about Screech, then asked if I knew *why* Dustin Diamond was working the inland Jersey stand-up circuit, since he'd been on a show everyone knows the name of and that still airs today.

Skateboard League) or USA (United Skateboarding Association) or NSA (National Skateboard Association) are dedicated to promoting skating, building parks, and organizing contests. They're nothing like unions, and in fact represent the businesses much more than the skaters.

Skating is also in a non-category that makes it especially buzzard-prone. The sports/arts/performers/music/concert audience puts skaters in no one category, but caters to and sells merch in all of these categories, which works well for the money people and not well for skaters.

The Department of Labor considers skaters to be neither athletes nor actors. Their contracts are viewed more as commercial sponsorship deals than movie or sports deals. A skater who rides for a company is less a salaried member of a team and more a product endorser. Skaters model equipment and apparel in advertising, use it in tournaments, and promote it on tours. It's the reason why top riders like Chaz Ortiz change shirts and sometimes hats during contests. Big stars earn royalty checks for equipment that's marketed for skate wheels or apparel. These contracts aren't covered by child labor laws.

Given all of this, it's actually a testimony to the general goodness of the skate world that such exploitation doesn't happen more often. Of course, it's the big sports that tell the best/worst exploitation stories, stories long known and rarely discussed unless something outrageous happens, like when point guard Kevin Ross graduates from Creighton University even though he's illiterate. Or recent reportage on overused rookie pitchers and what they're doing today. Look these stories up. They'll make you angry and break your heart in that special burning way that exploitation makes you angry.

# 16

# RODNEY NEARLY DIES IN SWEDEN, AND THE BEGINNING OF THE 1990S

FOR ITS BEST GUY, skateboarding's final crash was a period of exceptional darkness and light. Hawk may have endured, but Rodney nearly died before being reborn.

Mr. Mullen's plan backfired. Banning skating did not take Rodney's quirks away. It fed them steroids and methamphetamine, and in the long run offered proof that skating was the only thing keeping his son's neuroticism under control. Without skating, Rod couldn't sleep or eat or feel anything but terrible, all the time. He saw the world, he remembers, "through a filthy window." It made him so crazy, in fact, that he defied his dad and kept a board at the high school, putting an hour in here and there on the tennis court. That only made it worse, because he could feel the decay, and after three months without skateboarding, Rod was a starved, twitching zombie. It was so bad that Mr. Mullen retracted. Rod even remembers a sole note of pleading in his voice when he told him he could skate again.

Within a few months, everything was back to normal. It was still the '80s, and while Rod remained the weird guy flipping his tiny board off to the side of the ramp, he was still one of skating media's superstars. He had the top-selling freestyle deck and demoed around the world forty weeks a year. Being a freestyler, he was left in the middle as vert's popularity sank and street developed. At contests, his events had always yielded the smallest crowd anyway, so drops in attendance didn't matter much. Plus, he could go to both street and vert demos, store openings, parades, etc., and just skate. He retained his sponsors and continued to win every contest.

Things started to change after his second year at U Florida, where he was 4.0-ing his way through a mathematics and biomedical engineering double major. One day after a particularly bad blowup over the lawn mower, Rodney essentially ran away from home, leaving his dad a one-page note of thanks, telling him he'd make him proud someday. He sought out his estranged grandmother, who let him sleep in her basement apartment, where his dreams were a combination "of drowning and my father coming after me." He tied kitchen pans to the door and kept a length of pipe under his pillow, just in case. He also got asthma from the basement, and saw a doctor who remarked on his high blood pressure.

Around this time, Rodney's long-lost uncle moved into his grandmother's house. A famously anonymous figure in Rodney lore, his uncle was a prodigy like his sister, had become a doctor and inventor, and then developed such an interest in the medical industry that he frequently wrote governor Bob Graham, advising him on the state's health-care crisis. He talked to Rodney about everything, from the beauty of physical chemistry to what it felt like to have a true nervous breakdown, to how he had tricked the State into giving him disability checks now that he'd served his time for contempt of court. He had learned Hebrew and Greek so as to better understand Aleister Crowley, whom he called "the beast." Just before Rod moved out, he decorated the basement apartment with pentagrams and tarot cards, and his uncle called him a "worthy recruit."

Rodney found a $240-a-month place in a housing project, next to a cemetery and an early meth lab. He kept his windows covered with black paper. He owned a chair, his books, and his stereo, and he ate out of empty yogurt containers with McDonald's silverware, walking through the cemetery at night. Twice during shopping binges his mother emptied his accounts, spending $10,000 and $20,000, and both times Rod was able to put it back. In the summer of 1989 Rod accepted an offer for $800 a week and a free apartment to do demos around Norway, where skating has thrived since 5000 BC. It was a good opportunity because things stateside had slowed down. At that time, his board was selling thirty copies a month internationally, with diminishing sales. And though he was still number one, he'd kind of been number one for too long. At this stage, he admits that he was practicing not to foster his skating's evolution, but for contests, working four hours a day on joyless autopilot. There were a few meltdowns at signings, one on the tour bus, and one really unfortunate incident at a clothing store demo. A fan had given Rodney a metal bracelet that cut into his wrist. Rod was so programmed he didn't notice he was badly bleeding when he went into his powerspin.

Rodney imagined Norway as a great break from competition and World Industries, the new company he'd started with Rocco and Mike Vallely. But he was still tense and empty, reading Kafka and a ton of philosophy. He also stopped reading the Bible, and started collecting postcards of different fjords, which he planned to jump off of, preparing every detail, as always, right down to the prayer he'd say before he leapt.

He walked around at night, seeking out other strangers, which at the time didn't enrich him but further reinforced his belief that he's a freakish weirdo. He met a chess hustler at an Oslo bar who'd been an assassin for the Israeli Army before he was caught in Iran and mock-executed three times. (Real rounds; they just fired up in the air.) "It completely destroys you as a human being," the man told Rod. Another guy he met said he has to wear earplugs because unfiltered noise gives him a shock.

Rod slipped from anhedonia to depression to being full-blown suicidal. He even dated a suicidal woman, and during one scare called her parents, who told him that she always acted like this.

SUICIDE is something with which Rodney has long struggled, and it was a topic he brought up himself in one of our interviews. I mentioned Antwuan Dixon, a facially tattooed young black pro who keeps his arms at his sides while he magically floats over long sets of stairs. Mullen describes Dixon's skating as "stunning."

Dixon has said that his style comes from secret advice that Mullen gave him as a youth. I mentioned this, and it was the first Mullen had heard of it. He let out a soft laugh. "That is the coolest thing," he said. "And that's another beautiful thing about skateboarding, because I've always felt like an outsider. But what skater *doesn't* feel like an outsider? It's a collection of people who don't belong in collections. And in there, there's a sense of pure respect and camaraderie.

"I had a lot of suicidal issues, whatever. Maybe the way I grew up. Maybe it's in my blood. Maybe there's a gene."

"Your uncle?"

"Yeah. And it's something I struggle with. I'm all better now, but it's there. And I read that [Emile] Durkheim book [*Suicide*], and statistically, it's that sense of not belonging to anything. And that connectedness, to someone like Antwuan—and I'm pretty sure Antwuan and I don't have a lot in common, the way we grew up. But to me, that thing we share—that's the coolest thing. That we have such a connection. When I see him do stuff I made up, or do in a way that I could never do—that makes me connected to that, feel part of a whole, which means everything to me."

▲

SUCH CONNECTIONS (and *The Notebooks of Malte Laurids Brigge*, by Rainer Maria Rilke) helped Rodney off this path in Norway. He'd relocated to LA and now lived with Rocco and Vallely. He'd also been disowned by his dad at a recent family reunion, a weekend that ended with him and his mom fleeing their house and taking back roads all the way to the airport.

By 1990, vert was gone and skating's organizing bodies had fallen apart. At the final National Skateboard Competition, the freestylers were moved to an apron of broken asphalt next to a fishing hole. Most of the people watching Rod win were guys with poles on their way back to the parking lot. Shortly thereafter, his board was discontinued.

It didn't matter. Rod was done with contests. "I won by doing what it took to win," he says. "It makes you feel like a fraud." Today he doesn't know how many world championship contests he won. "Thirty six out of thirty-seven, or thirty-four out of thirty-five, whatever it was. And winning's not what you think— believe me."

At this time the industry was supposedly a fourth of what it had been during vert's peak. However, this fourth consisted of almost 100 percent hard-core street skaters, and with 2.6 million people still skateboarding, World Industries was doing well enough that they needed a team manager. Rodney took care of Jeremy Klein, Ron Chapman, and Shiloh Greathouse, who remembers, "I've never seen anybody look more stressed out than that . . . But he did a good job. Nobody died." Rodney handled World's accounting, and skated at night on what had become like a Wilson T2000 racket or a 1935 Epiphone Olympic guitar. Through the night, he chatted up homeless people, recording their conversations.

And while vert skating's line was all but flat, street skating remained strong, and the new company was picking up steam. World partner Mike Ternasky wanted to make a high-quality video, "the ultimate skateboarding video." To do this, Ternasky informed Rodney that he was going to street skate, use a regular board, and roll around instead of staying in one place. Rocco told Ternasky that he'd tried to get Rodney to switch over, and it wouldn't work, that "Rodney is a mule." Ternasky insisted he could make it happen. They made a bet.

It was 1990, and Rodney hadn't stood on a regular board in a decade. He wasn't only riding an old freestyle board, but riding with a noseguard and skidplate held in with seven tiny screws. Ternasky watched Rod remove them, and check his board routinely. (For the first couple months, Rod put them back in to skate at night.) He began skating longer, fatter boards, shaving down decks until they were a millimeter wider than the last one, one deck per week for twelve months.

Progress was slow. Rodney plowed into things and sometimes just fell over. But soon came the spike, and he started incorporating his earlier creations into street skating. He was doing his freestyle ninja tricks, but doing them on the roll. It wasn't quite either genre, but was way ahead the way his skating had always been way ahead, and soon word got out that the best freestyler in the world was becoming the best street skater in the world.

Etnies called and soon ran an ad to coincide with the buzz. It pictured Rod vertically sliding along a curb on the nose of a partly shaved board (aka, nosebluntside) with the caption JUST ANOTHER GAY FREESTYLER.

World's first video was called *Rubbish Heap,* and Rod's part begins with young pro Jeremy Klein running over and stomping his freestyle board in two. Rodney rides a freestylish board for the video, but does a lot more lines, ollie-ing into benches and double-tre-flipping off curbs. The director's a Maryland prep school kid who wrote for BMX zines before he started skating the Brooklyn Banks, sometimes taking pictures he'd sell to *Trans-World.* His name's Adam, but he goes by Spike Jonze.

But it was the next video that changed everything. "The greatest skate video ever made" is called *Questionable,* and is still on every skate nerd's top-ten list. The premiere was in London, and the auditorium was full of pros. Rodney sat next to Mike with his head down, embarrassed as always. The song for the opening credits is "Here Come the Bastards" by Primus. Everything in Rod's part is very, very different. He's on a street deck, the song is "What a Wonderful World," and eighteen years later, no one can do much of what he does in this video. His part ends with an adapted freestyle trick, a 360 casper slide, wherein the board's flipped upside down and slid on its tail, held at a 45-degree angle with one foot on each side. Rod rides up to a waxed concrete island, flips the board, catches it upside down, slides across, then tre-flips out and rides away. How many times can you say no one's ever seen anything like this? I don't know. No one's ever seen anything like this. No one's ever seen anything like this twenty years later. Everyone screams.

Ternasky grabs Rod by the head: "This," he says, "is the beginning." Ternasky sits back and smiles. Rocco owes him a dollar.

# 17

# RYAN SHECKLER CAN KICKFLIP AND HE'S SIX YEARS OLD

RYAN ALLEN SHECKLER was born on December 30, 1989, in San Clemente, California, where he still lives today. His parents are Gretchen and Randall. The family lived in a gated community ten minutes from the beach. There were three skate shops on the main drag of El Camino Real and several board shops that sold surf and skate gear. San Clemente has one small skatepark, but twenty minutes down Interstate 5 is the Magdalena Ecke Family YMCA, with a 32,000-square-foot skateboard megaplex Tony Hawk had been sessioned on ever since he'd sold his house in Carlsbad. The Y was also a stomping ground for a young snowboarder named Shaun White, who used the facility when San Bernardino's snow melted in the spring.

Ryan could walk at seven months, and at eighteen months his dad and pregnant mom noticed how much he loved to knee around the garage on Randy's old Powell board, a tankish thing with OJ-brand wheels. Hawk never had the conceptional moment that Rodney did with skating, and while no one remembers a single such moment with toddling young Ryan, things changed once Ryan and that board came together. Skating was Ryan's priority, his dad remembers, "from the time he was about two years old."

Aside from SoCal's surf and skateboard DNA, Ryan also had the Bam Margera thing, where he not only had a surplus of energy that needed burning, but also loved climbing and jumping off of things, like furniture, the dishwasher, and the roof of their house.

He later would be diagnosed with ADD, but he's never taken Ritalin. He and his two brothers grew up skating, surfing, riding BMX, Motocross, and playing paintball in their backyard.

"I didn't start seriously skating till I was, like, four," Ryan remembers. That's when he got his first board. A Woody Woodpecker model, he rode it for a year and learned to ollie in a week. His next board was a Tony Hawk. Within another year he could kickflip, and it's interesting that Ryan points to this as the first trick he ever learned, rather than the ollie, which he must not consider an accomplishment, at age four. He got the flip at the end of an all-day session, and was so excited he called his dad at work, who told him to keep practicing. He did, a hundred times a day, until he could flip as high as he could ollie—about 3 feet, which he can still do today.

That same year he broke his arm for the first time while trying to clear a picnic table on his skateboard. The break was bad enough that doctors needed to reset it—had to re-break this first grader's tiny broken arm. Ryan didn't cry, and in fact, that same year, he entered his first contest at the big-deal-in-skating California Amateur Skateboard League, and won. Tony Hawk attended his birthday party that December.

Unhappy skaters' parents were already complaining, but Sheckler was on a roll. He wasn't just better than everyone else—he was better in competition than everyone else, and while young Rodney had to practice routines so they'd be automatic and mute all contest pressures, early on Sheckler displayed not only a natural competitive streak but also a weird performer's talent where he was able to do especially creative, difficult, frightening, beautiful things in the same environment that makes other skaters cave. Like Alva or Hosoi, he shone brightest under pressure.

Sheckler's first flow sponsor was the nearby IWS Boardshop in Laguna Niguel, then shoe giant Etnies, then Volcom, who also sponsored a guy named Chet Thomas, a 1990s prodigy and still a force today. Ryan was eight. He was never tired and never complained and pretty much never failed to kick everyone's ass, all the time. His skating seemed incongruous with the body it came from. Ryan skated hard and fast and hit everything with fueled flare. He looked like a big toddler out there, yet he always had his head down, pumping between each landing to get that little extra bit of speed, and grabbing an extra foot of air, then kicking with his little legs to make his huge-looking board flip clean every time, then landing and bending his teeny knees to keep going.

Talk of a fearless, fat-cheeked, buzz-cutted kid spread through the community. The tone was heavy among skaters and breathless in boardrooms. At this point, he was still a tiny child, hidden in pads, with big brown eyes and a button nose. He wasn't distinct or photogenic yet—he was just too little. But everyone on the inside was talking. This kid could be the next Tony Hawk.

Rodney had heard the talk, but was filled in on Ryan sometime around 1999, from pro Chet Thomas, who rode with Sheckler on Volcom.

"You start hearing stories," recalls Rodney, sitting in his kitchen with a pot of tea. "'There's this kid, there's this kid.' The rare one that comes across. The Tony Hawks—though there's only one Tony Hawk. There's a Koston. Tony. Prodigies, like Caballero, or whoever of this generation, like Paul Rodriguez. And he is of that extremely rare caliber. 'And you should watch him.' I remember Chet saying that, and Chet never says it like that. And Chet was very much one of those kids, too."

He doesn't remember if he first saw footage or photos of Ryan, but does remember how he felt. "That's when it really registered," he says. "Wow, yep. You can see it. There it is. It's obvious. This kid was—born to skate sounds trite—but he does have that wiring. Somehow, some way, like in a Mozart way where it's second nature."

Ryan was banned from junior tournaments by age eleven. According to CASL, it was because he had too many sponsors, but it was mostly because none of the kids or paying-to-belong parents liked the idea that if Ryan showed up that day, their child didn't have a Mayor McCheese's chance in rat hell of taking first. In this way Ryan was just like Rodney and Hawk—whose scores were sometimes thrown out at contests—and almost the same age here, facing the same inevitable negative attention that comes with being the best.

Early on, he was still in the weird place where he was technically an amateur and not a pro, so his team couldn't cover travel expenses. Those were largely paid for by his dad, Randall, a mechanical engineer and very early proponent of Ryan's career. Short and stocky like Ryan is today, Randall built his son his own small backyard park after Ryan skated through a neighbor's ramp.

Randall has said that he worked not fourteen or sixteen but eighteen hours a day to help it all happen. How it happened is not important. Ryan was out there winning again and again and again, and it was only a matter of time because it was a mismatch everywhere he competed. No one was happy—not the other amateurs, not their sponsors, and especially not the parents, because if everyone knew who was going to win, then how could it be a real competition?

Hawk and Rodney comparisons fit here, but this was a different time; there was more risk and parental investment, and more money at stake. There was more bureaucracy and more security, and, for the first time, a small, consistent group of skateboard parents who—you got the idea from the way they stood and yelled instead of cheered—weren't there to support their kids, but rather to support the investment they'd made in what their kids were doing. It was nothing like the certain police-attended high school hockey, soccer, or football games, but these "skate moms and dads" were out there. Parents who sounded more like they were at a racetrack than at a sporting event, hopeful but not in a happy way, guarding instead of watching, like the spandexed mother who took her tiny-voiced son on *Rosie O'Donnell* to skate and introduce his clothing line.

THE FIRST TIME Rodney called Ryan's house, his dad hung up on him. But Rodney eventually spoke with the Shecklers and asked if Ryan would like to be sponsored by World Industries. With his parents' blessing, Sheckler joined the Am team, and at age ten, went on an international tour. Soon Sheckler was the star of demos in Spain, China, Dubai, and Australia, where the team was invited backstage to meet 50 Cent and Lil Jon.

Rodney remained part owner and a distant participant in World, and had little direct contact with Ryan until an American Sports Retailer trade show. "He didn't say too much, and he didn't say too little," recalls Rodney. "There was a little old man in that body. . . . I remember locking into him. The way he carried himself," Rodney continued. "He has this sort of stability that you rarely see. Especially when you're older and you have a name. Often when you first meet people it's awkward, and I know that—I lock up in front of Paul Rodriguez. I almost expected some version of that, but no, he was just so clear."

Here Rodney reiterates how often he sees ultra-talent in young skaters that goes to waste, because it's not recognized by them, or it's askewed because they're easily distracted or "they simply don't have the heart to pursue their talent." Rodney relays a story he heard from friend and '90s switch-stance pioneer Marc

Johnson, who says the best skater he ever saw still works at the gas station of his North Carolina hometown.

But Sheckler had none of these problems. "He seemed to know himself well enough to know what skating meant to him at such an early age," says Rodney. "It was like, yeah: That kid is a skater."

Sheckler's first pro model board featured World's famous Wet Willy logo, designed by artist Marc McKee. Ryan was thirteen, and was soon traveling five months a year, homeschooled by his mom, who was and still is his manager. Other talent surfaced: He was good at traveling around the world, waiting in airports, eating chain restaurant food, and trying to sleep and heal on planes and in strange hotel rooms. But he was always good at this, level-headed and uncomplaining, driving with his parents around California when he first began to dominate the local Am scene instead of the worldwide professional one.

He won for the first time as a pro at the still-important Vancouver Slam City Jam contest, and Rodney was there to watch him. Because of his age, both his new pro status and his victory were youngest-ever world records.

"He had this crazy run and I was so excited," Mullen remembers with a giggle. "And I ran out and I grabbed him. He was so tiny then. And he was just so calm, as if he were just skating the place for fun.

"He won that contest, and I was so proud of him. And at that stage, at least from my end, I thought, 'What a privilege it would be to have this guy around.' Engage with this kid, because he's special."

Mullen remained a distant partner in World, but he knew it was too big a place for a new skater like Ryan. At the time, Mullen rode for a small company called Enjoi with Marc Johnson, but when Johnson left the company, so did Rodney, forming Almost Skateboards with Daewon Song. Ryan was their first pro.

Ever since Peralta released *The Bones Brigade Video Show*, a skater's biggest exposure has come through video parts. Ryan's big video part debuted in Almost's premier video, called *Round 3*. The video featured full five-minute parts of each team member, including Haslam, Daewon, and Mullen (*Round 3*, remember, featured Rod's last full video part).

It was the first footage I ever saw of Sheckler, who'd just turned thirteen. He's seated at the edge of a fountain, chewing and looking at us through a hole in a potato chip. He's in a black shirt with a black backwards hat high on top of a bell of brown hair, and then there's a cut and we see Ryan shortly ollie onto a walkway and land in a rolling manual. His stance is regular and The Cure is playing. Ryan's manny is mellow, with the board's ends pointing at two and eight o'clock. His right arm, which is camera-side, is out and curved and about level with his shoulder. His left is up in a ta-da.

His front leg points to five but his back leg is straight, pointing to six, in a posture kind of like he's standing on one foot. His back sneaker's flat across the board and his front is up at the nose. His back knee's slightly bent, and he's leaning in such a way that his ass is farthest back and the tip of the board is farthest forward. The board's almost out in front of him, and as he keeps going the nose nods up, just under the control of his left toe. His arms go into two sickle shapes, one up over his head like a backwards dunk and the other to the side like he's petting something while his whole body stiffly shifts and the sidewalk goes *clack clack clack*.

He does one of the longest manuals I've ever seen, and I've seen a lot of them. Like Hosoi's airs and Jamie Thomas's ollies, it's so excessive that its unnatural beauty feels almost eerie, like a sea creature that glows in the dark. How's it doing that?

Sheckler cruises the whole length of the park until he reaches a three-set staircase. Staying in a manual, he hops off and rolls on in the same manual, does it again on another three-set, and, still on his back two wheels, rolls off a final set and touches down, riding on all four wheels for the first time since he ollied that curb 100 yards ago. He bends and comes up in a light squat like a surfer, then leans so the board makes a broad serpentine motion, then another, then he flips a longer set of stairs down into the bottom of what looks like an old fountain.

This opens a video of steadily more impressive tricks that ends with Ryan launching off a second-story balcony. Google "sheckler + gap" and you'll see. All of this thirteen-year-old's footage is pro level, with something extra. An extra set of stairs at the end of a line, an extra few feet of a drop no one else will try, a kickflip into a narrow and really steep drainage ditch, or over a rock and off a little cliff down on the street. There's a cut to the tour bus, where Haslam— in an Ozzy T-shirt—is shaking Ryan and saying he's had *enough* of this horsing around, young man.

It's really impressive, but it's also somewhat unsettling. Almost Skateboards remains an MIT of skateboarding, and when the video debuted, Ryan was their youngest rider by ten years. Haslam was twenty-four; Daewon, twenty-nine; and Mullen, then thirty-eight. They were all at that level where you almost have to consult other top pros to understand how advanced they were. Most of the team didn't compete because they didn't need to, or want to, because they'd been at the top-pro level for so long. Ryan was a decade younger than his youngest teammate, yet he had what they had—a versatile and dominant naturalness in everything we got to see.

Ryan's kickflip, the first thing he learned, looked evolved. He didn't and still doesn't really ollie, then kick. Slow or pause footage of Sheckler flipping and you'll see: He crouches down and pops the tail and leaps and kicks in one complex thrust. It almost looks like he fumbles it and ollies wrong, and he's going to lose control and flop it over. The board's already in a quarter rotation almost at the same time he drills the tail. Half a second after leaving the ground, the board's flipped over and Ryan's two sneakers are hanging at the same 45-degree angle over the hissing wheels. The rotation's done before his board's reached the ollie's apex, and there's this weird part of a second where the board stops spinning and goes up a final inch or two and finds Ryan's feet. He doesn't seem to need to put his sneaker down to stop the motion.* Everyone else does, but he doesn't. It's weird. He's weird.

In the footage I'm looking at right now, Ryan's on a steep hill, flying from a curve in one road, up over a dirt gap and onto another. He goes about 6 feet high and 10 feet long and falls hard the first two times, then makes it. He has a natural weird boost where it looks like something's pulling him from above, when he goes off ten or twelve or fourteen stairs and flips the board and catches it with an almost horizontal kick and brings it back under him and lands, then bends to about a third of his size so it looks like he's going to rip the ass of his pants out against the ground. But then he's up, riding away, fully intact.

Of course, this is all on a tiny screen. I hadn't seen him skate in person yet.

---

* For a very different but equally impressive flip, check out Lizard King, whose motion is analogous to that of a club and a scalpel and has a lot to do, one pro told me, with his roots in snowboarding. The King's build goes back and forth between really lean and chain-smokingly feeble, making it all the stranger when he cleanly explodes the board some 4 feet into the air. But he does, and the board goes basically as high as the King's legs will bend, and once at the top, I swear, the board hangs there for an instant, and that's when the King flicks his foot out like he's scraping dirt off home plate, and the thing neatly flips like a spit on a drill gun, and then he stomps the whole thing down, bolts. I once mentioned the King's flip to Rodney. He nodded and said, "The delay."

# 18

# THE 1990S REBIRTH OF TECH SKATING, AND CHRIS HASLAM MAKES P-ROD CRACK UP

PAUL RODRIGUEZ, aka, P-Rod, won the last Battle at the Berrics contest. He sealed his victory over teammate PJ Ladd with a nollie front-foot kickflip, a new rendition of a trick invented during the post-vert early '90s, when skating became purely technical.

P-Rod grew up in Anaheim, California, where he still lives today with his girlfriend and two-year-old daughter, Heaven. His dad is the actor Paul Rodriguez, and in 2010, P-Rod starred alongside Sheckler in an indie movie called *Skate Dreams*. He's a bit bulky for a skater, with a short beard and longish hair under a backwards and sideways Mountain Dew cap. P-Rod is a lot of people's favorite skater, including Sheckler—famous for his smoothness, his command of switch tricks, and his technical wizardry. He's so technical that he'll occasionally skip contests if the courses are too big, with the high drops and long stairs Sheckler loves so much.

And while he's won numerous other street contests, including the 2009 X Games, as of this writing P-Rod's latest achievement was winning the third annual Battle at the Berrics in 2010. The Battle is a 100 percent flatground contest and the most-viewed thing on the most-viewed skateboarding website. The contest starts with a pool of sixty-four participants who are paired off for games of SKATE, which is like HORSE in basketball, except with flatground tricks. Contestants aren't allowed to pick up their boards, like for a handplant or boneless, or touch down with their feet, like for a no-comply. Everything's done just off the ground.

P-Rod and I were seated at a cloth-covered round table in a humongous conference room at the Hard Rock Casino in Las Vegas, the last stop of 2010's Dew Tour. The room was empty but for a Chinese food station with those yellow heat lamps, and another round table where the PR people were working. They were in town from Chicago, and on the whole, really nice.

We were watching the Battle on my laptop. It was the finals, so there were big crowds on both sides of the flat area. Berrics skatepark owners Eric Koston and Steve Berra were in front of the crowd next to Hawk, who wore a Foot Locker referee shirt and had a whistle sticking out of his mouth. P-Rod took me through the contest, listing each trick—inward heelflip, 360 shove-it, nollie bigflip—and kept reiterating that he'd never once beaten Ladd in a game of SKATE.

After the Berrics video we watched the aforementioned Haslam part on *Strange Notes*, the switch frontside flip backfoot bigspin. It's a short video, with Haslam outside in a park somewhere, skating on black brick. He stands switch on the board, then flips it with a 180 rotation, so the nose of the deck goes behind him (frontside 180). The board is completing its 180 when Haslam, with what P-Rod calls "the ol' horse kick," uses his back foot to boot the board into another 360 degrees, and turns his body 180 to land in his regular stance.

It looks like two tricks at the same time because it *is* two tricks at the same time—one per foot, and both extremely difficult, done together in the second and a half that the board's off the ground.

P-Rod, polite and mild-mannered, threw his head back with a huge smile while watching Haslam. "He has *so* many tricks, man. And so many ideas," he said. "With guys like him, Rodney, and Daewon, you almost forget shit that they've done, because they've done so much. And it's just hard for your brain to retain it."

▲

AS USUAL, Rodney's stuff in the early '90s was oracley ahead of everyone else. This time, however, he was at the forefront of skating's new movement, instead of off to the side of the ramps, rolling around in a handstand with mummified fingers. This is because skateboarding now took to the street with the same fervor with which it had taken to the air a decade ago. It was as if the culture exaggerated the extreme downfall of vert skating. Participants were reportedly a fifth of what they'd been during the vert craze, but the ones who were still out there were playing a whole different game. Pioneers of street skating had been doing handrails and bouncing off fences and going really big five years earlier, but now everything was tighter and much closer to the ground.

This short but fascinating period was essentially freestyle skating. It was technical and abstruse, and often done on flat pavement and curbs, and yes, skaters at this point were rolling, but so was basically every freestyler besides Rodney. Nineties footage today looks odd. The pros look like beginner street skaters, but what they're doing is not so much small street as it is big freestyle. It's a very important baby step, analogous to the shove-off lip tricks Blender did on a halfpipe, or the high, hard turns Adams and Alva and especially Gelfand were making at the top of their pools' coping.

It had taken five years, but now pros besides Gonz and Natas and Vallely could get off the ground and flip and spin, and after some time, put these things together. A young pro named Jason

Lee seemed to just show up one day with a 360 kickflip. He had long sideburns and a peroxided buzz cut and could do it every time with clown-footed flair, and can still—many films later—land it today. Soon it was a staple, incorporated into longer, more complex lines, and soon after the pros started taking it off stairs, gaps, and even small ramps. (Today the 360 flip is more of an intro trick. It's something pros like Nyjah Huston or Chaz Ortiz do onto a handrail. The name's also changed, first to tre-flip, and then to tre.)

It was also a time of invention. There was a total obsession with a new move called the nollie. Never credited to one skater, the nollie (nose + ollie) happens when you're moving forward and then pop down on the nose and drag your feet back to get airborne. It's so much harder than an ollie, you kind of have to try it to understand.

There were new variations on flips and shoves and especially sequences, what today are called lines. Really hard, technical things went into even harder, more-technical things, like a kickflip to a 50-50 grind to a shove-it. Skaters also started skating switch, or wrong-footed, a trend picked up by vert's tiny handful of survivors and pioneered by a young Brazilian named Bob Burnquist.

Sequences got so complicated they turned to code, and for the most part stayed this way. A switch nollie, for instance, is the same thing as a fakie or backwards-rolling ollie, but with the board turned around. So a switch nollie flip would be easier for most than a regular nollie flip. See? Complicated.

And please note, unlike vert or more-flamboyant early street skating, this technical stuff guaranteed zero interest from outside parties, especially when the people doing the tricks were wearing outfits as strange as their skating: dress-like shirts and huge pants cut above the ankle and flat low-tops and bendless-brimmed hats that say FUCT, which we'll get to.

Designs changed too. Boards' concaves went from steep to very mellow. We started seeing scoop noses, then longer, more upturned noses, and when Mike Vallely's doubletail deck premiered, it was the top seller, copied by everyone for the next year, until the next and quintessential '90s shape came about, a shape similar to what we see today.

Shapes went from having wide tails and upper midsections to long, straight, narrow pellets with rounded ends. Tails became lower and smaller, and thus the trucks grew wider apart, creating a larger sweet spot on which to land. And as the nollie became a staple, noses just got huge. Gigantic. Like Steve Martin's nose in *Roxanne*. Again, you kind of had to be there. Prior to the doubletail, some of the decks still had two inches of flatness between the front truck and the end of the board. Now they were steeper and longer than the tail. When Hawk's new deck premiered, Powell ran an ad with a message from him, asking people to just give it a chance. An older skater on our street growing up said it looked like "an old Nash turned backwards." The whole pachydermatous nose trend eventually passed, but the basic shape remained: thin, low tail, steep nose, mellow concave. A freestyle board.

Risers disappeared and wheels went from cylindrical to tall and thin, then shrank to almost nothing, the argument being that a lower platform would yield a higher ollie. For maybe six months there was a what-next feeling as smaller and smaller wheels appeared in shop cases, finally bottoming out when Toxic Skates released the 39er—"39" as in 39mm, less than half a centimeter of urethane around the bearing, which made it like you were basically riding on the bearings. This was also when skaters began putting their wheels in backwards to hide the brand name—a trend that stuck. Eighties skateboarding had been turned literally inside out.

"Everslick"* was released but not patented by Santa Cruz, and within six months most every board had a sprayed-on coat of thermoplastic to aid in sliding. Rails vanished from skateboards, never to return. So did noseguards, skidplates, copers, and those grippy stickers you'd put on your deck's underside. Griptape's decorative patterns and bright colors vanished. The gap often left to expose the deck's top graphic was closed, as boards were covered in black. It became cool not to write or draw anything on top of your board.

One reason decks from the time were looking more like Rodney's was because he was making a lot of them. He'd become a shaper at World, "because it's what I liked to do." A skateboard engineer, he was designing the decks for the industry's top company during this strange incubatory period in modern street skating, and doing this while managing the team and learning to skate all over again.

We know that once he relearned how to skate, he did things no one has yet to duplicate, but I don't think anyone could have expected what he came up with next.

Like the kickflip, Rodney's next great invention stemmed from failure. One day his interest was piqued when he didn't get a flip trick around and the board slid away, wheels up. Sometimes he came down too fast and ended up standing on the wheels or trucks. He started to do this on purpose, with speed, and soon he could flip the board, surreally slide along on the wrong side of it, flip it back over, and roll away. He developed an idea Gonz

---

* Developed by former freestyler and NHS developer Tim Piumarta, Everslick was a quickly passing fad, and everyone soon returned to reducing drag with what skiers used for millennia and skaters still use today: wax. It goes on their decks, trucks, the inside of wheels, and whatever they're skating on. Companies even sell "skate wax" in goofy shapes. Wax from Almost is molded and colored like a big pink boob. Deathwish wax comes in these tan Atari Asteroid shapes and is packaged inside a paper chicken bucket. Most everyone, though, uses good old drugstore candle wax on everything. This is why skated curbs blackly shine.

had, where he did an upside-down railslide while holding on (aka, "caveman"), and in one videotaped session he could do it no-handed. The darkslide was born. First perfected on a ledge, he eventually brought it up to a handrail, once again kicking out a skateboard's ceiling.

▲

POSTSCRIPT, which if this reporter had greater editorial control would be printed in blood and bound on human skin, and why this skater deserves so much more than a footnote: Beautifully incongruent to this tight, technical period was a barely teenaged Santa Barbarian who still rode rails and whose pro model had a blunt nose and steep tail and a picture of a big bulldog head. He was Frankie Hill, and everything he did was just huge. He could clear tall fire hydrants, then do it again except ollie (not nollie) off the nose, which was unprecedented, and then do it *again* with a 180 in there. He could 180 shove at the end of a boardslide down a long wheelchair ramp handrail, and whenever he approached anything, he'd pump four or five or six times as if stomping on a loved one's assailant. Everything he did was hard and fat, down to the sound of his '80s fishtail slapping the sidewalk. If you skated back then, you know how his 1990 video part ends: He rides off a cliff. It's a dirt cliff at about a 70-degree angle, a steep no-man's space between two parking lots, but it's still a cliff. The shot opens with him overexposed and pumping wildly and smiling with his mouth open while he gets closer to the camera, then with a fat snap, he sails off and over the gap with about three holy seconds of hangtime, lands, and rolls away.

One of skating's most famous whatever-happened-to people, Frankie appeared on MTV Sports, rocketing around a skatepark and showing off the holes in his body. He had the top-selling deck in Canada, and his royalty checks topped $5,000 a month during skating's death days. But in 1992, he landed a huge handrail trick wrong and his knee buckled. His new deck had just come out—a more-stretched board with a graphic of a severed ear. But he was gone. Hill's gift was his hex. His talent demanded Sheckler-sized stunts that facilitated injuries from which his body eventually couldn't recover.

Or so we thought. Hill recently resurfaced on a team called Legion, and shortly thereafter Powell reissued his old bulldog board. As of this writing, he's bigger, with a shaved head, but still stomps instead of pushes his board, clearing handrails with the same loud fatness he did when small skating ruled.

# 19

# WAIST 66 JEANS AND THE RISE OF WORLD INDUSTRIES

SKATEBOARDING AS A SPORT changed during the early '90s, but the shift was minimal compared to the all-out mutation of the skateboard culture. This was true for the styles and attitude that have always made skating unique, but also for the $150 million business structure that was turned on its head by one man: Rodney's old nemesis and new business partner, Steve Rocco.

Like surfing, skating has always had more than its share of codes and jargon and styles that both celebrate itself and exclude nonparticipants. Fortunes continue to be made by selling the you-don't-understand-and-we-don't-want-you-to aesthetic that Stecyk pioneered in the early '70s. This proud isolation naturally intensifies as it does in any culture, and then can shrink, like the ska scene in Boston or go-go in D.C. But in this case it just fell off the deep end.

Skate culture turned aggressively inward and dark, and there wasn't always a jokey element to make it okay. It didn't last long, but the street skater's look in the early '90s was distinct and strange.

DayGlo and patterns disappeared, replaced by blank earth tones. Like decks, T-shirts started appearing not with swords or skulls or snakes, but with cartoons, and came in sizes ranging from XL to XXXL to XXXXXL. Pants were the same way. Made of stiff denim, often sewn with a different color thread and cut off just over the ankle, they were very, very big. It was a trend that eventually caught on when places like Chess King and PCH carried those giant JNCO jeans. But it all started five years earlier when skate companies made pants that looked like two skirts sewn together. Waist sizes reached 66 inches, and that's not a typo. One ad's catchphrase read: "Pants Big Enough for Your Friends," with a pictured skater and friends all standing inside of his pants. You can still watch video parts of riders like Alphonzo Rawls flappishly riding in $60 purple jeans that were triple-stitched with white thread and had a little round patch that said FUCT on the long back pocket.

Skaters wore caps but left the brim flat and grew sideburns and got buzz cuts, where every hair was the same length. I don't know if anyone did this anywhere else, but in Rochester, certain skaters wore little clocks around their necks, and those of us who couldn't grow sideburns grew triangles of hair just in front of our ears and combed the tendrils down our faces. Thick high-tops disappeared. Vans made "chukka boots" that looked like thin, three-quarter-suede clown shoes and came in maroon or blue that looked like velvet and dyed your socks when it rained.

And yet this particularly black period of skating ushers into the culture an age of cartoons and Technicolor. Natas released the same SMA deck, except the classic panther was a tiny, wet-eyed cartoon kitty. Rodney's full-size board graphic was a dog reclining in front of his house before a line of mounted cat heads. There was a new company called Acme, named after the catalog Wile E. Coyote orders from. Good old Alphonzo Rawls's board featured the Energizer Bunny. Silent Jeremy Klein released a deck covered with the running bomb creatures from Super Mario 2, and clown-shoed Jason Lee's deck featured the Cat in the Hat.

Names of pros or companies sometimes didn't even appear on boards. Another Rawls deck was totally blank but for the

Pillsbury Doughboy, the letters ALF on his toque. Vallely's dou-bletail board featured the famous "Animal Farm" graphic. Mike V was a vegan at the time and requested a folk-art design, and got back a whole animal collective hanging around the barn-yard. Another Klein deck was a Norman Rockwell spoof. There was a popular shirt that kids waited until they were at the bus stop to put on, with Pepé Le Pew blowing a kiss while 10-4ing a joint.

There's a *Huh?!* feeling to it all that the tiny, clinging group loved, and the industry responded by turning more intense.

One pro's T-shirt just said HUMAN RACIST across the back. Josh Swindell's board featured instructions on how to make a pipe bomb. Randy Colvin's two decks spoofed the Scientology *Dianetics* book cover and a blaxploitation velvet poster (Colvin is white), with fake velvet. The velvet deck recently sold on eBay for $760. One board copied (without permission) the old boxy New Kids on the Block logo and a color photo of the Kids.

Companies received cease-and-desist orders from Burger King, the Church of Scientology, and Dr. Seuss. Commenting on the latter, Rocco said, "What the fuck's he gonna do? He's like eighty years old." World Industries incorporated the legal notices into their board graphics.

Almost all of these were radiant, animated images with ironic or illegal subjects, and soon there was a running pornographic, incest, parricide, and racism theme to boards, like a calico, car-toonish country scene behind a Sambo figure, snoozin' in a watermelon patch. The culture was so tiny and insulated, and so few outsiders cared, that they not only got away with it, but they took it even further. Blind Skateboards released a series parody-ing the long-gone Garbage Pail Kids, with each deck designed as a playing card for each rider. The riders were characters like Jerkin' Jeremy (Klein) or High Guy (Mariano), with illustrations to match the names. What was probably thought of as the limit was a pornographic cartoon of a woman pleasuring herself that even in the context of all the other boards was such that World wrapped it in a dark plastic bag with a sticker that said: WARN-ING: CENSORSHIP IS WEAK AS FUCK. This deck hung unwrapped on Samurai Skate Shop's wall in downtown Rochester.

But the true high—or maybe the low—came one day when artist Marc McKee followed Rocco's instructions to "make some-thing that is truly evil." It's a famous image in skateboarding. And it is evil. Even today it's difficult to look at, the way a really distasteful joke is hard to tell. It was so harsh at the time that Jason Lee turned down a $10,000 check from Rocco (penned in red ink) to put the graphic on his board. As the story goes, Lee first took the check against the pleas of Rodney and the warnings of Gonz, but that night drove back to World's office and slid the check under Rocco's door. The next day, however, Natas walked into the shop, saw the drawing, and thought: "That would be a good thing to have on my board."

The drawing is a cartoon, and features the devil underneath a gallows in the shape of a cross, holding a headless infant in one hand and the infant's head in the other. Green pus instead of blood is oozing from its head and body, and the devil's hooves are crossed over a giant pentagram with 666 at the center, and one of the people hanging from the cross is the Pope, naked. The infant has a deep cut under its right breast because it turns out he's the baby Jesus. Natas took the graphic.

Note here that while the '90s was a different era, skating had also behaved with the same polarity during the previous decade. The skulls and swords and fire that accompanied the high-flying, high-paying, DayGlo-ing '80s; the fame and appraisal of the out-cast Dogtown guys by the uniformed, contest-going, skatepark generation of the '70s; and now this florid, not-caring, lovingly objectionable and sue-able period in the '90s. It was just a new extreme, obsessed with its own downfall, of the 1-percenter attitude we saw with that first *Life* article in 1965. No one could have expected these extremes to be successful, but they were. They sold so well that the industry was turned on its head, and the guy doing the selling was Steve Rocco.

IN 1998 STEVE ROCCO sold World Industries to Swander Pace Capital for $20 million. World was the first skateboard company to be sold on the stock market, and by then Rocco was already living in Hawaii, where Rodney would spend Y2K in fear of the approaching Armageddon. Almost single-handedly, Rocco changed the sport's business structure from corporate and huge in the '80s to skater-owned and small in the '90s, all the while building his own empire and keeping skaters in control.

It started in 1987. Sick of the corporate structure at Vision, Rocco quit after being fired and went into business for himself. As the story goes, he'd saved no money but had a calling card from his team manager days, so he reached out to a number of people, including SMA's Skip Engblom. Engblom showed him how to make money buying wholesale decks on credit, then selling them for double the price. He screened the boards with an SMA Rocco Division logo, and they sold well. The success prompted him to borrow $20,000 in a paper bag from a loan shark and start his own company. Sort of. By all accounts, including his own, Rocco just thought most of this up as he went along.

Rocco partnered with former Vision pro John Lucero, but Rocco's, shall we say, spending habits scared Lucero, and he pulled out. Rocco approached Rodney, then twenty-one, and asked him if wanted to become a partner in the company for $6,000. Rocco asked him this at the airport, as Rodney and Hawk were about to depart for a demo in Tahiti. Rocco had already borrowed money to pay not the principal but the interest on his loan-shark loan, and it wasn't so much that he needed a partner as he needed money *now*. Rodney complied, handing him the check, he says, through the gate on the way to the tarmac. World Industries was saved.

Somehow Rocco managed to be both an anarchist and a successful businessman. Part of it was that he came to the then $150 million industry when it was already in utter chaos. Vert skating was dying, and the five big companies had been upping their supply to match the demand that was totally falling off. Everyone knew Rocco from his days as a pro and a manager, and he was pretty recognizably the opposite of the big businessmen running the industry at that time—an industry that had become much more rigid and structured as it grew over the years, naturally repelling free-spirited skateboarders, who had started to pull away.

The first one was Mike Vallely, the top street pro in the world, which in 1989 meant the top pro in the world. Vallely was an inland New Jerseyan who dropped out of school to skate for industry giant Powell, and had become invested in '80s vert riders like Hawk and Caballero. As his sales improved and vert dropped off, Powell was suddenly and heavily reliant on Vallely. At this point Powell was still Powell-Peralta, with Peralta in charge of Vallely's video part for the upcoming *Public Domain*. It was the introduction to the corporate side of the world Vallely loved so much. The shots were rushed, and he was forced to run through the cemetery like an idiot, plus he was given the famous team rulebook, detailing dress and speech codes for all team riders. Vallely quit at a demo.

But Rodney was also feeling these winds of change. He and Vallely had an "If-you-will-I-will" conversation, and left '80s giant Powell-Peralta to join a company with no riders. It was a core-shaking occurrence, but was happening everywhere. Within two years Hawk had left Powell to start Birdhouse, and Peralta had left to work in Hollywood.

Vallely's doubletail board premiered the next year, 1991. It was World's first product and Marc McKee's first graphic. The board was a best seller and an instant classic. The mold was actually Vision's; Rocco bribed the shaper $6,000 to get it. The fine tuning was done by Rodney, who'd become World's shaper and worked with Marc. Together they "designed a huge freestyle board," since that was what everyone was doing then.

Within a year, all of the best street skaters came to Rocco, in part because he offered twice the royalties of anybody else. Jesse Martinez, Natas, Gonz, and Jason Lee all joined the force, and soon started their own companies under the World umbrella. Gonz started Blind as a response to Vision. He and Jason Lee were the two pros, and shot a really cool video in the plaza at the bottom of the Eiffel Tower. Natas ended up with full control of his own umbrella company that he was going to call 101 Dalmatians, but just called 101, sponsoring Jason Dill and Berrics founder Eric Koston.

Rocco either had the era's aggressively inward attitude, or else he knew exactly how to market it, because he came out swinging. He ran Z-quality ads promoting World's amateurs, taking very specific shots at Powell. Powell was so desperate they actually took shots back, which further confirmed everyone's view of them as AOL and World as a young Facebook. Rocco also ran an ad debunking SMA "special formula" wheels, informing readers that the only difference was the price, and that they said "special" on them. Engblom promptly pulled all backing. Now the company was just World Industries.

It didn't matter. Skaters loved World. By the end of 1991 the company reportedly had an unseen 80 percent of the market share, and Rocco moved everything to an LA warehouse. It grew into a cross between a skatepark and Warhol's factory, with ramps, offices, computers, and editing equipment. Everything was spray-painted and there were holes in the walls, and some rooms had bunks so the teenage skaters could live there.

It's here that Rocco once again followed the successful skate conglomerate model by founding a magazine. *Big Brother* premiered in mid-1992, published by World's own Dickhouse Productions. Rocco gave out 20,000 copies for free. Like the owners of *Thrasher* and *TransWorld*, he promoted riders and products from his own company alongside articles about sex, drugs, and all things objectionable. One color photo caught Steve Olson heelflipping over a pile of burning Bibles, but it's the "How to Kill Yourself" story that made the evening news. *Big Brother* was annoyingly aggressive, but a cool magazine. One early issue was spiral-bound. Another came in a cereal box. Another came with an audiotape.

The crew also made videos, first with skate footage, but then with content-related stuff to coincide with stories in *Big Brother*. One article/video combination was reported by a correspondent named Johnny Knoxville, who investigated what it was like to be TAZE'd and Mace'd and then stun-gunned. They hosted the Bong Olympics, which they shot and distributed. Rocco's brother Sal Jr. penned a weed column, got a lot of mail, and ran an early umbrella company called Bitch Skateboards.

In March of 1997 Larry Flynt bought *Big Brother*, because he "thought it was great."

Then one day, on a receptionist's birthday card, Marc McKee drew a smiley face with devil horns and pointed goatee. It was Devilman, and soon it was to the world of skate money what the Nike swoosh is to the world of sports money. A newly cautious Rocco had been wanting something for the upcoming age demographic, something kids would like and their parents would be willing to buy. He put Devilman on a board and deck sales tripled in one year. McKee made similar drawings, including a water-droplet version of the same figure. He was Wet Willy, the character on Sheckler's first pro model.

Rocco eventually become not just one of the industry's top power guys, but The Man. The ultimate powerful, money-hungry, money-guarding, yacht-owning, golf-playing *man*. He vaporized anyone who messed with World, including beloved '90s pro Simon Woodstock, who sometimes dressed like a clown and skated contests on boards with eight wheels, or boards made from an ironing board, or covered with carpeting rather than griptape.

Woodstock and pro Rich Metiver found this out the hard way when they ran an old Worldesque ad for their own company, with Devilman sodomizing a skater who looked a lot like Rocco under the words CONTRACT NEGOTIATIONS. Rocco hit him with a massive lawsuit, eventually dropping it under the condition that they pay him $100,000 and leave the industry forever, which they did.

# 20

# THE INSANE POWER OF TELEVISION

IN LATE 1993, encouraged by the healthy television ratings garnered by alternative sports shows like MTV Sports, ESPN began planning an event called The Extreme Games. The idea was to tap a new, young demographic with a weeklong alternative Olympics televised every two years. Sports would include skating, BMX, Rollerblading, street luge, freestyle bungee-jumping, bungee-jumping in kayaks, something called Eco Challenge, and the most forgotten anomaly of maybe the whole '90s: skysurfing.

It had been a rough few years for '80s skateboarders. Powell's sixth video, *Ban This*, premiered during skating's peak year of 1988. Partly shot at Hawk's home ramp on 35mm, Peralta needed so many lights he'd had to get a permit (he told the town he was making an antidrug commercial). The video did well, but the following year Hawk's income fell, and the following year it was halved. He would have made even less were it not for his contracts.

Next came that strange—and now, for skating—predictable period where supply was backorderly huge and demand dropped to nil. Contracts had stipulated prepaid international tours, still, but Hawk calls touring that year "a joke." Exhibitions by the best pros in the world, he said, were like a vaudeville act crossing Europe during the plague. Powell cut everyone's salaries, then reduced their royalties. Most of the people watching vert competitions were pros stopping over from other events.

Hawk flew to Japan with Bucky Lasek—probably the other best vert pro in the world—and thirty people watched them compete.

In 1991, Hawk became the National Skateboard Association vert champion for the tenth straight year. It was the only competition of the year. Everything else was a demo, which meant no prize money. Like so many teen pros in the '80s, he'd saved little and spent lots. He sold his Lexus to Cindy's parents and bought a Civic. Cindy was still a manicurist, and according to him cut his $5 food allowance in half because they needed the money. Things were so bad at Powell that they opened their warehouse park in a doomed effort to pay the bills. Peralta left Powell and went to Hollywood, officially ending the greatest company of the sport's greatest era.

Hawk left Powell too, which would be like Jordan leaving the Bulls if vert skaters weren't already like dodos wandering around the conquistadored island of Mauritius. He used the $40,000 from a refinance on his first house to start Birdhouse Skateboards. The next summer, Hawk rented a van to tour with a handful of vert's last komodo dragons. The following summer, with Cindy pregnant, Hawk took off for another tour where they'd stay five in a motel room doing the mattress/boxspring split, traveling from city to city in Cindy's minivan.

Things were bad, but if you're thinking that the financial darkness infected the sport or its participants at this time, please consider that throughout this period Hawk still hit the YMCA most nights, all the while inventing bigger, more innovative moves. His own thoughts on the famed minivan/boxspring tour: "The closeness on that team has never been duplicated."

In the spring of 1995 Hawk was twenty-seven years old, newly single, and making his living as a freelance video editor, much of the time cutting surf movies. He'd moved back to Carlsbad, had a roommate, and was the father of Hudson Riley Hawk.*

So when rumors about ESPN attention thundered through the industry, like everyone else Hawk took a great and wary interest. On the one hand he knew it would be a migratory work experience where all controlling bodies came not just from the corporate media infamous for misrepresenting skating, but from the corporate sports media. ESPN was going to send the same low-level reporters they used to cover the Special Olympics and beach volleyball tourneys to try to describe pros executing maneuvers they wouldn't even try to learn the names of. And no kind of dialogue was going to take place because the NSA was gone and the few skaters left had yet to organize. The Games would be a weeklong job, and ESPN needed labor.

But they had money. And Hawk ended up going because he knew he could win the $10,000 for first place and—because everyone was so panicked and broke—all the top vert skaters would be there. There were also very few big vert events those days, and Hawk, like Sheckler, had always loved to compete.

But it was worse than anticipated. Skaters were prohibited from displaying anything promoting their own brands, but would, they were told, wear bibs screened with the logos of the Games' sponsors during competition. All athletes were boarded together in a sort-of longhouse, with teenage bikers and climbers bunked with street lugers and professional people who did an obstacle course called the Eco Challenge. Also, because it was the summer of 1995, Rollerbladers were more in demand than skaters and treated accordingly by ESPN. The blader/skater tension back then is comparable to the skier/snowboarder tension today; none of the roller-skating roots they shared seemed to matter. The not-fresh air was thick. Hawk checked into a hotel.

---

* Now nineteen and a rider for Birdhouse, Spitfire, and Nixon watches.

The first Games were held for eight days around Rhode Island and Mount Snow, Vermont. About 200,000 people attended and it all worked out. Within a year ESPN would contract to broadcast the Games in 198 countries. Skating and BMX were the top-watched events and got picked up all over the place, from CBS and CNN to *Thrasher* and *TransWorld*. Hawk took first in vert and second in street, and later, with the camera crews at his heels, he dropped in on a quarterpipe, shimmied through the street course, hit another quarter, and launched long and smooth and splashless into Narragansett Bay.

The press wouldn't leave Hawk alone. Coverage of him was so homogenous that he met with ESPN brass to ask if they'd include some other skaters. They declined. Hawk was 6-foot-3, with a head of blond hair grown in California and a slimly muscled build he'd had for a decade and everyone knew he would have as an old man. Photographers took looking-up photos of him and his shins, which were layered with fat crosshatches of scar tissue and little holes and short wide slits forever trying to heal into dead skin. But standing on the coping, he looked powerful and strong and effortlessly in charge, pouring sweat while he rawly gazed into the ramp.

In competition he wore a watch and big black pads and breezily destroyed the top skaters in the world. He was never flamboyant; he just went a lot higher and faster and did much more technically impossible things than anyone else. His skating was systematic and controlled, but it was also giant in a freakish way that no can else could get anywhere near. His airs were higher and movements more complex than they were fifteen years ago, but his skating felt the same: Each trick was part of a much broader rhythm, and it was all so distantly ahead that it seemed slow and relaxed, with a power that was almost vague to us, like a fighter jet in the sky. Like a great artist or truly great athlete,

Hawk's genius drew in new people who didn't necessarily know much about what they were seeing, but they knew they wanted to keep seeing it.

That was the skating. Let's meet the skater: tall, thin, handsome, golden-haired, and speaking in a friendly, clipped, quotable, serious manner, glazed with a youthful SoCal cadence. In interviews he smiled and laughed off incredibly stupid, insolently naive questions about keeping his feet "on the skateboard." He was number one by far, but didn't seem competitive (maybe because there was really no one to compete with), and he was always praising other skaters from different teams, listing technical tricks but then explaining them, and winning new fans, including skaters, who worshipped his skating and now his ability to capitalize on the press who'd been sent to capitalize off of him. His business card reads MEDIA WHORE.

When he left the ramp, he took the hand of his cute blonde soon-to-be wife Erin and hoisted his cuter, blonder cherubic son on his shoulder. Crowds and cameras followed them like an aura, and when it came to autographs or shaking hands or giving away Birdhouse merchandise, Hawk worked just as hard with as much success.

SKATING WAS GOING to resurface anyway, but the new boom now had a leader who was a brilliant outside spokesman, a surfacing industry guru, and the sport's greatest athlete. That skating never again crashed as it did in the '60s, '70s, and '80s might owe a great deal to Tony Hawk, who, in addition to being the best at everything, is also by all accounts a really good guy, with a level-headed decency that comes across for the first time during those first ESPN interviews, making him a household name and making parents feel that he's a safe brand for their kids. That this is so rare in pro sports, I think, says a lot about skateboarding.

The Games brought about a new surge. In six months Hawk collected $38,000 in royalties from his new shoe by Airwalk. He was invited to do demos everywhere, including the Hard Rock Cafe, where Donald Trump shook his hand and said he was impressed with all that Hawk was doing for the industry.

ESPN changed the plan. The event would thereafter be called The X Games, to be held not only every year, but twice a year, because now they were planning a winter version of all new events to be held in Aspen. The next X Games were broadcast in 21 different languages. Selected events, like skating, aired on ABC, the way they did in 1965.

Skateboarding viewership was second only to BMX in 1995, so in 1996 it got more attention. ESPN pushed a rivalry that even most non-skaters knew was lame and false between Hawk and vert pro Andy Macdonald.

*The New Yorker* assigned what remains one of the only good pieces of outside reporting on skating, though the writer never stepped on a board until Hawk gave him one, which he nicely included in the story. This is also the year Board-Trac formed, an action sports firm who monitored not only the deck, wheel, and truck sales figures, but also figures on who bought them, and when and where and why they bought them. Board-Trac sold data to various advertising firms, who in 1997 convinced clients like Slim Jim and the Marines that they should put skateboarding and skateboarders in their commercials.

The 1997 X Games got double the viewing audience of the first. Everything was bigger and worth more, and they moved it to San Diego, skating's cradle of life. Hawk was made a consultant, though it still seemed that no one wanted to interview anyone other than him. More skaters were getting lucrative deals from non-skate companies like SoBe and Taco Bell that seemed mind-boggling within this industry, but in fact should have been for a lot more money.

In 1998, Hawk hired a manager, his sister Pat, former backup singer for the Righteous Brothers and John Denver. Pat knew a publicist in New York named Sarah Hall. She had been a publicist for a modeling agency before going solo, and had a website that could have been mistaken for a New Age bookstore and crystal shop in Taos or something, but it turned out she was married to the head lawyer for William Morris, who put Tony in touch with Peter Hess. Hess is still, as of 2011, Hawk's endorsement agent, and he's the guy who told Hawk he could make tenfold what he'd been making in commercials. Yet again, Hawk was trailblazing a new path in the sport, and others followed suit. Vert experts Danny Way and Bob Burnquist soon found representation, and Burnquist's guy is an up-and-coming extreme sports mogul named Steve Astephen, who currently represents Ryan Sheckler.

Through all of this, Hawk was still the greatest skater in the world while running a successful company that only makes skate gear. In 1998, revenues at Birdhouse reached $15 million.

If you don't skate, this was probably around the time you first heard of Hawk. He was a Got Milk spokesman, photographed by Annie Leibovitz. As the first pro skater with an agent, he was finally making pro-athlete money. He was also famously easy to work with, and soon stat firms were showing that he was more recognizable than most top football or basketball players.

Activision called him to develop a video game you might know the name of even if you don't play video games. Tony Hawk's Pro Skater went on to generate more than $1 billion in revenue and became the most popular game franchise of all time, and today Hawk is a video-game character in seventy-nine gaming platforms.

Work kept coming. Next up he was hired by Disney, who wanted to use his figure for the action sequences in their upcoming animated summer movie, *Tarzan*. When you watch Tarzan (voiced by Tony Goldwyn) slide down those huge vines with Jane (voiced by Minnie Driver) over his shoulder, that's actually footage of Hawk they've digitally washed over.

Hawk's next and nearly most bewildering accomplishment was the Loop. For a decade now, wallrides had been part of skating, and as vert developed, some ramps included an overhanging wavelike extension at the top that curled overhead. The extension was meant to serve as a meta-wallride, to challenge the very best skaters, but Steve Caballero did an aerial off one at the Kona contest in 1988, again stretching the plane. An unfindable centerfold from an '80s skate magazine featured the skater at the top of a wavelike indoor ramp extended with a stop sign, sandwiched upside down, riding the ceiling.

While no one had ever done a loop on a skateboard, like the 900, it had been on Hawk's mind. He got the idea for the loop from his childhood Hot Wheels track, and after discussing stunts for the new Birdhouse video, the loop was constructed in a bullring in Mexico in 1997.

Hawk calls the loop "a magnificent way to compress your spine," and in his autobiography he uses the stunt to open a discussion about his love for extra-strength Advil (a sponsor of the first Games), which he keeps all over his house and in his car (and he says was a major contributing factor the night he completed the loop).

"I have to get a rhythm going," he explains. "An unbroken pump so I can carve the loop in one smooth movement." He first practiced going halfway and falling down into gymnastics pads, then tried it once and fell off at two o'clock, landing flat on his hip. He worked for a half-hour, then nailed it. Then nailed it four more times. Yet again, Tony Hawk had achieved the unprecedented, a boggling high point in the techy world of vert skaters, and a simply astonishing visual feat that no one else could touch. It was the biggest roof-destroying accomplishment of his career, thus far.

TONY HAWK LANDED THE FIRST 900 at the fifth X Games in San Francisco on June 27, 1999. He'd actually placed third in the vert contest, behind Lasek and Macdonald, and then returned the next day for the best trick contest.

The 900 is two and a half aerial rotations, and it made international news when Hawk finally got it. The stories, of course, were all about Hawk, who'd become a risk-free, demographic-spanning pro athlete linked to that summer's big Disney movie. None of the members of the press really knew what they were talking about, or why it was such a big deal.

The 900 is a big deal. Hawk reiterates that skating has no one goal, but for years the 900 had been the holy grail of vert skating, and maybe all of skating, since street is so diverse and expressive that it didn't have one. The 900 punched out a ceiling the best pros couldn't touch for thirteen years. The very few good enough to seriously try and get close enough to see the whole trick said it was physically not possible. That to get two and a half rotations, you'd have to spin so hard there was no way you could stay on your board when you landed back on the ramp.

Hawk credits the 900 conception back to 1986, at a skateboard camp in Bourges, France. At that point he'd nailed 720s and naturally wondered about adding another 180. He dropped in, built momentum, and tried an all-out decontrolled spinning aerial, and came down on the coping. The coping landed over his shoes and under his knee pads and split both his shins open, then bounced him off and out into space, squirting blood while he rolled 12 feet down through the air and then landed on his back.

One of the big steps Hawk describes in landing the 900 took place on the famed Plan B ramp in 1996, at a session where he discovered the key was coming off the ramp at an angle, and pulling the first 540 with his weight on the front foot, and the next 360 with his weight on the back. He almost did it then. He went up, made the two and a half rotations, and landed, but was so front-heavy that he fell forward so fast, he couldn't slide out, and so hard the impact broke his rib. That's the other problem with the 9: Even the sport's Hercules, who was then thirty-one, could only attempt it every few months because of its physical demands, and its 100 percent rate of injuring failure.

It's worth stopping here for a second before the action to try and imagine this. To imagine putting on your pads for the thousandth time, or the first time you're going to try since the trick injured you, vert's greatest pro, to such an extent that you needed a month to heal. What kept him trying? Did he know it was there? How? Where?

## July 27, 1999: San Francisco

THE HALFPIPE is outside, and it's late enough in the day that they've turned on the big stadium lights. Hawk's at the ramp's lip, with one foot on the board, his hands folded behind his back. Foggy wind whips through the air and moves the ramp. Ramps shake and squeal when it's windy and rumble when good people ride. The grandstands are filled with thirty-thousand spectators. The San Francisco sky is the erased color of bright brushed steel and almost looks like the inside of a dome. The sun's just down but it's still light outside, which makes it the magic hour.

Time's run out for the contest but no one's left. The pros have surrendered the ramp to Hawk, who is feeling on top of the trick—specifically, the landing—and he's decided he's going to make it or go to the hospital trying.

He tries and falls for the tenth time and slides out and stands up and someone hands him his board. He's soaked. The edges of the ramp are crowded with people, and when he walks over to the ladder they touch his helmet. He's in black shorts, a black Birdhouse T-shirt, and pads by a small company called Pro Designed, which makes the bulkiest pads. His are double-capped. He's got a goofy purple bracelet they all have to wear and thick black shoes. His helmet has stickers from Birdhouse and Adio shoes and Club Med, and one from Hot Wheels. The hair on the back of his neck and his gray temples is wetted into little spikes.

Macdonald, Lasek, and Burnquist are up on the ramp. Lasek rubs his arm as he drops in. The announcer says, "Everybody picture it."

He crosses the ramp and moves up then off the opposite wall and grabs down by his huge forward-facing right foot. His left arm's out and his back is straight with his long legs bent, the way he's skated since fifth grade. He goes about 6 feet in the air but he goes long, spanning maybe 10 feet of the ramp to build momentum. He comes down and moves across the ramp, then flies up into a high slim arch.

He rolls down from the spot where he dropped in six seconds ago, crosses the ramp, and goes into a hard left-leaning ollie a foot under the coping. His head's already parallel with the board. By the time the tail's over the coping he's put his weight to the front. His right arm's holding on and his left arm's out at three o'clock. He's inverted for most of it and if you were on the empty platform below, his hand would be out over you and the rest of him would be out over the ramp. The first rotation is really close to a flip, and he starts the second rotation when he's at top height. It's here—you can see if you slow it down—where he squeezes and transfers his weight, because now he's in a little dark ball that almost instantly gets him 90 more degrees. He's got a 540 and he has 6 more feet and half of one second of freefall before the ramp. But he's made himself smaller and faster, and passes 720 and comes around facing the ramp as the lip comes up to meet him. He needs 100 more degrees and he's falling now a foot under the coping with the last 90, but you can see he's got it. It's the last part of a new sequence he's finally figured out, thirteen years later, this technician.

Coming around crouched, he's going to conjure the extra quarter second by keeping the board up and in a little longer and stomping out a little late, which he does. He's at the bottom of the transition on all but flat ground when he comes down, way forward and knock-kneed as he rides out across the floor, standing on the skateboard with his arm up, both of his eyes and his mouth in an O, his hand in a 1.

# 21

# MIKE V'S GREATEST HITS, OR HOW SKATING'S NEWFOUND SUCCESS WAS NOT SO SUCCESSFUL

THE SUCCESS of the X Games proved that extreme sports events could be rock concert–size profitable. Tickets, merchandise, concessions, and product-placing media coverage of the events meant big money, and by the summer of 1996, similar tours were in the works. Like the first Games, a few went overboard and grouped together things like motocross, Jet Ski, and snowmobiling the way the third HORDE tour grouped Rusted Root and the Allman Brothers.

All of the tours featured skateboarding. See, for instance, Tony Hawk's Giant Skatepark Tour, the Boom Boom Huck Jam Tour (with live music), the Dew Tour, Vans Triple Crown, Slam City Jam, or Mike V's Glory Bound Skatepark Tour that hit twenty-four cities last summer.

There were typical halfpipe and street courses as well as specific contests within the events, like best trick on vert, or a "jam" where skaters went in heats. All in all, there were more contests and more events and more people and more money.

So after a long and pretty flat line for skateboarding, there was new interest in the sport, and while it made sense that Sheckler was coming of age (like age ten) during this time, there was also the previous generation, some of whom had lost everything in the last crash, and some of whom were still there because skating was what they knew, and because they needed the money.

And at least for now, the money was there.

Street skating was still going strong, but this new wave of contests and skate events took place at bigger venues, and were for the first time planned by event people and staffed by big-venue security, like the kind who work casinos and arenas.

Skating still fit that non-category, and is somewhere between a sport and a dance-off and a rock concert and an all-day track meet. But there were more people and more security, and for these first few summer tours, security was often working a skate event for the first time. Which meant being a security guard within a skate crowd for the first time. Skate crowds were the biggest they'd ever been, full of mostly skaters, some new skaters, some non-skaters, and some industry people from the outside world.

Skating had had a menacing identity since its *Life* cover in 1965, but up until this point, the culture had been insulated by participants and repellent to nonparticipants to the extent that laws were passed to keep them from the public eye. No one wanted to look at skateboarding, let alone look inside.

Demos in the '60s and '70s were mostly held at shops and skateparks owned and operated by skaters. No one made much money, and while this changed in the '80s as sales increased, the community still remained largely insular, with most contests held at skaters' homes. Besides a few commercials and Hollywood projects, skating stayed mostly within itself. Skating was not yet seen as a sport, and especially a sport for TV.

This all changed with the X Games. Demos now meant big money, wide promotion, and a place to spot and show off talent. Both skaters and non-skaters liked this, and so for the first time skaters cautiously shook hands with big-money non-skaters, and started to skate in non-skate venues with non-skate media. As expected, there was friction.

At least this was the case in 1996 at the Hard Rock Cafe inside Universal Studios in Hollywood. It was a stop on the Vans Triple Crown tour with a vert competition with a street-course demo off to the side. Vallely was there. So was beloved new pro Chad Muska.

This is an odd example, and even though not a lot happened that day, how it's been retold and sold is important.

We were outside at Universal Studios in one of those non-areas where they always have street contests. Ramps and rails were set up on the pavement, surrounded by bulgingly crowded barricades, affixed with sponsors' banners.

Off to the side, Muska, a guy of a medium build in a gray tank top, who skates with his hand taped because he rips it open so often, was trying to flip off a launch ramp, flying up 8 feet in the air and landing in the tiny rounded strip of blacktop where the crowd was not standing. He fell twice, and when he fell the third time, Muska recalls, "Half my skin just came off my hand—you know—in my palm." He cursed in pain, and a security guard told him not to curse. It escalated, and soon Muska was skating away, yelling, *Fuckfuckfuckfuckfuckfuckfuck!* Soon after, the guard had Muska in an arm lock, and skaters and other security were running over, pushing their chests into the event's talent.

The security guards were the high-end kind, with brushy flattops and cheap dark sunglasses and outfits meant to look like police uniforms: shirtsleeves with patches and star-shaped badges, and a telephone cord that came out of the armpit and went up to the walkie-talkie that was buttoned into a shoulder loop so they could push the button and talk into it while I guess keeping their other hand free.

Not too much happened. Vallely was up on the ramp, about to take his run, when he saw the commotion. He hopped down and ran over and put the security guard into a wall of skaters. He pinned another guard in the process. The first guy let go of Muska and the other security guards tried to grab Vallely, but he spun out and shoved them all back and ran away. It doesn't look like anyone even threw a punch in the footage. But by now there was pretty much no barrier between the crowd and the camera crew and more security and a lot of other people, and it was whirling across the course, picking up size and volume.

One skater threw his board under a running guard and the guy fell on his face. Another slid along a high quarterpipe and kicked his board into a guard's head, and the guard just walked away. The Nevada State Police came. The unfortunate event planner, in a sunhat and dress, announced in a wobbly voice: "We're going to stop until we get security."

Again, nothing really happened. Vallely disappeared. Muska was led away and then came back. It was barely reported in the uber-reported world of skate media. The only reason skaters have heard of this is because it was part of a compilation called *Mike V's Greatest Hits*, an important artifact in what has emerged as a whole new genre in skate media: confrontation footage.

Almost without exception, since at least 1988's 8mm masterpiece *Sick Boys,* every skate video has a scene where a cop or store owner or asshole accosts a skater. They're as ubiquitous and important to the genre as the slam section, or a clip in a rider's part that has them taking a fall. They're there because it's part of the culture, and seeing these scenes helps skaters trust that what they're watching has been made by other skaters.

*Greatest Hits* rounded up all of these confrontations and cut out the skateboarding. The show is emceed by Vallely, sitting on the edge of a boxing ring, recalling his various security run-ins and ass-kickings. Each chapter opens with a title placed between two boxing gloves, and an iBand's dinging sound. You can watch it for free on Google Video or buy it on Amazon for $1.45. The video's scored with music by Vallely's old band, The Rats.*

Each segment consists of Vallely and fellow skaters talking about an incident, interspersed with little bits of poor footage, spaced out and repeated with quick cuts and thrashy music and shitty post-prod effects where they zoom in or slow down on a grainy piece of tape. There are a few skaters you've never heard of, along with young pro Bam Margera, who was on tour with Vallely during a more-important incident. Hawk even makes an appearance, in a T-shirt with a graphic I finally recognized of the monster created by Marvin the Martian in that Bugs Bunny episode where he goes to outer space.

It's rather low-budget and pretty boring, but the video does include the most famous piece of confrontation footage in skate history, of which there are a lot. It's a thirty-nine-second clip with no beginning that gave Vallely a new popular identity. The screen opens and we're in a dark parking lot, looking at Vallely's shaved head and huge back. In front of him are four roughly college-age men in a tight semicircle. The grainy footage is black-and-white, as if caught on a security or glove-compartment video camera. We're not a second in when Vallely gives two of the group a butterfly stroke shove. The circle loosens, then tightens. Vallely does it again. The guy who is going to run away when he gets hit has his arm up in a little wave and a big smile on his face. There's a few more seconds of exchange we can't hear, and then Vallely takes all four of them down. The last one, in a backwards hat and

---

* Vallely actually came to skating through music and remains involved today. The punk rockers he hung around with all skated, and he was kicked out of his first band in 1985 for spending so much time skating. He also posts and reads poems at open mics, and after starting The Rats founded his current band, Revolution Mother, which sometimes plays the skate tours where Mike competes. In 2003, Vallely was invited by Black Flag front man Greg Ginn to sing at a reunion show. Vallely not only obliged, but sang the entire *My War* album.

a Hawaiian shirt, tries to side-slap Vallely as he's wrapping his foot around the back of the kid's leg and cocking back his fist.

In the ever-video-watching world of skateboarding, the footage gave Vallely a new rock-star identity as the sport's destroying angel. He filled a long-vacant subcultural niche the way Hawk filled a major-media one—that of the skater who fights back. People still ask him about it. Various YouTubers have scored and re-edited it, slowing it down and even adding subtitles like MIKE VALLELY VS. FOUR RANDOM JOCKS and THEY CALLED HIM SKATER FAG. The clip was anthologized twice and ran on numerous TV shows, and actually ended up more than anything else being the thing that brought Vallely into popular culture.

Explained in the *Greatest Hits* compilation, all the other pros weigh in, calling the boys "dumb drunk jocks" a few different times. Vallely tells us the boys first said they were going to kill him, and then said they were going to kick his ass and his friends' asses. This is the only segment where Hawk is included. Prior to *Greatest Hits*, the footage was first distributed in a stunt video called *CKY* (or *Camp Kill Yourself*), which was eventually viewed by two of the boys Vallely hit, Tom Sayers and Adam Dailey. They sued for $10 million. Sayers went on the Seattle news, insisting they were coerced into fighting with threats, that they'd not even spoken to Vallely, and that he had approached them. Five days before jury selection began, the case was settled out of court, silencing all parties.

The incident happened outside a Seattle 7-Eleven during Tony Hawk's Gigantic Skatepark tour in the summer of 1999. One of the pros on tour was twenty-one-year-old Brandon Cole Margera, better known as Bam. Margera grew up skating in West Chester, Pennsylvania, and was sponsored by his local Fairman's Skate Shop at age fourteen. In early footage he looks about eight, and has huge cheeks and dyed hair and the thickest Pennsylvania accent I've ever heard and my cousins are from Pennsylvania.

Bam shredded with that particular East Coast gnarlment of skaters strengthened on years of cold air and torn pavement. He was good. He'd switch stances at the apex of a wallride into a blunt, and could flip up onto a long gravel-mixed bank made to discourage skating and then manual forever, smiling down at the glorious chunky purr under his feet.

He was also one of the first of a new generation that videoed and distributed most everything he'd done, eventually piecing together a series of skate and stunt videos into the abovementioned collection, *CKY.*

And they're brilliant, because Margera inverted the regular skate-video idea, piecing together stunts and confrontations and silly shit with bits of skating to help it along. It's Bam and the friends he grew up with, kicking footballs into passing cars, falling from deer platforms, or jumping off rooftops into aboveground leafy pools under the coldly crackled Pennsylvania sky. It was not a new idea, but selling it was, and it was a success.

They got a distributor, but the videos also spread virally like the Jerky Boys tapes did, eventually ending up with Jeff Tremaine, former editor of *Big Brother* and cofounder of MTV's *Jackass.*

Anyway, it was 2001, and Margera was the young guy on the tour. He held his own by doing things like skating off staging hauled up onto a mini-ramp. He had big bushy hair and a grinning young face and almost no tattoos. He'd been doing *CKY* for two years and was a longtime fan of Vallely; he told Vallely that before the tour was over, he'd tape him fighting.* It's all

---

* That's the story in the *CKY* video, anyway. There's an earlier and not-as-exciting video of Bam skating in a crowded parking lot. A passerby stops his S10 and chucks a Nerf football at him, calling him a name and driving away. But the guy shows up later on Bam's MTV scripted reality show, and in a Right Guard Xtreme commercial. He's Vincent Margera, Bam's uncle. And it was set up.

Bam's thirty-one now. His Sirius radio show, record label, and production company are all run from the Pocono Township of West Chester, Pennsylvania, where Margera lives in a castle on fourteen acres that house his own personal megaramp, at least two Lamborghinis, and that car Lurch drove on the Addams Family.

detailed in the *Greatest Hits* video, and detailed again when Vallely appears on *Viva La Bam,* a five-season scripted *CKY*-esque reality show that hit on MTV and got Margera featured in *Sports Illustrated, Rolling Stone,* and on ESPN.

VALLELY'S gone back and forth on the incident, and at the end of *Greatest Hits,* sitting by the boxing ring, he says it's bad to fight, and he hadn't been in any fights in over a year. But it turns out this message, however scripted or insisted upon, is nowhere near as popular as the fighting ones we see every night on SportsCenter, and it wasn't long before he was back at it. He discussed the incident again in 2007 on the *Tom Green Show,* I guess ignoring a court order and stating that he'd do it again—that "They got what they deserved."

HERE'S WHERE I'm going with this: A year later, in 2008, similar footage of Vallely surfaced. He's standing in the landscaped area outside of a mall, spray-painting a wall in broad daylight. He's without his board. Soon he's approached by a portly, mustachio'd security guard on a Segway and they talk for a second, the guy pointing and saying to turn off the camera, just before Vallely sprays him across the chest.

Because the community was familiar with Mike's run-ins, and because footage of these run-ins was so popular, most viewers weren't aware they were watching a commercial. The video was leaked just before the premiere of *Paul Blart: Mall Cop,* a top-grossing, PG "family movie" by the director of *Daddy Day Care.* Mike has a small role in *Paul Blart,* where he menacingly chases the same security guard on his board.

The video was (and still is) really bad in two ways. It was the worst (or maybe best) kind of commercial, because we came at it with our guard down. It's a video that pops up on YouTube with other confrontation videos, and our star here is not known for bullshit, and in fact has built a rare, heroic reputation for upholding his own ethics and honor with his fists, if need be. And while so many of these incidents that Vallely is famous for are legit, once our trust is violated, it's hard to not keep our guard up, even when we don't need to.

But maybe worse, Vallely had taken a (probably paid) role to play the hooligan stereotype that guys like him have always fought against. In the video he's not a skater who's just standing up for himself, someone who won't be disrespected, or someone grabbing his board back from a security guard,* or warning a soon-to-be-sorry landscaper, "Don't get in my face." Instead, he's a prick—a hoodlum displaying the same insolent, undeserving disrespect he himself is so respected for standing up to. He's playing a character thought up maybe by people who don't like skating, but definitely want to capitalize on it by selling the idea to the same kind of people.

This really isn't meant to single out Vallely, who in 2009 at age forty filmed a Berrics part that displayed the same dynamic board spinning and launch and plant maneuvers that made him famous as a teenager. It's meant to look at the slippery slope of the attention that's brought to skateboarding and skate culture. Attention that gives, yes, but wants something in return. It's a newer threat to the sport, and a threat that won't go away with a simple fistfight, since that's what sells today.

---

* To his credit, Vallely was the only skater of stature to speak out against Officer Salvatore Rivieri of the Baltimore Police Department, challenging him (of course) to a fight on *Tom Green*. A big guy, Rivieri made headlines in 2008 when a video surfaced of him threatening, headlocking, then throwing fourteen-year-old Eric Bush to the ground because he kept calling him "Dude." He was first suspended with pay, but the video and the force's disciplinary inaction got national attention, and Rivieri was eventually fired.

# 22

# THE BEST SKATEBOARDER IN THE WORLD IS A SEVENTH GRADER

RYAN SHECKLER was already the talk of the skate world when he turned pro at age thirteen, which made him a world-record holder and garnered the beginnings of the major media coverage that would make it one hell of a year for the youngest pro skater in history.

All longtime skaters know that contests are only a small part of their diverse, artistic, complex sport. Still, the 2003 circuit is legendary because Sheckler didn't so much arrive as invade. Now competing for money against the biggest pools of the best skaters in the world, he won the four big contests of 2003: the Dew Tour starting in March, Vancouver's Vans Slam City Jam in April, the X Games in August, and then the Maloof Money Cup in October. These four events had the highest viewership, biggest prize money, biggest crowds in the best venues, and the most competitors.

Ryan was thirteen, 5-foot-1, and ninety-seven pounds, with braces and a big bell of sun-kissed brown hair, and he beat the shit out of everybody again and again and again. And again. He won all four contests—which no one's done before or since—and won with runs that weren't just incongruously huge and technically perfect, but also wildly innovative. He wasn't only creating stuff that no one had ever seen before, but also finding new spaces and gaps in which to create the stuff no one's ever seen.

Footage from that year shows a young master hard at work. He does little things, like shoot between the not-meant-for-shooting-between space between two quarterpipes, building enough speed to launch off a hip and impossibly transfer to another ramp too far for anyone else to reach. But he also does moves all his own. One thing he does a lot is called a kickflip indy by the announcer, but is soon better known as his signature Shecklair: He rolls in off a ramp and tucks forward or pumps wildly on flat to get speed, then lithely flies off a quarter pipe and kicks both his legs out as the board flips up through his knees, 6 inches from his crotch. At peak height, he reaches down and grabs and sticks the board under his sneakers just as he starts to fall.

It takes a second for the crowd to go *Oh!* No one had seen an adult pro do this, yet there was a seventh grader who just rode up a wall at cyclist's speed, ollied about 7 feet into the air, then no-handedly shot a spinning six-pound board between his legs and was back on before he'd even started his descent.

It is a David Lee Roth–ish rock star move and a crowd favorite. It is also mechanically perfect and smooth, yet thunderously huge, and risky, and by the time he stands all the way up he is already pushing toward the next thing, a steeper incline he'll backside 180 over.

"What are we seeing here?" one announcer asks the other at X Games 13.

"What we're seeing here is a thirteen-year-old dominating the street course."

And we are. This is the way Sheckler skates. Tight and clean and microfine, but also fast and huge and hard. He wastes no part of the course, and whether he's just rolled in or just rolled off something he's always pumping his foot, and you don't see how fast it makes him go until he hits a ramp and goes, always goes, higher than anyone else.

He also seems to be having a good time. Whether he's moving down a packed barricade signing autographs with Tony Hawk, or accepting a trophy or giant check for $10,000, or up there on the ramp with the pros he's about to destroy, he's not just at ease but sometimes smiling or laughing or just plain goofy. He sometimes wobbles his head back and forth or makes a whistling face and slightly crosses his eyes, or does this exaggerated expression of being really scared, like Big Ern McCracken in *Kingpin*. Often when they stick a camera in his face just before his run he gives the same big lippy smile that Hawk used to do when he was flying so high he'd be level with the photographers' platform. Sometimes when way up in the air he puts his tongue in the corner of his mouth, like Babe Ruth.

He has a little androgynous voice more like a child's than an adolescent's, and in interviews he seems relaxed and happy and never exhausted or in pain, even if sweat has soaked his hair into cones that rustle down over his shoulders. He doesn't seem rehearsed and empty like a tennis player or bloated and autistic like a football player or mannered and disgusting like a baseball player. He seems excited to be having a new kind of good time.

"Being pro is awesome," he says in one interview. "All of these places that we go—we just skate all these spots you see in the videos and you're like 'Aww—I wanna go there,' and you go there, so it's fun." At the end of interviews, when the talent tells him they're done, Ryan says, "Sick. Thanks," and swings up his board and walks on to the next thing.

These interviews are also where we see his beauty for the first time. He's still a kid, and it will be a year or so before he gets that slight-toned adolescent look, but you can tell. He not just cute. His body, like his talent, is a gift. He has big shining eyes inside long-lashed, almond shaped sockets and full lips and tan skin and pink nails. His vibe is tranquil and peaceful and almost wise, and it's a sharp contrast to the berserk way he conquered the course fifteen minutes ago. That he doesn't need time to enter or exit that My Lai zone of a top pro athlete is a mystery, but he doesn't.

There was no seeming connection at first between this happy middle schooler and the way he was napalmingly winning a lot of attention and respect and money with a skateboard. Anyone who has been around young athletes dragged through a competitive circuit will attest to their general unhappy weariness when they're not wildly alive in competition. Nothing about Ryan suggested he was one of these. Like Gretzky or Pele or Beethoven or John Nash, he was just a nice kid, and something somewhere made it so that he ended up a channel for some huge force.

Or so it seemed. Pretty early on, Sheckler was the hit of the Games. He didn't generate the attention Hawk had nine years ago (nothing really could), but they filmed him pretty much all the time. You can still watch his competitive footage, and can also watch him just before competition, and you should. Because before he takes his run, Ryan looks different. Being so small, he naturally looks out of his element, and staring at the course his wide-eyedness might be mistaken for fear. But during his time on deck, that sixty-second interval after he pushes off the crowded railing and before the clock starts, something happens.

He moves into competition mode, which he'll tell you is his natural element—an element that again is only a part of skating but happens to be the part seen by most outsiders. He looks a little nervous, then aware, then empty for that minute, watching the course from under his black helmet. Six feet below him photographers are sticking their cameras out, and then pulling them back. Out over him is a video camera on a stick. He holds his board by the nose; it comes up past his waist. He's almost waddling up there, looking out then down at his little feet then out again, until ever so slightly he touches the tail's tip to the platform. He slides his toe over and lets go of the board and it falls forward onto its back wheels, sticking up at a 45-degree angle.

When they call his name, he step-slides forward and rolls the wheels over the coping and locks his truck into place. It's these seconds of bull-box time where you can see. He doesn't look distracted or nervous or even calm anymore. He looks like 5 feet of coiled spring. Small and sharp but also organically powerful in the emotionless way a hurricane looks moving toward your boat.

There's a famous early photo, taken with a zoom lens from the bottom of such a ramp: Ryan's face is serene and feral, like a quiet baby and an ageless old hit man. His shoulders are a little wider than his helmet, covered in bright stickers with a chin strap swinging between tinted locks of hair. His comp'd shirt fits him like a dress. The sleeves go down to the hard plastic on his elbow pads, which end by his wrist. His pink bracelet's too big for his tan hand.

It's the X Games finals in 2003, and Ryan has simply beat everyone's ass all year long. The buzzer starts and he drops into a tuck and before the sound stops he's out past the first ramp's lip, lunging with his little swinging back leg, his clothes flapping and everyone watching, like it or not. He flies off a bank and kicks his feet way out, flipping and then catching the board before he's even peaked. He's got it under his feet and gone into a crouch while still in the air, so he's already moving in the direction he wants before he touches the ground and shoots off the next platform for a 360. Then he turns and scratches his little nose before riding down to a hip that takes him into the air then into an uphill grind on a rail shaped like this:

His truck riding up the long steel cylinder makes an even, screaming *KAAAAAAAAAAAA* sound. Sheckler grinds in the angled
way Lizard King does, where his board is way out and his ass is
way back, like he's karate-kicking or riding a snowboard or leaning against a cool car.

▲

RODNEY MULLEN attends very few contests or promotional
events, but was there for one in Australia to coincide with the
video release of Almost's *Round 3*. He sat next to Ryan on the
plane and a woman asked if they were father and son. "I was so
proud," remembers Rodney. And I said "No, but I wish we were."

He didn't follow Ryan's sweeping record, but knew "that
yeah—he's killin' it." Contests have always been a divisive subject with Rodney. No skater won more world championships, but
no skater hated them more. Mullen could see early on that one of
Sheckler's many talents was to perform and perform well under
the pressure of a contest environment. But he also recognized
the dangers.

Before the famed tour year, he took Ryan aside and told
him: "I know what contests are and what the expectation can be.
Losses will define you more than wins, and at some stage that
is all that is left for you—after the consecutive wins. And other
people will define you. And the second that your skateboarding
is defined by external things, such as media coverage and what
number [is] associated with your name and the other guy who
came up second—just like Tony and Christian, that battle—then
you're the loser. And you become a slave to what you love, and
soon you will come to hate it. And that will be the biggest loss."

Rodney told Ryan this after he'd gone over to the Shecklers'
for dinner. "They have the greatest family," he remembers. "His

little brother was *so* funny." After the meal, the two stepped outside.

After Rodney spoke, Ryan thanked him. "So I remember telling him that, and he just took it and was quiet. Like, 'Thanks.' "

▲

RYAN WAS A HIT—consistently the highest-scoring competitor and crowd favorite. Other skaters called him a peer, I think so they could feel better about themselves and have proximity to the person they knew was this new wave's rock star. Vallely said Ryan is "making life difficult for guys like me," adding that he was a good kid, respectful, and that he represented well.

Press stuck to Sheckler because they knew they had something special, and because they hadn't found a competitive replacement for Hawk since he'd retired in 1999. ESPN ran a segment on Sheckler when he won the X Games, and so did NBC. The NBC thing was type-A mass-media skateboarding coverage, pointing out Ryan's unprecedented four-contest victory and trying to narrate over footage of one of his lines, describing tricks they didn't know the names of, informing us again and again that this thirteen-year-old was a top competitor in "skateboarding, and especially street skateboarding."

None of this bothered Ryan. He seemed to naturally have Hawk's learned thing of just rolling with the outsiders and getting it done. And like Hawk, he'd point to other skaters and would shine for the community he was now, like it or not, representing. Asked about his various records, given his age and many wins, or the fact that he was officially the best skateboarder in the world, he just smiled and said, "I got lucky."

Sheckler was already endorsed by top skate companies and some companies that associate themselves with action sports:

Almost and Ethika and Etnies and Oakley and SoBe and Tensor and Volcom. That was about to change. Panasonic and Red Bull came calling, which was important because they'd never before called a skater.

On the Internet, videos from the Games, or Almost, or early footage of Ryan started getting exponentially more hits than anything else skate-related. Some popped up off the side of your YouTube window because so many people had watched them. And there were comments now by probably non-skaters:

*OMG I DIDDNT KNOW HE WAS SO YOUNG!*

*He is sOsO cute!*

*MMM, MMM, MMM*

People started making their own slide shows of Sheckler, posted with similar comments. Some photos have hearts Photoshopped around his head.

*love ryan sheckler alot im the biggest number-one super fan ever! he is soooooooooooooooooooooooooooooooooooooooooo oooooooooooooooooooooooooooooooooooooooooooooooooo damn hott*

Ryan did not shy away from the attention. He did every interview he could, often citing Rodney as his mentor. The *LA Times* came to his house for a profile. So did *MTV Cribs*. He showed them the fridge where he kept his sneakers and the freezer where there was a frozen pizza covered in Volcom stickers and a brick of skate wheels in the ice drawer. "If you keep your wheels in the freezer they'll last ten times longer. Rodney Mullen taught me that," he says. "Shhhh . . . It's our secret."

But here's another Shecklerism: While his audience was expanding outside the sport, he was still not just a skater but *the* skater, repeatedly beating pros twice his age. He'd been doing this, but what else surfaced during this time was a work resolve not unlike his skating: mature and level-headed and way ahead of everyone else. The things that stirred Rodney the first time they connected.

Fuel TV did a special on Ryan, a few-days-in the-life-of feature called *First Hand*. Sheckler was fifteen in the footage, still small, with narrow shoulders and messy hair and deep olive eyes. The crew followed him to an office park where he was going to jump a gap. Sheckler narrated the special, saying, "It's always important to get the photographer out there because getting the picture is what it's all about."

The gap was massive and hard to even reach. It was at the end not of a sidewalk but of a wall, and to get there, he was going to have to ride along the *top* of a stacked stone wall, with all of his wheels on either edge of the top of the wall. (The other pro I've seen even try something like this is Mike Mo Capaldi, big-tech genius and the first Battle of the Berrics champion.)

Please note here that we were not in a park, with perfect transitions of smooth concrete. It was a street spot: unintentional and raw and on private property, and it demonstrated Sheckler's versatility as a young master.

He walks up to the gap before the attempt. He'll need to launch off the top of the wall he's riding on, sail down over a drop wall and a patch of landscaping that's sticking out at the top of another short wall. He'll need to get about 5 feet out to clear it before the 8-foot drop to the pavement.

"This should be easy," he says, then merrily sighs. "But nothin's easy till it's done."

He tries a pop shove-it, a basic board varial/180 without spinning his body, but something goes wrong and he barely clears the first wall, falling forward and down with his toes almost catching the second ledge. He lands with his wrists out and rolls into a pile, then gets up fast and says, "I'm done."

"Yeah, that was bad. That hurt a lot," he tells the camera. "If I'd been ready to fall it would have been easier to fall, but I kind of just had to stick it out and roll with the fall."

The day's a washout, and Sheckler, sounding like a seasoned director, explains: "It's a bummer when you don't get anything done. But it's part of skateboarding. You can't go out every time and expect to get five tricks. [He means magazine shots of five tricks.] It's just the way it is. I've kinda learned to deal with it."

Besides seeming to have a full understanding of the products and promotion and performance of what he was doing, Sheckler just continued to get better on all fronts and still seemed to have a lot of fun. At his local skatepark, a connected white floor of pools and steps and hips, he teamed up with a friend for a double line, where two skaters ride the same space, sometimes flying over one another. It's a bit like couples figure skating and high hard art when it's done by Bob Burnquist and Bucky Lasek. Sheckler and his buddy went up a ramp together, locked their tails in the coping, and kicked out to give each other a foot-five, the way Kid-N-Play used to do. Then, ready for something new, Sheckler wove through the course and shot out of the little bowl, tucking his legs to fly up over the 6-foot skatepark fence and land on the sidewalk.

On July 1, 2005, Sheckler flew to Germany for the Munster Monster Mastership World Contest, where he'd placed fourth two years ago. It was a huge contest, so big that the winner was declared world champion until the next season. The course took up the whole arena floor, and from one end you could hardly see across the gray wooden sea of banks and drops and rails and stairs.

He was down there practicing when a stray board hit his shin. Ryan was sent in one of those Craftmatic Adjustable Bed stretchers to the hospital, since he couldn't walk. One doctor told him it was a fracture, and one doctor said it was not a fracture. Whatever it was looked like a scalpel scar or fat pink worm down the bottom of his shin. "I couldn't move my foot," he said.

But Sheckler was going to compete anyway, not because he felt he had to, but because he wanted to. It was another thing we were seeing about him, and maybe the reason he was so good and happy and relaxed at contests: He liked them.

"I'm a competitive person," he told me. "I've always been a competitor, which plays out in my skateboarding. I mean, if it's a contest, I'm going to try to beat you." I asked him about contests versus the expressive side of skateboarding. "Personally, I like contests," he answered. "There's something very rewarding about perfecting a sixty-second run. If you work on a run for a week, then bring it to the final, and you just nail it, there's nothing that beats that feeling. It's an adrenaline level you can't match skating on the street by yourself."

Now in his runs, you could see his thirst for the win and the need to push his limits. He had long bounced back and skated with injuries, but now outsiders were seeing this for the first time, since everywhere Sheckler went camera crews went with him. He'd skate through anything. And he'd skate through anything hard, because he wanted not to compete but to win. At the hospital, orderlies put a foamy sticker over the broken-skinned bruise and wrapped his leg in gauze.

"I woke up and didn't know if I was gonna be able to skate because it was hurting a *lot*," he said. He went anyway. "My heat came up and it was all or nothing." Just before his run, he touched the toe of the injured foot to the ground and started working the ball and socket joint to loosen up his ankle. "I didn't care. I just started skating. I didn't think I was gonna be ready for it. I was ready, though."

He wasn't only ready, he was in his mode, hitting every inch of every rail, getting an extra 180 in when he flipped up over hips, pulling a Shecklair to the great pleasure of the crowd, and then sailing off a drop much like the one that had wrecked him on Fuel TV, a little cliff about 8 feet high that he ollied off of, picking up his knees to fly, landing with his ass almost touching the ground, then standing as he yanked up his pants.

He took third in the world, behind Brazilians Daniel Vieira and Ricardo Porva. He won $4,000. "The money is great, of course, but I don't worry about money at the contests," said Ryan. "Just being considered number one, that's what's most important to me."

Sheckler flew home to heal for forty-eight hours, then flew to Denver for what was officially called the Right Guard Open at the Pepsi Center, the second of five stops for the Dew Tour. Sheckler took first, beating out top pros P-Rod and Jeremy Rogers and then laying in the bottom of a quarterpipe with his knees bent and his hands over his face. The following month he would go to Portland, then San Jose, then Orlando, his point total taking overall first place by the end of the 2005 Dew Tour.

His talent and his brand were both growing, and when he took the gold and $75,000 at the Tour's end, capping yet another extraordinarily successful competitive year, it was going to be a smaller version of the Shaun White phenomenon, where *Thrasher* and Grind TV but also NBC and *Seventeen* had good reason to do segments on this talented young man.

He missed about half of his middle-school days due to travel, but by the time he was fourteen, he had won so many competitions that he would only need to compete in the big ones, like a top tennis player. With his dad and manager mom, Ryan made a doomed plan to have a normal high school career, with no more homeschooling and less travel.

"I just want to get back up with all my friends and start doing the social thing again," he told the *Los Angeles Times*. "I just want to go to high school."

He lasted a year.

# 23

# RODNEY RIDS HIS BODY OF SCAR TISSUE, AND THE FIRST STANCELESS SKATER

ALMOST'S *ROUND 3* premiered in London in 2002. Rodney Mullen sat with Ryan Sheckler and his teammates, watching his footage and harboring a hard, dark secret: Skateboarding was over for him, yet again. Halfway through filming, Mullen's right leg—his ollie leg—began to work improperly. First it was aches and cramping, followed by full-time seizure and near-constant pain. Rolling out of falls became difficult, and he found it hard to sleep through the night. Due to temperature change he couldn't sit in the window seat of the plane while the team flew from the United States to Australia to Europe to promote the video.

From Tony Hawk's sports medicine doctor and the man's brother, an East Coast radiologist, Mullen learned that years of skating, specifically years of his back foot slipping off the tail, had built up scar tissue that over the decades had wound through his right leg and was now pulling his femur into his pelvis. He started feeling a grinding sensation every time he stepped out of his car. Doctors explained that the ceaseless grinding was due to his bones producing calcium, and that as the condition worsened, the head of his femur would be ground off completely, and the bone would eventually fuse to his pelvis. This would shorten his right leg; he would walk with a cane. Doctors said the unremovable scar tissue resembled that of front-end-collision victims whose legs had been driven back up into their hips.

"I couldn't tell anyone because I knew this was it," Rodney remembers. "And my skating, very much like we talked about with Ryan, it defined who I was, and it's pretty scary—even being as old as I am—I mean I'm a grown man, and I shouldn't have to rely on my skateboard like it's Linus's blanket, carrying it around for security. But that's all I've ever known. And that's been me so long—to take that away . . . there's a lot of unknown in that."

Mullen knew he couldn't top what he'd done in *Round 3* to his satisfaction, and he could never be "that ugly old guy people feel sorry for because he's holding on to a dream. So let it go. Just be a man and let it go and disappear. Essentially that's what I tried to do."

Mullen told his sponsors and coworkers he was going to take some time off, but soon found himself stretching and "prying myself apart," trying to rid his leg of the binding tissue he could feel inside of it.

"You get a sense of what's foreign in you, holding you. And you know it's in your muscles—and when you're stretching it that far, you do sense that foreign thing." Mullen wrapped himself around fire hydrants so their stems would dig into his tissue. He twisted his leg into the wheel well of his car, and used screwdrivers or knobs atop chain-link fence poles to apply pressure to the scar tissue before he'd stretch against a shelf or shopping rack. It was the chemotherapeutic idea of destroying a little of the person and a lot of the toxin. Little by little, he began to remove the scar tissue.

"It tears out like chewing gum that's kinda old, dry, and it'll stretch and stretch and stretch and that's when you're just giving up—and then [there's] a 'pop.' If you've ever broken bones you get a heat sensation, then a little nausea, then you get this crazy high."

Every time he tore out a piece of scar tissue, Mullen says he would find himself a bit more free. He went on for three years, pressurizing, stretching, tearing, then trying out his balance on his board. Sessions were always at night and lasted up to six or eight hours. The process improved his flexibility but also freed his leg of scar tissue, which Mullen refers to as "material." As the material was flushed from his body, he would wake up sick and dehydrated with chapped lips. He urinated frequently, and it always smelled terrible.

His flexibility was improving, but he says his hip still felt like a stick shift instead of a ball and socket. A turning point came one night in the valley around 1 a.m. Mullen was under his car with his leg in the wheel well, twisting so hard that he was up off the ground, "bouncing," he says, on a specific area of pain in his hip. "You have to get to that stage where you don't care. And that's when you make it. And guys like Ryan and Jamie Thomas and Jeremy Wray and Bryan Herman, they're all ninjas at that stuff."

Suddenly Mullen heard a loud *POP.*

"It was like when I broke my ankle," he remembers. "Like a tree branch. And my body hit the ground—not all of it, because I'm stuck in the wheel well, but the rest of it. And I looked up, and there was snot and tears on my hand. And I got that crazy high and I pulled myself out the best I could, lying on the ground going, 'God, what'd I do, what'd I do, what'd I do,' and I got up. The pain goes away in twenty to forty seconds because you're numb. So I get up slowly, and for the first time in four years, three years, I felt it move like a ball and socket."

He'd broken the bit of calcium that had formed between his pelvis and femur, which was keeping the two from moving like a ball and socket. "I got on my skateboard and was like 'I did it! I did it! I did it!' I went home, slept for fourteen hours. I vomited. And at that stage, I kept going."

Mullen tore out the remaining scar tissue, and by 2007 was skating at his "normal level" again. But by then he'd lost interest in adding to the dizzying, unique lines exhibited in *Round 3*. Flipping a different way out of a primo slide (when the board's sideways and the rider's on the wheels), he said, was just diminishing returns. "Polishing a turd." But the past three years had given him a revelation: So much scar tissue had grown in his right leg because of the asymmetrical nature of the sport. His stance is regular, and so he was disproportionately using his right leg, where the injury occurred. Now that he'd undone the nature of his stance and was starting clean, he planned to approach skateboarding not with a new stance, but with no stance at all.

"We're flesh and bone, and the flesh wraps around your bones like a thick wetsuit," he explained. "And if I can rotate or change the way my flesh is around the bones by manhandling it—again, I'm not a tough guy, but I've got my pain threshold—then I can change my stance."

Mullen began only skating switch, goofy-footed, doing hundreds of thousands of switch tic-tacs, and he says, forming two right legs.

After the plateau there was, again, a spike, and Mullen found himself doing things in his switch stance he could never do regular, "because my center was at a new place."

One example of this is the switch one-foot nose.

He also found himself remembering tricks and sequences he'd done in his old stance, and could quickly nail them switch, because "If my body is in the exact same position in the opposite stance, then my brain already has that knowledge, so everything I've learned—it's no longer switch. Switch is an entirely different trick. But this is just like regular. It's like remembering, and I'm already finding that's the case."

▲

I KNOW this is a little confusing. I was confused at first too. Mullen doesn't want to simply (and revolutionarily) relearn everything switch-stance. He's already done that. He wants to have no stance, to freely rotate between switch and regular, where each stance is equally proficient, canceling the other one out, so that, in fact, he has no stance at all.

He points to the Group Theory branch of quantum mathematics—cutting out calculations that go on forever because they're symmetrical, thus simplifying the equation. He points to P-Rod, who, like many skaters of his generation, grew up skating both stances. P-Rod's position over the board in either stance, he says, is almost identical. That's Mullen's goal—to skate identical regardless of how he's standing. To have no forwards or backwards. To be the best in the world, regular and goofy. To be the first stanceless skater.

After developing ollie power in his left leg from skating switch, he said he needed to break that down so he could rotate between the two, a task that took two more years of nightly practice. His progress was encouraging, and in 2008 Mullen filmed and released two five-second parts. Each part features a sequence of tricks done on a drainage ditch. His stance is goofy riding up into a baffling sequence (half cab impossible late flip, nollie impossible late backfoot flip) and regular riding back down.

They're tricks that would never work switch, he explained, because of the natural leverage a stance builds into a skater.

"My goal was—if you can change that, you can come from behind the curtain."

# 24

# LIFE OF RYAN

IN EARLY 2007 I pitched *GQ* a profile on Ryan Sheckler to coincide with the premiere of his reality show on MTV. A kind man named Joel Lovell liked the pitch, helped me rewrite it, and then brought it to the magazine's brass, who, in the end, decided they weren't sold on a skateboarding story.

*Life of Ryan*'s first episode ran on Monday, August 27, 2007, just after *The Hills*, and was MTV's highest-rated series premiere that year. It averaged 2.3 million viewers per episode and captured the time slot's twelve- to twenty-four-year-old demographic, the same advertiser-coveted demographic that *Jersey Shore* captured two years later, and a demographic that MTV's pretty much owned since its inception in 1981.

The show's intro mixes calico-cartoony footage of Ryan skating with shots of him in crowds signing autographs and climbing onto planes and hanging out with his friends and family. Over a pop-punk theme song we hear Ryan's voice telling us that he's trying to be a normal teenager, but it's hard when you're a pro skater. It's a good reality show. Executively produced by Ryan's mom, each twenty-three-minute episode is well scripted with a lot of drama, some of which is about Ryan's quest to find the right girl or a new best friend, but some of which centers around his parents' recent divorce and the toll it's taken on Ryan and his brothers, Shane and tiny Kane. There are girls who never wear much anyway, but show up in a lot of the beach scenes. Ryan cries a good amount of the time, but he always endures.*

He does his freshman year at San Clemente High and even joins the wrestling team, but he's still missing too many days of class and transfers to Futures, a $10,000-per-year "school for young professionals," whose alumni include Olympic figure skater Sasha Cohen. Ryan attends classes once a week for three hours, meeting one-on-one with instructors in a mirrored office building off the San Diego Freeway.

At 16 he buys a red-rimmed black Range Rover with a stereo so impressive that *DUB* magazine puts him on the cover. So does *Sports Illustrated Kids*. More stories follow, and helping to green-light major magazine coverage of this teen skateboarder is the fact that Ryan doesn't look like a little kid anymore. He still looked mostly like a child at fifteen, big-hair-headed and small all over, even though he'd started to stretch out. But his teenage body appeared the next year, hard and tubular over his golden skin. Those days are gone. He now wears the unskaterly build of an Abercrombie model. He's not just sculpted, but jacked; his body tan and V-shaped, and displayed prominently over a two-page spread in a *Rolling Stone* package on extreme sports.†

---

* It's no accident that Sheckler's good on camera. He has experience. Apart from the interviews and short specials he's been doing the last few years, Ryan's first TV appearance was on *20/20* when he was a ten-year-old skateboard prodigy. The next year he appeared in a direct-to-video movie called *Most Vertical Primate,* where he had a dual role as a rival skater and stunt double for a chimp. The same year he filmed a skate-lesson segment with Johnny Knoxville. All this required both on-camera talent and representation, which he's always had in spades.

† The same issue of *Rolling Stone* includes a profile of Philadelphia blacktop genius Stevie Williams. It remains one of the only major magazine profiles on a skateboarder who isn't Sheckler. The angle was that Williams is "skateboarding's first gangsta hero, and he's taking the strength of his street knowledge global." Big press, of course, is famous for not getting skating, but the piece is particularly insane and insulting and wrong, and pretty much resembles a paint-by-number where the numbers are filled in with different kinds of shit. I hardly exaggerate. By all means check it out: *RS* #1032, August 9, 2007.

A lot was happening to Ryan, and a lot was also happening to skateboarding. He was both a top contender and fast becoming the sport's second-most-recognizable figurehead. Sheckler has always been a divisive force in skating—beating people a lot older than him, bringing his mom on tour because he was thirteen, getting more inside exposure because he was thirteen—but skating had never had this kind of a young celebrity before, let alone a sex symbol.

Tony Hawk was different. He was a family guy and longtime businessman and longer-time vert champion of the universe. Hawk's pop appeal was his safeness. Unquestioningly respected within the community, his physical genius was the type that brought outsiders in, coupled with the fact that he was *not* a kid, and that you probably wouldn't want to see him with his shirt off anyway. Hosoi's image is enough of a sex symbol today that they made a movie and he's writing a my-story book, but he peaked during skating's last inward phase, when outside coverage didn't exist and all athletes and almost all fans were male.

Also, Sheckler was still a comparatively new pro, and while he often held a top ranking, he was not always number one. It's hard to love getting your ass kicked by someone half your age, especially if that person was just on the cover of a magazine that represents every kind of commercial conformity your culture is traditionally supposed to despise.

Stoking further fires in the community was the fact that Sheckler didn't simply abandon skating for reality TV and celebrity. That would be too easy. He had also been advancing his skate career. He also left Almost to join Plan B, an old Rocco project resuscitated in 2005. The team includes serious young talents like Pat Duffy, PJ Ladd, and P-Rod, but is run by still-competing longtime pros Danny Way and Colin McKay. Plan B is maybe the most successful skate company as far as managing both a massive following and a ton of skate press, while maintaining the industry's respect and an insider attitude.

There's a team deck that throws back to an old NWA T-shirt and reads:

PJ&
PAUL&
TOREY&
RYAN&
PAT&
DANNY&
COLIN.

Mullen knew much of this was going to happen. While elite, Almost was a small company that could never match what Plan B or others would eventually offer. And he told Ryan so early on: "I said this to him on a couple of occasions, but one in particular," remembers Rodney. "You will have opportunities that I never had, nor anyone of my generation. And there'll be opportunities that I can't match, and no matter whose company you're riding for—know that I'm always there for you."

He remembers this time as a "blur," seeing Ryan only once at a video-game commercial shoot with Bam Margera and Tony Hawk, where all four guys were dressed as pigeons.

"He'd gotten so big so fast," remembers Mullen. "And he was just very much his own man, and at that stage I was just sort of watching it."

The year 2008 was even bigger than 2007. Like skateboarding itself, after consistent momentum, a lot seemed to happen at once. Very quickly, Ryan was both a top skater and a recognizable TV star. Little by little, tween magazines were giving Ryan space, but now there was no risk. The magazines wanted the TV numbers. And stories abounded.

*Life of Ryan*'s already-rolling second season was as successful as the first, with more drama around the parents and more talk about Ryan getting his own house, which he finally does in the last episode, putting an offer down on a mansion in a nearby gated community the day he turns eighteen. A third season was already in the works, executively produced by Ryan. There was also detailed talk about another show, conceived by Sheckler Inc. that was sort of a skateboard *American Idol*, where Ryan would be a panel judge in the search for the next great skateboarder.

In January, he went on *Leno* with the Jonas Brothers. In February, he went on *Ellen*. In March he signed a death and dismemberment clause and became the first street skater to land the mega-ramp.* There's video of the jump, and even Sheckler seems a little nervous, up at the top of a wooden mountain he's going to ride down at 55 miles per hour.

"It's mellow," says Danny Way, up there with him. "It's just like bombin' a hill."

"But not. Like that. At all," says Ryan, just before he starts to roll.

Ryan got the cover of *TransWorld* that April, flying backwards over a handrail, and then the now-coveted cover of *Skateboard Mag*, puffing out his cheeks and floating over his board that's over a fence at the top of a 15-foot drop into a parking lot below. It doesn't look real but it's real, and the teaser is about how a reality TV show can't define Ryan Sheckler. In July he was on the

---

* Ryan's teammate Pat Duffy made the jump, but then fell on the quarterpipe and broke his tibia in three places. Other mega-ramp alumni include Danny Way, Lizard King, who did it without elbow pads, and Hawk, who executed a 360 over the 50-foot gap, rolled down the hill, then flew a 30-foot backside air over the quarterpipe.

cover of *ESPN* magazine, teasing the story I pitched them the year before. He's shirtless, holding his board and looking over his big, shapely shoulder. He has sideburns and a huge rock in his ear and those weird dimples over his ass and a 2-foot tattoo that says SHECKLER across his back.

The same month he reportedly broke his arm, again, and four days later competed in a black brace at the Maloof Money Cup in Cleveland, then had reconstructive surgery on his elbow. He took fourth that day. The only other people who could beat him, with one arm broken behind his back, were young prodigy Nyjah Huston and the two best competitive skaters in the world: Chris Cole (second) and P-Rod (first, winning an unprecedented $100,000 purse).

Invincibly, he didn't stop competing. Before contests, medics covered his torn and trying-to-heal elbow with thick plasticky bandages wrapped with tape, which he'd always sweat and bleed through.

The crowds grew. They grew because while Sheckler was and still is a great athlete, he is, like the greatest athletes, a longtime performer who is very in sync with his crowd—and his crowd was changing. For the first time in history, a skater's fan base was non-skater and female. He'll tell you this, and it was maybe the biggest deal of Sheckler's whole career so far. "Sheckler fans" attended contests, and it was a little weird because they only wanted to see him, and they were often young teens, and they'd scream and there were a lot of them. This added to the rift his person created in the skate world, to which we've dedicated the whole next chapter.

As usual, Sheckler incorporated. He thanked his fans in interviews, signed autographs, changed shirts in front of everyone, and posed for pictures while people yelled and grabbed at him. In August he won the X Games yet again, and three weeks later showed up at Paul Revere Public School in downtown San Francisco to a street contest hosted by *Thrasher*. Sheckler's celebrity had been hated by a parcel of his community, and some of this group also pointed out that he's only good at park skating, the environment for all the major contests. Park skating's sometimes looked down on as easy and pussified by street skaters, the way New York skaters will judge their SoCal counterparts.

The Bust or Bail contest consisted of a big loud crowd and a set of sixteen stairs over weathered asphalt, and even though pro skaters were competing, it took a while for anyone to even land an ollie. The force was pushing guys down so hard that the energy bounced back up through their boards and feet so they lost their balance, then kind of fell onto their boards and the pavement. One guy decided he'd do the incredibly steep rail first try, and halfway down lost it behind him so that he got the rail in the nuts with enough time to bounce forward, his hands up in surrender, and roll through the air just enough to land on his head, then back.

In the middle of everything, a portly guy dressed as Paul Revere walked down the steps and the announcer yelled, "Who *is* that guy?! Get *out* of here!"

People started to feel it out, and soon it looked like lean and mean Andrew Reynolds had it. He skated high and hard and clean and began with a flip, then a hardflip over the rail, then a tre-flip down the stairs. It seemed like the crowd couldn't scream any louder until Sheckler showed up and won with a backlipslide (backwards slide), then a three-flip (a flat 360), then a tre, then a hardflip, then a backside flip—where he and his board do a 180 and land rolling backwards.

"That was the best day of my life," he remembers.

And the whole time Ryan just wanted to do more. He told me once: "Nothing's too much," and I think he believes it. He had a top-selling board and was dealing with brands that had never before touched a skater: Axe Body Spray and JCPenney. Ryan dumped his old sponsor SoBe for Red Bull, and the company built him his own custom two-story skatepark full of ramps made for his steroidic approach.

You know the park if you skate. It's a lot like his skating— gigantic and creative, full of excessively huge gray ramps and banks and red rails and drops and platforms you have to jump to, which Sheckler likes to do, except he lands on one foot, or lands sideways and slides.

And on top of it all, he was on top of it all. He was accommodating and getting bigger in every way and proud of it. He did an Oakley commercial where he shirtlessly skated into the frame up to the edge of a skatepark and clocked in. His voice-over says: "People don't think skateboarding is my job, but it's what I do." He's got a shoelace belt and high white underwear with black elastic. "People just don't realize that yet. Someday they will."

He founded the Sheckler Foundation, and with his new super-agent Steve Astephen hosted an annual celebrity tournament at Donald Trump's $264 million golf course. The SF, like a lot of foundations associated with pro sports, has vague goals about giving back to communities while they write off millions of dollars and whose partners are all Ryan's sponsors. The one other skateboarder with a foundation is Tony Hawk, but his foundation has raised millions to build municipal skateparks, and Ryan's hasn't yet.

Come December, Ryan was slotted for inclusion in *GQ*'s Man of the Year package. Other MOTYs were on the four fat covers: Obama and Phelps and Hamm and Leo. They even sent a crew out to San Clemente to get a shot of him on the beach in jeans and no shirt, amber-eyed with a gold aura of fuzz around his wetted crew cut, glaring rocks in his ears and a gout of foam swinging off his chin. Word was that Tony Hawk was first approached to provide a quote, then Johnny Knoxville, but in the end the photos were blurbed by a nice associate editor who didn't know slippery sheep shit about skating. The package was cut, along with the photo, but upon release Ryan was invited to the Chateau Marmont to party with Megan Fox and Zac Efron.

NONE OF THIS rising superstardom and mogulism and photo shoots and charity events and reading scripts (one based on Avril Levine's "Sk8r Boi") seemed to harm either his skating or his competitive career. In fact, as his brand and now female crowds grew, so did his ability. And it's at this time that his ability left its normal superhero level and jumped into a surreally huge while technically razorous category heretofore unforeseen in the sport.

In an interview with *Thrasher's* Jeff Phelps, he confirmed that he'd backside-flipped El Toro, a twenty-stair railed cliff and the most terrifying natural obstacle in skateboarding. Footage of the jump has yet to surface, but the cameras were rolling during the AST Dew Tour in Salt Lake City, the best example I know of when Ryan achieved the superhuman.

It's late afternoon and Sheckler's already won with an 89.5. Time's up, but he's cruising the course. The crowd has not dispersed. It's a street course, with platforms and rails and quarterpipes. He fires between two quarters and heads up the roll in towards the start platform.

The announcer is one of those people they use for extreme sports whose voice sounds like he's sick. Sheckler pops his board into his hand and steps up the roll-in onto the stage and turns around and stands there for a second, with his back to the camera, staring out at something.

He drops in and rolls down the steep transition and when he comes out, he's moving fast, leaning back on his board so his head is at one o'clock and his feet are at seven, and by the time he reaches the two ramps at the center of the course, he's pushing again with his arms at his sides because he has to go between them.

"*Awwwwwwwwwwww, full-speed attack!*" yells the announcer. Sheckler pumps again on his way out of the gap but doesn't come up. He stays in his crouch and turns just as he hits what from here looks like a big bright wall. It's the highest quarterpipe at the other end of the course, ablaze with afternoon sun, and in a quarter of a second he's up it and into the air in a frontside grab. He pulls hard and leans back and very quickly his head is the closest thing to the coping 4 feet below.

Things already seem set for something special. This is his native turf, like Nadal on clay or the Packers at Lambeau when it's five below zero, and he's at the peak of his celebrity, and his fans are even louder than the really loud crowd. But still, if you watch the footage, you can hear the collective scream's shock at what happens next.

He's about 6 feet in the air, upside down. His periphery is full of sky, and it's here at the apex that he somehow halts his momentum and somersaults the second half of his rotation, then drops down onto the stage. A backflip. Maybe the first in street contest history, and definitely the first I'd ever seen. Sheckler lands on the platform and stays on his board even though the impact snaps the deck in two. You can hear someone off camera say "No" just before the audio nearly drowns out the visual, the image of the sky and the sun and the crowd and the course shaking, because even the cameraman is screaming.

# 25

# "I HATE SHECKLER," AND THE EXPLODING OF RYAN'S RIGHT FOOT

I HATE SHECKLER is a current marketing campaign for Oakley sunglasses. The company's been taking out skate magazine ads featuring Ryan in what looks like a garage silk-screening posters and T-shirts that say I HATE SHECKLER. Sheckler says the campaign was his idea, that he originally wanted to sell the shirts, but only a few were made for the photo shoot, and he gave those to his friends. They sometimes wear them when they come over.

"He gets a *lot* of hate," Mullen said the first night we hung out two years ago, when Ryan's celebrity and skate status were at their peak midway through 2008.

And while Sheckler's been a divisive force ever since he started competing and winning at age six, 2008 was when the really hard talk started, the year he got rich and famous and simultaneously became a pop star and a young mogul. It was also the year he won several big contests and nailed unprecedented feat after unprecedented feat, clearing huge drops no one else had, and then clearing them while adding a flip, and dominating skate-media coverage, and achieved the status of bona fide celebrity, which always factored into the skate-media coverage.

His brand followed a common curve: Early attention generated more attention and brought about a short golden time where he was *it*, and then the natural reflex was to want something new. To not see Ryan everywhere. Comments like SELLOUT and ENOUGH ALREADY and SHEKLER [sic] WAS RESPECTABLE TILL THAT SHITTY SHOW had long been posted on the Internet under his dynamic skate footage, but now it amped up.

Someone made a looped video from a competition clip in which Sheckler flies up and comes down and falls backwards off his board. His head is the first thing to hit, and then the rest of him flips over and his shoulder and body and legs slam into the ground and he lies there very still. The title is RYAN SHECKLER GETTIN' A CONCUSSION. It's looped over and over and over with the caption THAT'S GOTTA HURT.

One former teammate posted an early acne medicine commercial starring Ryan. Another pro posted Ryan's Axe Body Spray commercial on his own blog with the caption WHAT THE FUCK IS THIS? For a scene in an upcoming video, *Thrasher* filled a newsstand entirely with Sheckler-covered magazines, some real and some not. On the fake cover of *Cat Fancy*, Ryan's sipping a little cup of milk with the caption MEOW, MEOW. The fake cover of *Seventeen*'s teaser reads RYAN SHECKLER: BEAUTY SECRETS.

It was mostly just talk, but it was a new kind of talk in the community. Trash talk is integral in team sports and highlighted every night on ESPN. Although it's less a part of individual sports, of course it still exists in competitive tennis or skiing or gymnastics or ballet or theater. Skateboarding, however, was such a small, disliked, illegalized, persecuted, prosecuted activity for so long that its community formed a bond unlike any other in sports. Thus, talk like this wasn't just rare—it was previously unheard of. Skaters don't hate other skaters.

He may have opened himself up to some of it. Whether *Rolling Stone* worked up to getting Ryan posed the way he was, I don't know, but the photo is Lolito-ish, and looks like the opening image of a teen-themed pornography sequence. He's on a top bunk, shirtless on a country quilt, in front of striped wallpaper with cartoon flame trim, a boy's room. The elastic of his pulled-up underwear has a star front and center, right over his penis. Affixed to the bed rail is a mini Nerf hoop from Chuck E. Cheese. There's a short prodigal write-up, then a mention about girls on tour. Sheckler's closing quote is: "Let's just leave it at that."

He was a new Got Milk spokesman, but his ad was nothing like Tony Hawk's, who was shot by Annie Leibovitz in cloudy midair, upside down in a folded kick pose so you didn't know which way was up. Got Milk? was on there twice, once upside down. Sheckler, on the other hand, is on his board in a nonsense nose wheelie, wearing black and holding a glass with a long Photoshopped white arch shooting out of it. It's a shot—not a spill. Globs and ropes and drops of white are dripping from the main arch. Ryan's in a *Wassup?* pose.

The big one, though, was for Axe Body Spray, one of the many commercials he's done and one I bet he'll never forget. Unlike, say, Mountain Dew or SoBe, Axe had no prior relationship with the skate community. They've become a leader in the billion-dollar male-grooming industry, owned by product/food/beverage giant Unilever, and their ad firm had found something in Ryan that they thought would resonate with their target audience.

The commercial was part of a seven-minute skate video Axe made with Plan B pros Greg Lutzka, Jereme Rogers, and Sheckler, who is shirtless almost throughout. It's shot in high definition and the footage is better than what you'd see in a lot of skate videos. It's the kind of thing you see in cereal commercials where the product is everywhere; the spray is on the coping as they're grinding, or they're carrying it around as they skate, spraying it like air freshener. They say *Dude* and get chased by an actor on a Segway dressed as a policeman (whom Sheckler ollies over), but mostly they just do a lot of pro-level street skating.

But the famous highlight comes when Ryan announces he's

going to attempt the "double-pits-to-chesty." Towed by a van, he gains speed, then fakely ollies up over a golf cart driven by Lutzka and Rogers, spraying his pits and gleaming chest. The effect I'm pretty sure is purposefully bad and low-budget, like in *The Boy Who Could Fly* or the Springfield Elementary School movie where Jebediah Springfield tames the land cow.

The Axe segment was all over skate sites.* One poster called it "the single gayest thing in skateboarding." Another wished Sheckler "double cock to anal penetration." It was bad, but worse was the pin-in-the-candy message so prevalent in modern advertising. Axe was trying to sell their brand to a younger demographic using young talent, in this case, skaters. But because they were using skaters, there was a smiling nod to both non-skaters and their older demographic that Axe was being disrespectful without the disrespected being aware of it. You'll see.

Their first target group is young men who maybe skated, but they were not after just one target group. They wanted to reach an older group (see Axe's long criticized sex marathon ads), and they do this by sending a message that they at Axe also looked down on these young idiots riding skateboards, and I think it's why out of everyone else on the team they picked Jereme Rogers, who happens to be a ginger kid with acne vulgaris and a treble clef tattooed one-sixteenth of an inch from his eye.

What they're also selling is their aboveness to the sport, and their ability to mask it, to fool the youth they're selling to. Watch; all the big brands do this. Even Nike's 2010 high-definition skate video, with baffling parts by newcomers like Daryl Angel and

---

* The community's reaction was so famous that the ad world eventually incorporated the backlash itself to target a similar demographic. This one was for Power Balance, the plastic mood bracelets everyone wore on the 2010 Dew Tour. Their site has a scripted talk-show series where a pro athlete like Shaq or Sheckler sits behind a desk and menacingly interviews himself as a guest on the show. "I saw your Double-Pits-to-Chesty," says the host Sheckler. "What did you think about that," asked the guest Sheckler. "Well, after I vomited, I was very angry at you."

Theotis Beasley, ends nearly every segment with the crew smash-ing a window or tipping over a garbage can, then skating away.

Skateboarding is no stranger to disrespect. What was new in these ads was that members of a group so strongly bonded by persecution had, with ad money, been moved outside, and prob-ably unknowingly taken part in that disrespect. That was previ-ously unheard of in skateboarding, and that was why it got the hate it did, and that's why I'm spending so much time talking about a stupid commercial for scented water in an aerosol can.

AS IS BY NOW standard operating procedure, Sheckler adapted and incorporated. He wouldn't even look up when someone yelled "Douchebag!" as he signed his way down a barricade outside of MTV. He wanted to work as much as possible, be it at perfect-ing his runs or auditioning or launching an extreme sunscreen with soccer star Mia Hamm. He was not just unapologetic—he was enthusiastic. He told reporters, "I'm going to capitalize on everything I can." Hate, he said, is just more fuel. "Every time somebody calls me out or tries to start something, it's motiva-tion . . . I want to give them reasons not to like me."

And there were. Because Sheckler, smart and business-minded as he is, is misbehaving. Not much more than your aver-age popular jock-y eighteen-year-old, and probably a lot less than someone that age getting the hate he did. But he also tends to fight back a little. And not just by saying that insults are motiva-tion. He's never been arrested or even cited with a violation, but occasionally, as happens with celebrities, someone starts some-thing and Ryan responds. There's a fight or two, and a picture of Sheckler hitting a kid at a Red Bull event spreads all over the Internet.

And it wouldn't matter so much if he hadn't become famous for being a physical genius who happened to be an adorable but especially level-headed kid, with a cool Hawk-like earnestness that gave skateboarding a better name in the public eye. He was, of course, not that kid anymore, but in addition seemed to have developed that macho high-schooler's attitude you just roll your eyes at and hope is a passing phase.

At least, that was the vibe I got when we first met at Conde Nast for lunch with Astephen and Co., wherein impressions were pretty uniformly negative. In the cafeteria, he hit the wrap station and said "I'm gonna rock this sandwich" at least five times and then didn't eat any of it because "I realized I'm not hungry." His pants were all the way off his ass and he walked on the leather booths and he'd cough and text when anyone but Astephen was talking, and told stories mostly to Astephen about various friends of theirs, one of whom was getting married for money—which he said he supported—et cetera.

I don't blame him. At this point he's traveling up to 240 days a year and he's been meeting and greeting constantly since he was about twelve. He was also covered with black scabs and holes and scalpel and pavement scars. His right arm is deformed from breakage, and both elbows had what looked like golf balls underneath the tan skin. The bulging elbow balls were also covered with scars. I don't know what they are. The insides of his arms read FEAR and GOD, tattoos you could tell were new because they hadn't been scraped yet. He brightened a bit after we'd dropped off our trays and were all walking down the wavy, walled mirror outside the cafeteria. He ran his hand over the glass. "How fun would it be to ride on this?" he said.

SHECKLER put a down payment on a house the day he turned eighteen. It was a house you or I might occupy were we teenage millionaires with sixth-grade educations: a three-story oceanside Mediterranean in a gated community that looks flashy and grand but quickly feels boring and minimal and hollow and a little scary. You can take a tour on YouTube. There's large pillowed furniture and mood lighting and the only thing on the walls are TVs, one of which is 103 inches long. The pool table has balls that say RED BULL and RYAN SHECKLER. In the basement is a boxing ring for his newfound and lately backed-off-of fight club. He has two dirt bikes and one of those Jessica Rabbit–looking motorcycles you see on *American Chopper,* a Black Series Benz V12, a white Escalade with an S in the grill, and a 550 diesel engine Dodge Ram with high suspension and three bumper spots inside of a white grill.

*Life of Ryan's* third season appeared in April 2009 and made as great a proclamation as any that he was a rock star. He's eighteen, in his new house, and in fact states in the opening that "Me and my friends are loving the rock-star life." The show lasted six episodes and was kind of a mystery to begin with. The leaked trailer—designed, I guess, to get people to watch it—features Ryan picking a used condom up off the floor, then one of his hooded and sunglass'd friends saying that he's sorry, dude. In the episodes, we see the gang hosting naked parties, making out with girls, fistfighting, and Ryan riding a Harley and being an asshole to his mom, agent, friends, and girlfriends. We watch him not just putting holes in his wall and then saying "It's my house—I can do whatever I want," but saying it to Steve Astephen, and then adding, "This conversation is over."

How scripted it was, I don't know, but with handlers like Astephen, it's a little confusing. The fact that Sheckler was an executive producer of the show suggests that this stuff is more unfiltered and natural, but who knows? There was talk that it was canceled midseason, but MTV did this thing I never heard of where they premiered the episodes back to back to back to back to back to back, in a "full-season marathon," except that the entire season was a mere three hours. Then they went to DVD. Like the sophomore year of *Real World*, even with digital cable the episodes are hard to find, though as of 2010 the show still runs in Europe, where Sheckler says people recognize him the way they used to in the States. He also says the decision to kill the show was "100 percent mine," that it was interfering with his competition schedule. At this point he was the money guy, so it's possible. MTV won't confirm or deny. Regardless, he's no longer a reality TV star.

In 2009 he appeared in *Tooth Fairy* with the Rock and the ever-smiling Billy Crystal, which would be one thing, but he just so happens to play a young, cocky, disrespectful pro athlete, and they use all these weird angles like they do in a more-recent *Cribs* appearance to make him not look so short. There was a new trailer for his upcoming Plan B video, where he's doing smoky dough-nuts in his truck, smashing up a hotel room, then footage of the same session on the *Skateboarding* cover, where he flies through an intersection, up onto a sidewalk, and flips over a fence and down a 15-foot cliff without blinking an eye.

Then he gets hurt.

It happens at the finals of the 15th X Games in Los Angeles. It's the end of the Games; over 200,000 people have attended the events and 44 million have watched on TV. Axe Body Spray has scattered prostitutily uniformed female employees through-out the crowd, where they wave signs for Ryan and Axe. Over on the street Shaun White takes first on the halfpipe. Over on the street course, Nyjah Huston and newcomer Adam Dyet are both on a tear, but P-Rod is in one of those modes that makes him everyone's favorite, skating not only huge and clean but also switch, and rather than the typical switch tricks that look a little more abstract and wonky, his are near-identical and look almost weirdly, reflectively cleaner, the way the T-1000 looked next to the regular Terminator. His tricks are relaxed but also radiate great power, much like their author. He switch-front feebles the twelve-set rail, switch-flip slides the rail, switch-grinds the rail, and then 360-flips the set.

Now to Sheckler, who's wearing a backwards red hat and red Etnies shirt with a white band over his elbow. He had won the gold the previous year so got to skip all preliminary rounds. The weekend before in Boston he had unprecedentedly won his third Dew Tour, then flew back to Los Angeles to go on *Jimmy Kimmel* and talk about going for his third gold at the X Games that weekend.

It's the jam run, something invented by a non-skater where five people go at the same time, so Sheckler's doing tricks and then popping his board up and running to somewhere else on the course to do another one. We don't get to see him do the fast creative lines he's famous for. He does a backside flip over a deceptive seven-stair that's three steps and a platform, then four more steps, and then he comes back for a full cab to backside lipslide. That is, he sprints up to the steps backwards with the tail facing the stairs and crouches, his body in a zigzag and his arms at four and eight o'clock, looking over his shoulder at the steep yellow rail. He pops up and spins around 270 degrees, so he lands in the middle of the rail with his back to the stairs, arms out and his legs almost together like a diver. Then he slips and suddenly the board is upside down over to the side. He's moved his left hand over his groin and his feet touch down, but his whole body swings back like fulcrum, and he hits his tailbone and almost rolls over up onto his head, clutching his back with his legs twisting outward. He gets up and tries it again, spinning off the stairs to land solid on the rail, backwards, before he flies off and skates away clean.

Then it happens. He backside-flips over the twelve-stair, lands wrong, and pretty much explodes his foot. In real time it looks like the board got out from under him and he landed and went cleanly down. But he doesn't get up, and before he even starts to writhe, he pulls off his right shoe and sock, then grabs his leg and starts shaking his head.

Tony Hawk's the announcer: "It looks like his back foot was coming off and [he] just sat on it. All of his weight going into that ankle as it rolled on the ground."

The other announcer goes "Whoa."

The sports doctor runs out with a big backpack. Ryan can't stand up, and is helped from the course to a waiting golf cart, taking tiny steps with the foot that's still intact.

He keeps saying, "It's broken, it's broken, it's broken, it's broken, it's broken."

# 26

# HEALING AT THE BERRICS

EIGHT MONTHS after he got hurt, a new video appeared on the Berrics website that included Ryan not looking much like himself. He was sans jewelry, slimmer, wearing a shirt, and skating without a brace. It was a video called *United*, and featured new short parts from the Plan B team. Ryan got the least time of everyone, though the little of what we do see from him is maybe as good as every other pro there, if you don't count PJ Ladd's head-clutchingly difficult low-rail and ledge tricks.*

Sheckler moves into the frame and the camera follows as he hits a bank then flips over a gap. Here the camera stops and he moves away, shrinking as he goes high up the transitioned wall and comes down backwards at about twice his original speed. He fast approaches the camera, all the while edging his sneakers up what's now the front of the board. So it's going to be a switch nollie or fakie ollie, depending on what you want to call it. They slow it down here. Sheckler's in his coiled stance long before he approaches the gap. He blasts off and does a backside tre, but as the flipping board 360s, so does he. It's a backside tre with a full-body varial, two independently spinning things in flight that are going to need each other to land. His body's in kind of a lunge and his bad foot's kicked out and his good foot is pointing down

---

* Patrick John Ladd grew up in Rockland, Massachusetts, and is a stronger technical skater than teammate P-Rod. That's according to P-Rod. Ladd skates few contests, speaks in a reserved manner with a thick, "r"-less Massachusetts accent, and is especially famous for his ledge tricks, a slide or grind on a bank or coped box, and the maneuver done onto and then off that rail. In this particular video he'll pull a switch kickflip into a backside tailslide and pop out with a 270 shove-it. Holy shit.

so the sneaker's black toe is almost keeping the board in place on an axis, like spinning a basketball upside down. Both toes find the board and he brings it all together, then down, whipping his front half around to catch up with his legs as he sails off an angled sheet of Masonite.

IT'S A LOT to say the X Games injury was the worst of Sheckler's career. Any dedicated skateboarder will tell you that injuries are part of the skater's evolution and progression in a sport of balance done at high speeds over hard ground. The people who push the most get hurt the most, and Sheckler's the best example of this, breaking his arm for the first time, you'll remember, when he was six. As of this writing, he's broken it nine more times, and the last time he needed a piece of his wrist grafted into his elbow because there was almost nothing left to heal. Aside from the various lacerations and a bendy right arm, he has a tweaked back and neck he's always cracking. He nearly didn't compete in X Games 15 due to back pain.

But this was the worst. When Sheckler rolled his right ankle, he snapped the first metatarsal, the pencil-sized ligament that comes up from your big toe when you flex your feet. The pressure of the impact popped it like a rubber band. "Exactly. That's exactly how it felt, too," Sheckler later told me. "When I tried to stand up, it folded over itself, so I knew it was fucked."

Arm and hand and teeth injuries are one thing in skateboarding, but foot injuries are another. They're like a sprained ankle for a runner, and they're not surprisingly common for big-tech skaters like Sheckler.* Still, Ryan hadn't badly hurt his foot

---

* Skate shoes often look clunky and sloppy because they're so thickly padded. This is to help protect riders' feet from the heavy board and the shock of hard landings. Shops sometimes sell Velcro ankle braces, and recently Supra shoes introduced a

since he'd stepped on a hibachi grill in 2006, then competed at the Dew Tour with second-degree burns and won. It's also not just a foot injury in a foot-based sport, but it was his ollie foot, where he generated all his firepower. This was bad.

Like most bad first metatarsal injuries, Ryan's required surgery and a long rest period. His foot was screwed together for six months so the ligament could properly heal. He describes the recovery process as "horrible." But it's Sheckler we're talking about here, and like everything else, he hit it hard. Every day he drove his Mercedes to a strip mall in San Clemente and crutched into the South Coast Spine Center for physical therapy. Some of the therapy, he says, was more painful than the injury, since now everything was tight and his foot was broken. Sessions involved long periods of stretching, standing on a wobble board, and something called cold laser therapy, which changes the cellular metabolism with desk-light-looking things that crosshatch lasers over a targeted area and speed up healing. They also used it on his neck and elbows.

Ryan was still spending hours and hours and hours with his leg elevated, but soon he began swimming, and eventually replaced the crutches with a black walking cast. Cold laser therapy is common with pro athletes, sometimes halving recovery time, but even so, his rate of recovery was miraculous.

"It's a healing ability I've never seen in any patient before," said Dr. David Sales, who was in charge of the rehab. "Leaps and bounds."

Unless you count the first eighteen months of his life, Sheckler had never been off his board this long. And it was a strange time. What does a physical genius do when paralyzed? When the

---

line of sneakers with reinforced ankle panels and removable straps. Two high-flying street riders suffered similar injuries around the time Ryan got hurt. Lizard King tore two foot ligaments, but was soon skating in a black-and-purple walking cast. Antwuan Dixon wasn't so lucky. His ankle injury put him in a wheelchair.

portal through which his genius manifests itself—something he's pretty much always been able to open and feel by hopping on his board—is suddenly closed?

Sheckler hung out with friends, watched movies, sat around a lot with the foot elevated, and redesigned his skatepark to more resemble a street course. He wanted to skate less in the big-park style he'd come to dominate and more in the close, technical style he was not as good at, compared to, say, P-Rod, his favorite skater.

"I made it smaller and a lot more technical so I could work on my nollie and my switch and ledge tricks and my lines," he told me. He also, quite openly, credited the change to criticism he'd read on the Internet about the park being too big. "I want to have a bigger arsenal of tricks. Yeah, I can jump down anything you put in front of me, but I want to also have the technical skills."

Like the old one, the new park was spending-someone-else's-money awesome. There is a twelve-stair and maybe the longest ledge I've ever seen, and a coped bank that slides out from under the ledge like a trundle bed. Another thin grind box is somehow laid vertically into a ramp, abutting another one at the top, which sounds unreal but it's there. There's a ramp at one end of the complex, and at the other, the floor curves up into the wall and there's a cave hole to skate over. The new space is an ambidextrous runway, symmetrical and perfect for switch skating.

Ryan started making appearances again. He videoed a visit to the construction site of his new park and made a short movie on the Ethika site about his physical therapy. In the summer of 2009 he and P-Rod threw out the first pitch at a Dodgers game.

Seven months after the accident, Sheckler took off the walking cast and stood on his board for the first time. "It was like learning to skate all over again," he said. With his new tech goals in mind, he started skating switch more, focusing on nollie tricks that were kinder to his right foot. Three weeks later he filmed the Berrics part.

Quick-healing bewilderment aside, the little we see in the part is a distinct change from the skating we've come to know from Sheckler, famous for the huge magazine-cover-getting stuff that exploded his foot and broke his elbow so many times that they had to replace it with his wrist. This new small part is less vertical and more horizontal, less pyro and more technical.

Top technical people traditionally don't skate well on big courses, and while Ryan will admit he's not in P-Rod's* or PJ's category, he had just shot a short technical video part with the best pros in the world. He also, for all intents and purposes, just started skating again, stepping on a board for the first time a month prior after a half-year hiatus of sit-still suffering. And if Ryan, with freshly unscrewed holes in his foot, could not only relearn but learn a fakie tre with a full-body varial, I wonder what technical places this former world-champion-at-thirteen will reach by the time he's twenty-four, twenty-nine, or thirty-eight, like Haslam, Daewon, and Mullen were when he joined their team.

He was, and still is, working on it, and there is no one on a skateboard who works harder than Sheckler, who has always had what Rodney calls a "ten-pound heart." Sheckler said he was skating the new park every day, and that future plans, at least for the following year and a half, would focus only on skating.

That Ryan wanted to skate smaller might have been due to his injury, or because he had somewhat exhausted the medium of huge street skating; he couldn't drop much higher than 15 feet since his skeleton is calcium and not Adamantium. He would now focus on the technical stuff. But his interest in fine-tuning also

---

* P-Rod attended but didn't compete in this year's Dew Tour finals. Instead, he went to a skatepark to perfect Haslam's switch-frontside-to-backfoot bigspin. When he landed it, he sent me a message from his phone: "so psyched."

didn't mean he'd abandon his old style. As this book was being completed, a video from his new park surfaced, wherein Ryan was skating with Chris Cole, the best all-around guy in the world, who skates in the big way Ryan did pre-injury and has technical chops that approach those of Daewon or almost even Mullen. And even if it's in a short Internet video, the fact that Ryan's both skating and skating *well* with a balletic linebacker like Chris Cole suggests he'll bring these two things together. Ryan's skating will grow bigger and broader and finer. It will be more *more*.

# 27

# TO TRY AND TALK TO SHAUN WHITE AND RYAN SHECKLER

IN 2011 in America, 8 million skaters will spend a projected $7.3 billion on skateboarding. Two hundred new skate parks are built every year, and skating now quietly boasts twenty times the participants of Pop Warner football. Once a Pogo-Ballish relic of the sport's past, the longboard's sales increased 43 percent in 2010's first quarter. In 2009, Powell-Peralta reissued Kevin Harris's deck, the first freestyle board on the market since Rodney's was discontinued in 1992. Most research firms estimate that 12 to 18 million people ride skateboards all over the world.

And at the top of this strange mountain of ever-changing statistics and factoids is Ryan Sheckler.

At thirteen, he was competitively determined to be the best in the world at a physically hard, technically infinite pursuit that had just started to be worth a lot of outside industry money. And despite endless travel, capitalization, ten broken arms, and legions of haters the likes of which few pro athletes have ever seen, his skating not only continues to win contests, but also to grow with the same clean, creative hugeness that first put him on network TV in 2003. Today the skating comes from a twenty-year-old person who is a top-grossing athlete in an industry worth a half million more than Major League Baseball and a half million less than the National Football League. He's an actor, investor, and mid-level celebrity involved with outside industries worth much, much more than skateboarding. Anything with his name or image or quote on it or in it gets traffic and is worth money. Appearances and face time are worth the most money, since he can't be working elsewhere when he's giving you face-time. And like Mullen, Hawk, now Hosoi, and maybe Vallely, he'll probably write his own book someday.

All of this makes him hard to talk to.

## Interpolation

FOR THE RECORD, it was almost easier to talk to Shaun White, who was in Vegas for the Dew Tour when I flew in the fall of 2010 to stalk Sheckler, and whom each press person got to interview for two minutes about his thoughts on the vert competition. Press members were led into one of those nervously anonymous sign-in-type rooms while unbelievably cliché camera guys who were both named Rob set up all the wires and lights and cameras and battery packs from black foam-lined plastic luggage written on in silver Magic Marker.

When White walked in, they told everyone who was not with NBC to wait outside. He looks just like he does on TV. He's maybe 5-foot-9 and thin, in a light denim jacket and a gray Mickey Mouse shirt and a pull chain around his neck adorned with a rib-boned pendant that looks like an old war medal. He's wearing two big rings and silver bracelets, little black socks and black slim-legged pants. His teeth are white and his laugh is wonderful—a big shucky, gulpy thing that sounds like *huggahuggahuggahugga*. And his hair. His hair's flaxenly waved and full and silky, neither wet nor dry, with slightly surfaced locks that split and rejoin the big red waterfall framing his face.

We really do each get two minutes. He's seated on one of two stools in front of a bright backdrop and is pretty tan for a ginger kid. Rob is moving around with the camera and bending over like he's taking a giant shit in a hole. While his leg bops constantly,

White's neither rushed nor tired-sounding as team after team after team come in and get their tape. They all ask the same questions except for the MTV Rock-n-Jock guys, one who is thin and blond and nasty-looking and one who is short and fat and has an Amish beard and an open, sleeveless red wool shirt with nothing on under it. DIRTY LIFE is tatted across his big belly and the I in LIFE is a forty-ounce bottle of malt liquor. He's also wearing the same pulled-up Ethika underwear as a lot of the pros, including Ryan. This guy sits on Shaun's lap, and their whole segment is Shaun rubbing the fat guy's back while the blond guy makes fun of the publicist telling them to hurry up.

When it's my turn, I bring up Lizard King's thing about how he kind of snowboards when he skates, which was stupid because White gives me a gentle uh-*huh* look, and I've already used a fourth of my time. I ask him if he started skating and snowboarding at the same time, and he says yes, around age six, in the spring when the snow melted. I ask what the sports have in common and the publicist makes a tumbling motion with her fingers.

He sort-of answers: "They go hand in hand, and there are vast differences that make it difficult. The snowboard is bigger, conditions change—the snow and the sun—and as the day gets later and the snow changes, the speed changes. In skating, the walls are consistently there, but you're not strapped in. Surfing is the hardest because the water is moving and the whole battle is getting up on your board and staying on."

The publicist is all but perched on the end of the camera now—and I'm sorry, but did anyone else notice she's wearing one of those stomach shirts and jeans that barely cover her labia? I know. I'm sorry. I took this out once, and the editor hates it, but it's going to bother me forever if I don't say anything—so I ask him if skateboarding informs snowboarding for him.

He doesn't really answer: "It's strange if you know about the stances. A lot of guys will snowboard goofy and skate regular. I can tell right away when a snowboarder skates because he does all of his tricks backwards. It's like cheating."

PUBLICIST: OK!
ME: OK. Thanks.
SW: Thanks.

## End Interpolation But BTW

EVER SINCE Shaun White became famous, for some reason the press has paired him with Tony Hawk, as if the two were married or related or at least business partners, which they are not. It reached a point last month where Hawk posted a request for media *not* to contact him if they wanted White, to harness the powers of Google and the telephone and contact White directly, please.

TALKING TO SHECKLER is about the same, and actually weirder. Like a regular star athlete, phone interviews are requested through an assistant, confirmed through an agent, and after an autistically long time, set up through that assistant again, albeit with stipulations. For his interview on the X Games, the topical criteria was skating only. No questions about girls. Later, when I mentioned I was writing a skateboarding book that included Sheckler, and asked if I could watch Ryan skate at his warehouse, the assistant wanted to know if they'd have final say over what was printed, and said we'd talk later, which we never did. Anyway, Ryan called me. When we chatted about his X Games victory I think he was in a car, and his cell number actually appeared in the little window of my desk phone. This isn't always the case, like with Sarah Hall or a certain *New York*

*Times* editor, whose numbers comes across as RESTRICTED, or (000) 000-0000.

But meeting in person was a whole different thing. Instead of just going to the street course, where I *knew* he was, I had to wind back through the casino to the huge press room where I met P-Rod and find the corresponding PR person. There was a cellphone exchange, and one of them walked me down to the Joint, the auditorium where they've built the street course. Sheckler was actually walking off the course as we walked in. He knew the PR girl and gave her a hug.

This is when Steve Astephen stepped from the shadows. I don't know how I didn't see him because he's tall with spiked hair and a bright yellow shirt, and because he's the kind of guy who, when he's in the room, you know he's in the room. If this were *Entourage*, Astephen would be Ari Gold. He is the most powerful and sought-after agent in extreme sports, which is why Ryan signed with him in 2008. He reps three other skaters: Lasek, Burnquist, and Jen O'Brien, Burnquist's partner.

One of five kids raised by a single mother in gnarly outer Boston, Astephen finished high school in 1988 and took a bus to Beaver Creek, Colorado, where he worked as a liftie. Within a year he co-opened the resort town's first snowboard shop, and while interim details abound, after that things pretty much just snowballed. In 1994, he became a marketing manager for Lamar Snowboards in San Diego, and the following year started Familie, representing skateboard, snowboard, and BMX (then later motocross) athletes. In 2005, he finalized the sale of Familie to Wasserman Media Group, though he still retains full control. Familie now reps a small number of top extreme athletes who, once they're with Astephen, stay with Astephen,* whom you can

---

* The one athlete to quit Astephen due to "personality differences" is Shaun White, who was repped by IMG before leaving in 2010 to join Hawk, LeBron, Hanks, Spielberg, Will Smith, et al. at CAA.

read more about in *Forbes*, *Entrepreneur*, *TransWorld Business*, et cetera.

∧

SHECKLER KICKS out his feet and makes a deflating sound when he sits down. We're in the long, tall hallway outside the Joint, seated in two tall easy chairs placed under a long line of framed concert shirts from Christie's. Astephen is leaning on a nearby vased table with his Blackberry. He is at least 6-foot-4, thinner than when we first met, and still has pen-and-thumbtack-looking tattoos, though a big one I remember on his forearm seems to have disappeared. Back in the low, dark bar area where we met five minutes ago, I'd asked if we could go somewhere quiet, and Astephen suggested the stairs up to the first mezzanine, which weren't out of mic shot from the thundering course. There was luckily a guy vacuuming the steps with a tank on his back, so we came out here.

Ryan's height is 5-foot-8, according to ESPN's profile page, but it's really more like 5-foot-5. He's chiseled but nowhere near as big as when we met two and half years ago, and though he was just running a pro course under stage lights and will compete in three hours for $25,000, he looks bright and clean and eager. He's not wearing his rings or Liberace watch, but he does have rocks in his ears that were glinting every color of the rainbow out there on the course. His buzz cut and mustache are brownish-gold, and his eyes are a washed-out olive hazel. All his clothes are new.

The goiters are gone from his elbows and he doesn't have any fresh cuts on his hands, but his arms are covered with scars. Some are from concrete and look like they were put there with a sandblaster. Others are from Masonite ramps and look like giant eraser burns. A few are from scalpels. His right arm has a thin, pale, raised line coming out from his T-shirt sleeve that curves down past his swollen elbow, a scar from the full-reconstructive surgery last year. Some of his older tattoos are nicked and smeared with unhealed skin, but inside his right forearm a big red ruby shines unscathed.

This is my third interview with Sheckler, and I'm pretty sure he doesn't remember me, though he's nice and looks me in the face and shakes my hand, like someone you suddenly look forward to working with. His grip is firm and his palm feels dry and sharp, and right away I remember that he's always been good at this kind of thing, too.

I asked about his foot: "My foot is 100 percent," he says. "Spent a lot of time working with Dr. Dave Sales, in San Clemente. And got physical therapy on it every day I could, and I still go get preventative measures done on it. So Dr. Dave Sales got me in perfect condition. Real fast."

If the therapy was a daily thing: "Yeah, it was a daily thing. It had to be. I wanted to be serious about it. To come back and be able to compete at the highest level again. I separated the first metatarsal in my foot and had to get screws in there for six and a half months."

His answers are less like responses to questions and more like sound bites for the topic he's waiting for me to bring up, and they usually consist of a statement and then an anecdote to illustrate that statement. Which actually is perfect, since we only have fifteen minutes, though I don't know that yet.

I ask how he chooses his affiliations: "It's just if it's good for my image in skateboarding. Like when we did the TV show. At the time it was a good idea. And then the backlash we got made me realize I definitely need to think through the steps I'm gonna take, and what I'm gonna do that the public sees. It's all good though."

I ask if the show changed his life: "Yeah, it changed my life. I don't like saying that, but yeah, it changed it. I've got more fans. More people know. The show still plays in Europe, so when I go to Europe it's like I never left America. It's pretty cool. It's different. I had to deal with it, though. I enjoy it. I don't know anything else."

It's not a great conversation, and I wasn't expecting one. Since he was around ten, Sheckler has been interviewed and photographed and written about, and like anyone pressed enough times, his answers tend to sound hollow, like a rock star promoting a new album. But he's also an industry guy, and so his answers also tend to have a capitalizing meet-and-greet feel to them. His favorite skateboarders are always guys on his team (P-Rod's his favorite skater because they're teammates and because "He's always been super nice to me"). He also keeps plugging that sports doctor, and says his fans were the reason he competed at the X Games last year. That despite terrible back pain, he couldn't let them down. Like Shaun White, he'll sometimes give answers to different questions or will kind of make a statement or answer even though no question's been asked. A few of his answers nearly match quotes from other reporting.

All this said, Sheckler's at work, and work's something he takes very seriously. How direct and engaged he seems during our interview, despite the fact that he's done this five thousand times, speaks loudly to his talent and power. There's just (of course) a feigned monotonous feel to the whole thing, until he looks up over my shoulder and says: "What's up, Smootchka?"

Greg Lutzka's standing there. Twenty-five, but looking like every kid ever kicked out of a parking lot, Lutzka grew up in Milwaukee and abandoned hockey for skating at age thirteen. At fifteen, sponsored by Beer City Skateboards, he placed third at the internationally important Tampa Am contest, and won his first world pro contest three years later. He was second only to Sheckler in the 2007 Dew Tour, and is a big street guy with something of a frontside 360 specialty. He rides for Almost, Rodney's company.

Lutzka's voice and demeanor have a general soft niceness to them, a kind, light goofiness that's nothing like his skateboarding. Sheckler's suddenly more animated. Smiling.

"What did you do last night?" he asks.

"I went to sleep."

"You're a liar."

"I did. I went to sleep."

"You're a liar."

"How was the flight back?"

"Flight back?"

"Flight."

"Flight. When?"

"You didn't fly home?"

"No. I flew home on Tuesday."

"Oh. Your dad told me. What up, man?"

He extends his arm. His hands are soft. They talk some more.

"It's gnarly out there."

"The course? You skated it yet?"

"Me? No."

"Enjoy it."

"Yeah. I'm gonna go out there. I'll let you finish up."

HIS MENTOR excluded, like all great athletes Sheckler can't explain the height and depth of his gift, or why he looks not just relaxed but serene when a flash freezes him over a cliff with the board upside down under his sneakers. Or why he looked like a puppy with its head out the window at the end of *Round 3* when he flew off a drop that broke another pro's arm. No one put skating in Ryan. It was already there, and continues to manifest itself in illustrious, complex ways that do not and could never match the persona of their author, a trait Mullen remembers well from their Almost days.

"Ryan was never emotional—he's always just been very clear. And that doesn't make him businesslike or unfeeling," he recalled. "It's more like 'Hey—get to the matter, and don't get wrapped up in it.' Which is such a sign of maturity."

This quote comes to mind while listening to Sheckler's interviews, but so does his exchange with Danny Way back on top of the windy mega-ramp. Ryan stood there quietly with one foot on his board, while Way gesturingly explained the best approach to being hurled at the speed limit off a wooden mountainside. Ryan cut him off: "Just go," he said. And went.*

But Ryan's also knowledgeable about all things skateboard. People and contests and sponsors and injuries. I bring up Mullen's scar-tissue-welding-his-leg-to-his-hip story, and Sheckler says he's heard about it, then shakes his head and sighs. "He's awesome."

He asks if I've talked to him face-to-face. "He's eccentric. Real smart," he says. "Always says what he thinks about. He's so in-depth."

I mention our first late-night visit and trying to stay awake as Mullen got more wound up. He nods. "Yeah. That's when he skates," says Ryan.

It's wrong to fault Sheckler for not being a great conversationalist the way it would be wrong to fault your grandmother for not being a great architect or something. That he's nothing like

---

* Sheckler's words to Way on the mega-ramp nearly match Tony Hawk's instructions to Margera on the Loop, which he finally nailed in 2008: "Just keep going."

a normal twenty-year-old U.S. male is . . . quite normal. Skateboarding has been his lifeblood since he was two. It's given him the closest thing mortals have to superpowers like flight, as well as fame and millions of dollars. It's also broken his arms, denied him of little more than an elementary school education, and kept him in planes and cars and hotels a reported eight months a year, so he can travel the world to competitions, where his best skateboarding has always come out.

Thus, maybe closing arguments don't matter. What matters is, you should see him skate.

And you should see him skate.

# 28

# DEW TOUR FINALS 2010

SHECKLER was in town for the Dew Tour finals, the last stop on a seven-part tour that takes place every year from June to October. Dew Tour offers the biggest prize money in action sports—$3.5 million—and is broadcast to 280 million people on NBC and MTV. The networks dually own Alli, the action sports conglomerate that created the Tour. Similar events include the Gravity Games, Vans Triple Crown, Slam City Jam, and of course, the X Games, all of which Sheckler's won at least once.

The 2010 Dew Tour finals took place on October 16 and 17 at the Hard Rock Cafe Hotel and Casino in Las Vegas, a block from the strip and across the street from a large gentlemen's club and a Johnny Rockets.

The casino is giant and windowless with a four-story neon guitar out front. I realize the guitar is the one Danny Way dropped from a few years ago at an event emceed by Bam Margera. There's a U-shaped driveway made of cobblestones and through the big glass foyer and little hallway the sunken casino veers off in all directions. The walls are decorated with quality prints of classic rock moments, and throughout the place are big glass boxes full of famous rock-star paraphernalia. The first one at the end of the entryway has Slash's Les Paul top hat, and the denim vest and leather jacket he used to always wear. These dioramas are every-where, and there are some really good ones. Santana's snakeskin suit, boots, and trench coat; the black pants and gray jacket Elvis wore on *Sullivan;* a few of Britney's early outfits; and all the masks that The Clown wore on a particular tour with Slipknot. Next to the check-in desk is a long wall box dedicated to Shaun White's win at the Beijing Olympics. It has his white snowsuit, iridescent goggles, American flag jeans, and the crispy, liquefied snowboard he burned for the *Rolling Stone* cover.

Besides the casino, this big black building is full of various themed night clubs, billiard rooms, sports bars, a pretty good Mexican restaurant, a John Varvatos store that's full of music equipment (but none of it's for sale, and the store is always empty except for the seven or eight architect- and Ramones-looking guys who work there), and the tattoo parlor where Sheckler got his famous SHECKLER tattoo. The hallways all seem curved, and there are no signs anywhere. The publicist actually got lost leading us around, but soon you can tell we're near the registration room for the athletes.

It's down a long and actually glass hall that faces the backs of the poolside tents and leads through a café where Greg Lutzka is having lunch by himself at a little table. Past the cafe the room is crowded with motocross, BMX, and skateboard competitors. It's easy to spot who's who. Motocross guys are the closest thing to biker guys, with blanket tattoos and piercings and leather and this general loud attitude you can pretty well feel. BMX guys are much closer to motocross guys than skaters, but have more of the skaters' lean build, and I personally think a thing for wearing their hats backwards and sideways but not pushing them down. Also a lot of tattoos. BMX guys' girlfriends tend to look kind of hot, whereas motocross guys' girlfriends look kind of pornographic. Most skaters don't have girlfriends or they're married.

You can spot skaters because they carry their boards. At the airport, on the shuttle, at the sign-in, skaters carry their boards. Always. Once every decade someone makes a doomed effort to sell some kind of skateboard carrying case, and one pretty shaky skate treatise says '70s pros not only used different boards in contests, but carried them all in a special quiver. I doubt this. Burton and Volcom make backpacks with straps for boards, but the only kid I saw using one in Vegas was very young and pretty portly and didn't skate at all. I think they're more for snowboarding.

Yes, so skaters carry their boards. Some hold the tip with their thumb and forefinger and dangle the tail just over their feet as they wait in line, standing the tail on their toe when they're stopped. No two skaters toe their boards exactly the same.* Walking down the carpeted halls, I notice that a few carry them under their arms, and most hold them by the front truck. The griptape is all black, and there's a slit near the tail or a marker of some kind to differentiate the front from the back, like a word or a cross painted in Magic Marker, or a logo pressed in the tape. Lutzka's board is leaning against the booth and the left edge of the griptape is worn away from flip tricks. The wear is less so on the nose and less than that on the tail. He's eating tacos.

You can tell the skaters who ride loose trucks because those riders' decks have little blurred spots of speed just over the wheels. Some carry what looks like a thick board but is actually their board with a new deck on top of it. This is in case the one they're using breaks during competition. One skater carries two full boards with the wheels locked over each other. Recently there has been a resurgence of popular '80s graphics, so a few of the decks feature classic V. C. Johnson images in various stages of smearment.

---

* It's such a ubiquitous little skating quirk that eventually Chris Haslam incorporated it into a trick. How he does it I don't know, but you can watch him pop his board from the ground up into a vertical 360, catch and balance it vertically on his toe, do another 180 rotation, and catch it again, then hop on and roll away.

THE TOUR'S events are vert skating, street skating, freestyle motocross (where they flip on their bikes), and three kinds of BMX: dirt, park, and vert. The motocross and BMX courses aren't finished yet, and there are fences and dust and bulldozers plowing what look like temples off to the side of the building, next to the village where all the promoters have their tents.

The street course is inside at the Joint. The vert course is out back behind the casino's main pool, a branched, multilevel, stone-patioed thing with private little tents stuck throughout its various enclaves. Outside one of these tents is Sheckler's dad, Randy. He's in a Sheckler Racing T-shirt and has STRENGTH tatted on one forearm and HONOR on the other. He's got Ryan's short, stocky build and a gleaming bald head with a spherical blond goatee and no mustache. He's accompanied by what I sure hope are female friends of Ryan, who I don't think was there, though I only walked past the little tent twice.

THE VERT RAMP is built on a lattice constructed over a fake lagoon where people are laid out on the sand. It's a little smaller than the motel down the street, with two elephant-width ends covered in black canvas and connected with a long Masonite floor. Vert skating is a totally different animal, about which your correspondent has little business writing—although I do have a press card, so I can walk up the two-story stairway and stand on the crowded platform with the guys. Some stand back and lean against the railing. Others put half their boards over the coping and tap to either applaud or tell someone to get off the ramp. Some just do it nervously. The thing's 12 feet high and at least 60 feet wide.

Bucky Lasek's up here with curls sticking out of his helmet. So is Chris Miller, a top '80s pro who is little and elfin like Sheckler. So is Andy Macdonald, who was up on the platform with Bucky when Hawk did the 900 ten years ago. One guy who is really good and no one knows the name of is skating without elbow pads. There's a kid up there in a shoelace belt and green helmet who is maybe in middle school and silently airing and grinding and sliding out, then doing it all over again.

Everything's bigger on vert. Most pros are in a helmet, full pads, gloves, and have solid, fit builds and not particularly young sweaty faces. (Bucky and Andy are both thirty-seven; Miller's thirty-five.) Decks and trucks are really the same, but vert riders use big angular wheels that have a slower hiss when they spin in the air, and these guys all stay in the air forever. You don't even hear their wheels rolling over the coping because they're airborne before they hit the ramp's lip. They don't ollie into it either. They just sort of lift off, and once airborne will spin or twist or sometimes flip while they baton-whirl the board in a 180 or 360, sometimes in the opposite direction. They land with kind of a silent whizzing slam. Lasek's doing 10-foot-long, 6-foot-high aerials without touching his board. He's also sponsored by Ethika.

The coping on this vert ramp looks about as big around as a softball and the grinds have a long, clean, steel-on-steel sound that's almost like sharp surf. The platform's crowded with skaters and their backpacks. There's a death box, an empty panel of space under the coping that's a '70s throwback from when skaters would grind over a pool's filter. Even a foot from the edge, you can't see down the wall. To see down you have to stand on the coping, and it's like looking down a cliff, and it sets off your heart rate and rocks your whole gyroscope in an awful, sickening wave that takes a few minutes to subside.

The ramp's also always moving. A constant shifting from the wet desert wind and a soft ongoing quake of the riders skating over the damp Masonite panels, punctuated with a jolt every eight seconds when that rider lands a trick.

Shaun White is not here practicing, but will later win the contest, again, for the third time. He'll place first for the whole tour. There are reports of Shaun sightings and a lot of people saying, "Where's Shaun White?," but no one sees much of him until the finals, when he shows up in a tank top and black cutoffs and destroys everyone in the Hawkish way he had in Beijing. He does sequences only he can do, doing them higher and faster than anyone else—if anyone else could do them, which they can't.

Some of the crowd stands in the water to watch him skate.

He's ahead the whole time, but his last run is the best. White drops in at the ramp's green edge, moves along the floor, and comes up for a high backside 360, landing forwards, crossing the ramp again, and flying sideways with his back foot off the board. He does it again, then on the other side of the ramp stays low and 180s and slides about 10 feet, his board even over the coping and his body stretched far out over the ramp. He does two more flip-your-board-up-into-your-hand-while-you-spin tricks, choosing these maybe *because* it's windy, and no other pros are doing them, since wind makes tricks like these especially hard.

He hugely heelflips and lands fakie, rolls up the wall and backwardsly does a frontside 540 (where you spin away from the direction your feet are pointing). He lands, rolls across, then does a backside 540, spinning the opposite way. He's crossing the floor in a recovery stance when he starts to roll up the opposite wall, and, standing basically upright, does a 720 about 10 feet over the coping. "No one else can do that combination," says the announcer. He lands with his fist in a pump and then rolls up and does a sideways 360 move I've never seen, where both his hands grip the board behind him, back arched like he's about to turn inside out.

The crowd's still roaring from the 720. White approaches the 2-foot extension at the ramp's edge, but doesn't roll up it. He goes to the lower left spot on the ramp and a foot before the coping he steps off and flies a few feet up to the high little platform, then grabs his board from the air as he steps down, his hand in a V.

MAYBE you didn't know that Shaun White was a top competitive skateboarder. You're not alone. A three-time Olympic gold medalist and *Rolling Stone* cover at nineteen, and then again at twenty-three, he's been known to the world as a snowboarder. It's ironic, but also, as our unlikely history shows, maybe perfectly appropriate that he is the best candidate to take vert skating's next giant leap. Tony Hawk landed the first 900 in 1999, a target he'd been after for thirteen years. And it's Hawk who has said vert's next step is the 1080 (three full rotations), and that the one to take it is probably Shaun White.

White grew up in snowless San Diego and had two corrective heart surgeries before he turned one. His five-person family liked to ski, however, and by the time he was four White displayed that interestingly off-putting characteristic of a kid who's obsessed with something in a way that spells Hard Wired. The official version is that his parents were so freaked out that after two years they switched him to snowboarding. Within a year he won his first Am contest, then placed at a National in the top thirteen, and was promptly sponsored by Burton Snowboards. He was seven. He won five Am titles, turned pro at thirteen, won his first pro contest at fifteen, and has really been winning ever since, with more medals and sponsors and coverage and much, much more money than anyone in snowboarding's history.

But White's almost always been that good at skateboarding. He was nine when he caught Hawk's eye at their local Encinitas skatepark, fifteen when he joined the Tony Hawk Tour, and seventeen when he turned pro. This was 2003. In 2005 he won his first Dew Tour gold medal and a silver at X Games 11 in 2005. The silver was for the vert contest. For the best trick contest that year, he used every run to attempt the 1080, and kept trying after time ran out.

He's never landed a 900 skateboarding. And while Giorgio Zattoni, Sandro Dias, Alex Perelson, and Bob Burnquist (on the mega-ramp) all have, they're not as likely candidates for the 1080. "The only guy capable of that is Shaun White," says Hawk, pointing out that White's both landed it in the snow and made the three rotations on his board. White tried again at the next X Games, and continued, after he had healed and rested, to try and try again, rocketing up in a tight, red-edged spiral that he holds through the air's apex and down into the bottom of the ramp. He needs to keep the board almost at his side to spin fast enough to get three, then he has to get the board under him before hitting the ramp's floor. He's done this. He spills again and again and again, but he spills with the board underneath him, and I'm knocking wood right now, but you can see—he's taking that step.

# 29

# WATCHING SHECKLER SKATE

THE DEW TOUR FINALS STREET COURSE was finished at four this morning, and by ten, most of the pros are here skating. The area is covered with platforms and rails and drops and abutted ramps of different angles, but on the whole is cross-shaped, made up of main lines that run north to south and east to west.

The north-south line spans the length of the standing floor and continues to the end of the stage. At the back of the room is a long, tall pitch ramp that reaches the second mezzanine. Skaters roll down this, hit a flat, then launch off a shorter angled ramp over a "death gap." On the other side of the gap is a lower-angled landing ramp, then a flat, and then another launch. This one is guitar-shaped, and, sticking out where the neck would be is a long square pole. The pole goes over a second gap, then there's a low landing ramp into a flat area and a small curved wall at the back of the stage.

The east-west line consists of two huge, tall quarterpipes at the sides of the floor that are mostly walls. The idea is that skaters can drop in on these and then launch off various ramps and fly over the runway or through the gaps of the north-south line. The edges of the gaps through the north-south line are all affixed with coping, and additional rails are everywhere. Off stage right, leading down to the floor are steep angled ramps with handrails. Off stage left leading down to the floor are two different sets of stairs separated by a foot-wide flat rail called a hubba. The stairs are between the guitar launch and a tall box of green plywood where paramedics are storing a gurney.

Sheckler's at the top of a tall quarterpipe wearing khakis, new red sneakers, and a Plan B shirt where the "P" and the "B" overlap and look like they are made of mesh, like a football jersey's numbers. He's riding seasoned red wheels and a contractually questionable Danny Way deck. His black trucks look gnawed on. His sneakers' laces are white but his shoelace belt is red. He's chatting about his mustache with someone in the crowd while he looks down into the course, waiting for a break. People are skating the east-west line both ways and angling off onto the north-south line. There are a couple of near-collisions, but everyone can stop on a dime and they often pat one another when there's a close call.

Ryan drops in with the easy slow-motion beat he always does, and follows the 70-degree arch of the board down with his body, so he's crouching by the time all four wheels hit the ramp's surface as he moves down the wall. It doesn't seem like he's going that fast until he hits the thin metal plate between the ramp and the floor. There's a hard cymbal sound and then he zips over the hardwood and onto the hollow plywood launch with a BOOM, then lowly clears the gap without holding on and starts for the opposite big ramp at his left.

He's crossed the whole venue's floor in about three seconds. He's tucked and trained forward, and a half-second from the ramp when he decides it's not right, he steps off the board. He steps to the right. The board rolls shakily up the ramp's wall and Ryan takes about ten blurred stuttersteps to slow himself down. But he's still going too fast and there's not enough floor to stop— just a wood-paneled wall and an emergency exit. He runs up that, takes about five quick steps till the momentum leaves him, then turns, standing sideways 6 feet over the floor, and drops back from the Y to the X plane. Then he finds his board and pops it into his hand and jogs up the ramp to try again.

Pretty much everybody's here. P-Rod and Lutzka are over by the stairs, hand-grinding their boards up and down the rails. Chaz Ortiz is practicing the north-south line, and when he lands short a plume of sawdust shoots up from the first platform. Fabrizio Santos, thirty-two, is here, with dreads tied back past his waist and two adorable huge-haired daughters running around in the stands. Frenchman Bastien Salabanzi is here, and fourth-ranked Mario Saenz from Mexico, and Adam Dyet, who, like Lizard King, is thin and tattooed and flamboyantly grubby, and also from Salt Lake City. A slight blond boy from Rochester, Minnesota, named Alec Majerus, age fifteen, just floats over everything. Everyone has a shoelace belt and no one's wearing pads or a helmet.

It's also loud in here, like a jobsite. The PAs in the casino and pool and the Joint are always playing fairly loud, hard-rockish music (they're playing Alice in Chains right now), but the skating's a lot louder. Every time a skater rolls over onto a ramp there's a quick *BA-BOOM* noise through the hollow space underneath. Someone's also drilling somewhere inside one of the platforms.

The edge of the first big launch is lined with a metal 2-by-4, whose top 2 inches are flush with the plywood. Skaters ride up the little side ramps and fly up 4 feet onto the metal 2-by-4, producing a hard *chink* followed by a fine grading hiss.

Inside the 6-foot death gap is a curved round rail about level with the ramp's edge. Skaters fly off the launch and land on it. Everyone takes turns over and over again. They sail up without touching their boards and land with the rail pinched in the corner of their wheel and truck. Pros mostly ride loose trucks because they turn fast and give more when they land. It's no exception here, and when the trucks meet the rail they bend so that the wheels nearly touch the board. The sound's a louder, amplified version of the 2-by-4, kind of a washed SHHAAAAAAAAAA. If a skater just taps a rail, that rail makes a *binngggggg* if it's thin and a *rinngggggg* if it's thick.

When they fall or lose control and shoot their boards way up in the air, you can hear each oiled spin of the bearing on its axle, four clean hisses that sound odd against the pained cries of someone down there, twisting on his back. You can hear the same sound when they go smooth over a gap, a kind of *wshhhh-hhhhhhhhhhhhht,* then a clean *pop* when they land all four wheels on that hollow platform.

At the bottom of each ramp transition and the floor is a sized thin metal sheet that makes an abbreviated four-part cash-register noise every time a skater rolls over it. The floor is a compacted and glazed kind of hardwood, like a dance floor, and underneath all the loud noise is a symphony of squealing urethane.

Sheckler's the first one to hit the guitar rail. It's long and square and angled up like the barrel of a tank. The wide square shape is bad for grinds (and better for slides), so he loses it the first couple of times. But then he comes down from the first launch and rolls loudly up the second and takes flight, falling hawkishly forward with the barrel passing under him. His arms are out and his head is down, and at the last perfect second before the rail disappears he taps his truck like a timpani mallet on a xylophone's big c.

The rail's hollow and open at both ends and lets out a long loud *WINGGGGGGGG.*

WATCHING the warm-up is like watching a three-ring circus without the rings. Everyone's skating, but everyone's also just kind of walking around and hanging out. One of tomorrow's emcees is a hefty, buzz-cut guy with glasses and a stocking tattoo, who meets and greets but also skates the course. Charlie Wilkins, a former Boston pro who designed the course, is here, and says it cost $15,000 not including man-hours, and that it has to all be torn out after the finals tomorrow night to get ready for a Godsmack show that weekend. He nicely explains that the course is gray because the plywood is Baltic birch, super-smooth and $100 a sheet, and that everything else—the neon green of the steps and the Dew logos covering the tall quarterpipes are just big stickers.

One of the Globe pros is complaining that the roll-in is too high. He says it's "scary." There's another young blond flying kid out there with a mom who's a little older than me. It seems rather icky but the publicists all confirm and then one Tweets that they've mopped the ramps with Mountain Dew so it's easier to stick tricks.

Most every corner and out-of-the-way surface, including on top of and underneath the quarterpipes, is piled with coats and sweatshirts and backpacks and boards. Some piles are in random spots on the floor. There are also little knobs of wax all over the place. They're many-sided and the color of ice and as big as your thumb, hidden like Easter eggs in the way that once you see one, they're suddenly everywhere. They're on the tops of 2-by-4 railings and just inside the coping and on chairs and ledges and shelves and next to backpacks and spare decks. Some skaters palm them as they skate. They all wax all the metal surfaces over and over and over again. They wax the tails and noses and trucks and insides of their wheels and the convex undersides of their decks. They descend the stairs carrying their boards and hand-grind the rails back and forth, then ascend the stairs doing the same thing, then do it again.

Meanwhile, everyone's still skating. The camera man stays menacingly close the whole time, waiting next to but sometimes *in* the gap when skaters fly up to grind. On the ceiling, some of the spotlights are outlined in a spinning halo of smaller lights that look a lot like a ball bearing with the shield pried off.

The skaters' focus now seems to have moved from the ramps to the stairs. About forty skaters are pouring down and around the two flights of stairs again and again. At the bottom is a piece of the hardwood floor that the course doesn't cover. It goes to the edge of the first barricade where everyone's parents are. There's not enough room for skaters to turn when they come down over the stairs or off the rail, so they have to slide out to stop. Most land and turn their boards from a straight twelve- and six-o'clock direction to eleven- and five-o'clock, with a quick squealing sound. A non-skater working the venue has uncommunicatively placed four big LCD screens along the edge of the course facing the stairs, and lost boards occasionally shoot out and hit the screens with a sharp crunch. Every skater has the same bewildered look of concern the first time it happens.

When Sheckler lands he slides out but also puts his tail down if he wants to really stop, so his board tilts up at 45 degrees and there's a squelching from the quarter-inch of sneaker sole he's dragging on the floor. The small technical rail tricks haven't traditionally been his specialty, but he won last summer's X Games with that backside 270 spin onto a rail in a similar setup, so he's by no means out of his element, and of course is going huge every single time, losing it once on the hubba but regaining full midair control the way the best pros can, landing feet-first and bend-turning into a clean slide straight on his back, eyes closed and hands clasped, muttering.

THE ACTUAL FINALS aren't much different. They let mostly young people in to fill up the floor and amp the music and turn all the swiveling, churning spotlights on at once. Cameras on long metal poles wrapped in wires loom out over the course. All the TVs loop this one video-game trailer, because it turns out a huge part of this demo was paid for by a gaming company called 4mm to promote their latest incarnation of an online skating game. A guy here from the UNLV *Rebel Yell* thought he was covering a video-game expo.

The floor's front section is still reserved for press, family, and nonparticipating pros. Jereme Rogers is here, and that treble clef tattoo is basically in his eye. Lutzka's mom and dad and brother and cousin are here, and all look *a lot* like him. Young pro Chaz Ortiz keeps skating over to change shirts and swing his little cousins between his legs. His whole family is here. Brothers, Mom, Dad, and a really nice young grandpa who just smiles, then comes over to introduce himself. When Ortiz goes back to skating, his cousins play tag with Santos's two kids.

Front and center are Sheckler's youngest brother Kane and his dad. Ryan's mom and brother Shane aren't here. Shane's now eighteen and sponsored by Volcom and could maybe go pro one day, but still, it's gotta be hard.

The lights go down and the crowd roars and the skaters all change their shirts a final time, popping tags off before they skate up to the stage to all get in a line. Both the emcees are in black. The camera guy's going to move down to film them one by one while the guy in a booth I can't locate introduces them. Lutzka gets the loudest roar. When the cameraman comes to him, Sheckler strokes his mustache. They're playing office-planned "extreme" intro music that's metal-guitar-heavy and a lot louder than before. In the dark I can see the builder's trigger light under the box by the handrail.

After everyone had been introduced, the lights start flying around and they make the athletes skate the course in the dark. People are bumping into each other. Lutzka rolls over the camera cord and falls forward. After a hefty tre-flip down the seven-stair, Ryan slides over and tags his dad's hand. The huge roll-in has no ladder and now has *another* roll-in on top of it, a 4-foot angled box painted the same neon green. But the new one is actually steeper, so now the whole ramp has two angles, like an A-frame's roof on top of a regular roof.

The contest begins. It's a thing where the guys go in heats of four skaters each, and every skater gets sixty seconds on the course to rack up points (like four points for grinding a rail). Two rounds of this, and then there's the Jam contest, where heats of five skaters all compete at once. Different contests have different point systems, most of them invented by non-skaters and not that well understood by any of the pros I talked to.

Sheckler doesn't traditionally drop in. He starts in a disaster. That is, he starts with half his board over the edge of a two-angled cliff so if he even steps on it wrong he'll fall. He needs to keep purchase on his back wheels as they roll over the lip but he also needs to keep everything even so he can skate down a 4-foot wall onto the steep roll-in that sends him over the death gap. He'll need to lean forward to get himself started, but for now he waits, two stories high over the course, watching.

Sheckler ollies the gap. He doesn't need to. He would have cleared it anyway, but instead he slaps his tail just before launch and smiles hawkishly as he sails over and down with a smooth rumbling break, then off the guitar launch, hitting the rail with a *wangggggggg*. Then he's up the quarterpipe, turns 180, and does the whole thing again, in reverse. He goes off the short ramps meant for landing, clearing the first gap and flipping the second, until he's back to the top of the first roll-in, the board running out of energy, and he steps off and pops it up and hops up on the little box again. Then he goes down backwards.

Partway through the evening Sheckler takes his shirt off. His body's flat now, with skip-stone muscles and STRENGTH & HONOR tatted around his collarbone. He has good runs both on the ramps and on the rails, and off the stairs, including a full cab (or 270) to backside boardslide down the handrail—the same move he'd won the X Games with two months ago.

But today belongs to Chaz Ortiz, who is sixteen, with thin sideburns and a digital watch and a woven hat with a black snowball on top. He started skating at six and was winning everything as an Am by the time he turned pro at thirteen. Then he joined the Dew Tour, and not only beat out Sheckler, P-Rod, and Lutzka at the Salt Lake City contest, but also won the whole $100,000 thing. He was fourteen. As of this writing he's a junior in high school, living with his family in Carpentersville, Illinois. Today he's going to place first and win $25,000, with Lutzka in second and Sheckler in third.

Ortiz is P-Rodly smooth in just about everything he does. All his stair and ledge tricks are top-notch. He no-handedly 360s the death gap, and then on another run tre-flips it. He flies off the same launch again, but instead of hitting the guitar platform veers right and flies up above the whole course. It's about 10 feet down and he lands in the little hardwood floor of space between the high quarter and the stairs, nearly taking out a camera as the crowd erupts.

That's not his best. This is his best: Ortiz drops in from the top roll-in and flips the death gap, lands in that slow-motion way Ryan does and then goes off the guitar and blindly backslides the rail. He straightens out when he lands, rolls up the quarterpipe, 180s, and locks into a noseblunt. He pops out of the blunt and fires down the ramp toward the stairs, but he veers to his left and ollies onto the steel edge of the box where they're hiding the gurney. He grinds the full distance on his back truck, stepping on his tail to stop about 1 centimeter from the box's edge. It's 6 feet down, and his whole board and three wheels are hanging over. He's stopped. Then he whirls 90 degrees and hops the truck around the corner onto the uncoped side of the box. He stays there, stalled, with his arms out on top of what looks like a big green refrigerator.

There's a *Wow!* look on his face just before he drops to the floor, clean. Everybody screams. Sheckler shakes his sweaty head. Papa Ortiz leans over. "He's been doing this since he was a little corn flake."

# 30

# WATCHING RODNEY SKATE, OR SWITCH NOLLIE LASERFLIP AT MIDNIGHT

RODNEY MULLEN SKATES every night from about 11 p.m. to 3 a.m., but has a warm-up routine that begins shortly after he wakes up around sunset. The last night we met he was limping hard on his left leg because he'd doubled his skate session the night before. We talked at the same table in his kitchen, with books like *The Force of Symmetry* and *Son of Hamas* and *Unified Theories of Cognition* stacked at the other end. In the open living room, sticking out of a metal bin by the fireplace, was one of his old Uber Light decks—a pricey but ultra-strong technology invented and patented by him. Marred with fat blurred lines from boardslides, like his other old decks this one had a cross and a note written in Sharpie: 5/10/08 MADE IT!

I asked about the date, and he said it was the night he first landed a goofy nollie laserflip. Since Rodney's original stance is regular, some would consider the trick a switch nollie laserflip, a maneuver long deemed impossible due to general mechanics and simple leverage. No one had ever done one. Not until Rodney erased his stance and could approach the trick not "switch" but goofy-footed, once again landing the unlandable and yet another golden link on skateboarding's evolutionary chain. Now he can land them consistently, and it turned out to be the one thing he agreed to show me.

It's a prohibitively complex trick. A laserflip is a 360 heelflip. The board spins a complete rotation in the direction the rider's heels are pointing, and requires a different task from each foot. Usually the rear foot rotates the board with a push-in motion, and the front foot spins the board with a downward punch of the heel. Both actions need to be done simultaneously for the trick to work, and a skater's legs have to first lift up and then catch the board after one rotation.

The laserflip surfaced during the technical time of the early '90s, but was so seldom landed with any kind of grace that it wasn't considered an actual trick. Like the player's rach 3 or the gambler's center deal, so few people had ever witnessed such a thing that for years the laser existed in the mythology between the sport's past and future. Stories and then video surfaced in the 1990s of one Ronnie Creager cleanly landing the trick, but his microfine ability was so freakish that almost no one caught on for another fifteen years, until P-Rod and Torey Pudwill could command lasers with the grace that's so important to skateboarding. They were further pioneered by macrotech genius Chris Haslam, who executed it switch stance over the famed Macba drop in Barcelona. Flash pictures of pros laserflipping well-demonstrate the sport's balletic mechanics. The skater looks frozen in an exaggerated backward skip, front leg bent over and in, back leg kicked out, arms in the air like an inspired puppeteer.

Done with a nollie, or off the nose, the laserflip takes on baffling new problems, including height (which means time), since almost no skaters can nollie as high as they can ollie. Still, a few can do them, and the best example is probably Prince Gilchrist, who has an Antwuan Dixonian gift of keeping balance with his arms at his sides.

Nothing in skating's five thousand year history and fifty year literature ever suggested rumor of a switch nollie laser. It was not possible. Not until May 10, 2008.

MULLEN ALWAYS has and still skates alone. He'll occasionally session with teammate Chris Haslam, who can land switch tricks like a 540 flip, but otherwise he's allowed three people in five years to watch him skate. After detailed and mutually uncomfortable negotiation, I became the fourth.

We met two hours later at around eleven o'clock down the road at the Globe Warehouse. Globe is the sneaker company that runs Globe TV, the website that released the last bit of Mullen footage in a series called *United by Fate*. Skaters' parts are interspersed with the team driving a big black van to skate spots, and when I pulled into the big parking lot the van was parked out front, next to Rodney's green Toyota. He limped out of his car in a knit hat, T-shirt, big pants, and torn sneakers. He carried his board under his arm, decorated on the bottom with a cross and a peeling I VOTED sticker. Both the nose and tail were equally worn, as were the outer sides of his shoes.

He unlocked the door to the warehouse, a high, open, lit space with cubicles and painted beams. One office cleaner made his way through the cubes, while another worked around the long gourmet coffee and tea station in the back. Above the front desk, a giant Almost ad hung on the wall, featuring Rodney's partner Daewon and Chris Haslam, the team's second pro after Sheckler. In the photo, Daewon's holding a board upright at the lip of a mini-ramp, wheels facing outward. Haslam is frozen in space above him, his back wheels riding up the nose of Daewon's board.

Rodney turned a corner and walked down a suddenly cold hallway and opened a door. We went up a short flight of lumber steps and walked out onto the platform of the mini-ramp, facing the garage side of the Globe warehouse. The ramp was long and changed heights three times, going from 5 feet at one end to 6 then

7 feet at the other. Rodney took out his keys, wallet, and iPhone with an Ed Hardy bulldog cover and dropped into the ramp.

The stanceless way Mullen rides the board is unlike anything skateboarding has ever seen. His body is centered with feet somewhat wide, each shoe a little closer than normal to each end of the board. His legs are ovally bent in the demi-plié stance of a ballerina. He rolls back and forth and at first doesn't turn; he moves up one side of the ramp, shifts his stance, and turns his head, then rolls back down. Sometimes he'll roll halfway across the ramp then evenly slide 180 and cross the second half in the opposite stance. Or not in the opposite stance, since he has no stance.

Soon he starts making slow, exaggerated surflike turns with his wheels high off the ground. He makes the turns in both directions, and points out that such turns would pull a normal skater off the board because of the sense of balance that forms with either particular stance. Erasing his stance, he says, gives him leverage on tricks that could never be done switch or backwards, simply because the mechanics wouldn't work against a skater's asymmetrically ingrained balance, like the switch nollie laserflip.

In the flat of the ramp, Rodney tries twice and then executes the move he said he would: a goofy nollie laserflip. He slows it down so I can see. He rolls forward, mouth underbit and eyes on the spot where he'll land. I don't even hear the nose touch down. He seems to just inhale and extend his arms and lightly kick, so the board whirls around his toe until it's back under his feet. He does another one in his regular stance, and another goofy. A switch nollie laser. Which is impossible. Or not impossible, since he's got the trick. And not switch, since regular or goofy or for that matter forwards and backwards don't exist for him anymore.

He does another one and nods, early sweat glistening on his temples. "That was a good one."

It's all he'll show me, and while he's willing to explain it over and over, once caffeinated, Mullen turns into a waterfall of complex information, listing numerous people and videos and dates and tech tricks and their evolution over the years. He points to P-Rod, whose shape over the board is almost identical in both stances. Mullen says that he can tell instantly from a photo if someone's riding switch or not. He brings up Group Theory again, explaining the symmetries in crystals, the perfect balance of pluses and minuses that make such intricate, beautiful, exacting shapes.

"We have those symmetries within our bodies," he says. "It is insanely complex. And that's where I say there are so many people that could be great, could be top pro skaters, but they're just lacking a few of those symmetries. And now that I see with this hindsight, I see things I never knew, which has been part of the joy for me—of understanding my skating, and why it's worked."

There are few people to talk to about this, since no one is more authoritative and passionately articulate about skateboarding than Rodney Mullen. One reason it's hard to explain is because it's a completely different kind of skateboarding or even sport, or non-sport, since all board sports are nonsymmetrical. You either ride regular or goofy; not both or neither.

What Rodney does then almost isn't skateboarding, which is asymmetrical by nature. It's a complete re-creation, the product of a decade of obsessive work by one man, who, starting at around age thirteen also forged the building blocks of that original creation. You kind of have to see what he does. And you will. A month after we met, Rodney began filming his first full video part in a decade.

Mullen walks me to the warehouse exit. It's a cold night and he gives me a black sweatshirt with a heavy patterned lining and a gold zipper. Later I noticed that the zipper's tongue flops over to either side of the slider and that the sweatshirt is reversible. Ha.

The last time he saw Sheckler was a year ago at a Denver trade show for a retailer called Zumiez. Ryan was still in a walking cast. Rodney says he literally bumped into him. They chatted, and the next time Rodney saw him was on the 2010 X Games, when Ryan came back and won. Mullen rarely follows contests, but that day remembers watching Sheckler skate with the same "insane will" he saw in footage ten years ago. Since then, they've texted a bit—there was talk of a meeting when Rodney drove to visit the Navy SEAL base near San Diego— but otherwise haven't been in touch.

WHAT ELSE can you say about skateboarding? What is it? A sport? An art? A dance? All? None? Some? Whatever it is, it's never belonged. Not with surfing or scootering or roller or figure skating. Not on sidewalks or in parking lots or streets or public parks—until 1993. As a result, it draws people who don't fit into these places either, and organically nurtures them with a sometimes lifesaving sense of belonging. At least, that's the case with Rodney, the most important skateboarder in history.

"Skateboarding's given me so much, I could never pay it back," he said. "And I'm not trying to make some big—it's everything I have, who I am. It's all come from this."

Mullen says to think of the ollie as symbolic for skateboarding. A push-pull motion where one foot falls and the other extends. And if its past is any indication, like the work of Rodney or Ryan, skating will continue to push and pull as it moves in all directions. Though long persecuted and now publicly diminished by outside parties looking to profit, the ranks continue to grow. Industry people all say they'll be surprised if skateboarding isn't an Olympic sport by 2014—not because the committee will finally see past the sport's outlaw image, but because they want the sport's traffic. Turning Olympic would mean a whole new level of money and attention and celebrity and corrosion, but also new participants, respect, and, in the likely event an American comes home with the gold, maybe even a new figurehead. A new Tony Hawk. Or a new Shaun White. Or a new Ryan Sheckler.

But there won't be another Rodney Mullen, who simultaneously has given everything and taken everything from skateboarding, and faced true blackness when he thought he might lose it—be it due to outside pressures, interior damage, or the realization that he was only pushing what he already knew.

That Mullen, at age forty-four, was the one to deconstruct the essence of skating makes sense, since he's the one who built it in the first place, first bringing the board off the ground, first flipping the board in the air, first winding the board around his foot, which everyone said was impossible. The question is: What's next? And the answer is: He's not sure, since he's only just reached his goal, and everything's now new again.

"There are corridors after corridors I can go through," he said that night. "I remember the hardest class I ever took, Number Theory. And it starts you off with, 'One is a number. Zero is also a number.' And by stating the obvious, you don't understand the profundities beneath. And that's what this has been—this glorious process of understanding why this has worked. That's been me."

Mullen moves through these corridors every night, all night, in a cold warehouse or an isolated parking-lot spot he's hunted down around Redondo Beach. Tonight he'll skate with no front, back, left, or right, moving alone through yet another plane he's created, his brilliant desperation synced and racing for four hours, until he's emptied and soaked and limping again. And when it's done, he'll put his board in the car and drive north towards Ojai, where his wife, dogs, cats, and horse are waiting, where he'll go to sleep as the sun comes up.

# MANY THANKS

Keith Wallman: this book's heroic, fearless, persistent editor—Keith, thank you. Kristen Mellitt: this book's kind and patient project editor. Jacquie Simone: research. Will Louison: tech support. Marie and Angelo at Board-Trac. Everyone at *GQ*, especially Luke Zaleski. Alan Gelfand, Rodney Mullen, Thom Denick and Ji Young Hwang, Dard Miller, Rose Scilla, Gerald Leichman, Mark Anthony Green, James Sigman, Katherine Wiley, The Peasall Sisters, The Pelham Family, The Louison Family, The Krause Family, Curt Louison, Margo Louison, and Nanny. And Linda Louison-Krause, who still says "I love skateboarding." Thank you, all. This book would not exist without you.

# NOTES

## Epigraph
ii. ". . . all I will ever care for": Louison, Cole. *GQ*, December 18, 2009. www.gq.com/
blogs/the-q/2009/12/stadium-style-who-the-hell-is-richie-jackson-and-why-do-i-
want-to-dress-like-him.html

## 1. There's This Kid . . .
1. ". . . rerun of the X Games": Mullen interview, December 1, 2010.
1. "8 million": shared data, Board-Trac.
1. "There's this kid.": Mullen interview.
1. "Sheckler's at the edge": ESPN. August 3, 2010.
1. "382 million": www.espneventwrapups.com.
2. "Get to the matter": Mullen interview.
2. "Nyjah Huston": *New York Times*, July 17, 2006.
3. "Twenty-five years ago": Mullen, p. 127.
3. "he was six": *ESPN Magazine*, July 16, 2008.
4. "frontside—meaning" Warsaw, p. 34.
5. "ABC and ESPN and ESPN2": www.espneventwrapups.com.
7. "foot exploded": *Los Angeles Times*, August 1, 2009.
8. "new skate footage": *United by Fate*, Episode 3.

## 2. An Easy History of Skateboarding, Then Another One
11. "The Roller Derby": *The New Yorker*. July 26, 1999.
11. "Val Surf shop": Booke, p. 26.
11. "Makaha Skateboards": Brooke, pp. 22-24.
11. "Hobie Alter": Brooke, pp. 28-31.
12. "first skateboarding competition": Cassorla, p. 10.
12. "Davey Hilton": *The Quarterly Skateboarder* Vol. 1, Issue 1, Winter, 1964.
12. "50 million": Cassorla, p. 12.
12. "Pat McGee": Brooke, p. 27.
12. "Portland, Oregon": Ibid, p. 13.
12. "National Skateboarding Championships": Cassorla, p. 11 and Brooke, p. 32.
13. "a new medical menace . . . banned in 20 cities": Ibid, pp. 12-13.
14. "the week, if not the day": Brooke, p. 24.
14. "Mullen was born": Mullen, p. 5.
14. "I called Michael Brooke": *The New Yorker*. July 26, 1999.
15. "group around Glendale": Cassorla, p. 9.
15. "Jim Fitzpatrick of San Diego": Brooke, p. 40.
15. "summer of 1904.": Cassorla, p. 9.
15-16. "You could say that . . . cold cases": Smith interview.
15. "Skate Designs": www.skatedesignsinc.com.
16. "Skeeter Skate": www.jimgoodrich.net.
17. "Roller-skating's famous debut": Trap, p. 1.

17. "John Joseph Merlin": Leinhard, blogpost.
17. Footnote: Latcham, 298.
17. "James Plimpton patented": MacClain, blogpost.
17. "bike races in wooden velodromes": Guttman, p. 197.
18. "Roller skates weren't mass produced": BBC 'I Love Toys-Rollerskating' blogpost.
18. Footnote: Mullen, p. 132.
19. "archaeologists exploring Russia . . . Formenti": *National Geographic News*. January 4, 2008.
19. "the word *skate*": Oxford English Dictionary, p. 2844.
20. "the term *board*": Oxford English Dictionary, pp. 952-954.
20. "at least 3,000 years": Britton, blogpost.
21. "supreme pleasure": *New York Times*, May 30, 2008.
21. "God-loving missionaries from England": Warshaw, p. 387.
21. "a local named George Freeth": *Los Angeles Times*, July 21, 2007.
22. "surfing on land": *Honolulu Star News Bulletin*, July 24, 2005.
22. "Stone's injuries include a . . . broken neck": *Associated Press*, May 25, 2008.
23. "Turks were cruising the snow": *Ski Magazine*, April 2010.
23. "Gunnar Burgeson": *Transworld Snowboarding*, February 11, 2010.
23. "Michigan engineer named Sherman": *Smithsonian Magazine*, February 5, 2010.
23. "the Diegueños": McCarthy, p. 301.
23. "own online publication": www.sandboard.com.

## 3. Rodney Mullen's Genius Roots and Femoral Anteversion

24. Family details: Mullen, pp. 5-14.
25. "You get one no": *Thrasher Magazine*, July 9, 2010.
25. "*femoral anteversion*": *What is Femoral Anteversion?* John Hopkins Orthopedic Surgery website.
26. "before he entered kindergarten": Mullen, p. 17.
26. "accused him of plagiarism": Ibid, p. 147.
26. "general number theory": Ibid, p. 137.
26. "fell off his horse": Ibid, pp. 16-17.
27. "panic rooms": Ibid, p. 15.
27. "dental floss": Ibid, p. 201.
27. "I didn't break this pattern": Ibid, p. 17.
27. "Wizard . . . Jack": Ibid, pp. 22-24.

## 4. Tony Hawk Doesn't Know When He Started Skating

29. "Tony Hawk's memory": Hawk, pp. 24-26.
29. "I don't know. It was fun": *The New Yorker*, July 26, 1999.
29. "'My life began'": *Sponsored*, 2000.
29. "As soon as I got on a board": *Rising Son*, 2006.
30. "Skateboarding saved my life": *Jimmy Kimmel Live!*, July 29, 2009.
30. "unlimited possibilities": Mullen, p. 25.
30. "Greg Weaver": *SkateBoarder*, Vol. 2, Number 1, 1975.
31. "Rodney's maternal grandmother": Mullen, p. 19.

31. *"Hell no!"*: Ibid, 27.
32. "mink coats": Ibid, p. 29.
32. "New Year's Eve": Ibid, pp. 29-31.

## 5. What're Ya Cryin' About

34. "Inland Surf Shop": Mullen, pp. 32-33.
35. "handstand": Ibid, p. 36.
35. "okay at home": Ibid, p. 17.
35. "Tony Hawk and Mike Vallely": Hawk, p. 38.
36. "broken his elbow ten times": *Jimmy Kimmel Live!*, July 29, 2009.
36. "capped teeth": Hawk, pp. 53-43.
36. "What're'ya cryin' about": online interview with Ninja Studioz. October 25, 2009.
36-37. "building a ramp . . . better than all those older guys": Mullen, pp. 37-39.
37. "cardboard ramp": Ibid, p. 42.
37. Footnote: *Transworld Business*, March 3, 2000.
37. "GO FOR THE LONG BOMB": Mullen, p. 42.
37. "pothead": Ibid, p. 24.
38. "mom rarely went to church...": *Thrasher Magazine*, July 9, 2010.
38. "so much as a school dance": *The New Yorker*. July 26, 1999.
38. "Vallely": *San Francisco Bay Guardian*, May 1994.
38. "Gator": *Stoked*, 2002.
38. "Hosoi": *Juice Magazine*, July 2004
38. "Danny Way": *Men's Journal*, July 28, 2010. www.mensjournal.com/danny-way.
38. "Margera": NBC Philadelphia, July 20, 2009.
38. "Jamie Thomas": *The New Yorker*, July 26, 1999.
38. "the rest cascade": Dissent TV, December 30, 2009.
39. "five consecutive 360s": Mullen, p. 41.
39. "Pros like Antwuan Dixon": Havoc TV, July 2010.
39. "Every motion would be taken apart . . . kickflip": p. 42, Mullen.
40. "Stacy Peralta Warptail": Ibid, p. 43.
40. "Peralta": Brooke, pp. 100-101.
40. "Kissimmee": Mullen, p. 45.
41. "flawless forty-five-second run": Mullen, p. 48.
41. "Tim Scroggs": Ibid, pp. 48-49.

## 6. Rolling Into Stacy Peralta, and the Strangest Day of My Life

43. "rolled into Stacy": Mullen, p. 51.
43. *"Charlie's Angels"*: *Charlie's Angels*, November 14, 1979.
43. "Dennis Martinez": Mullen, p. 50.
43. "approached by Bruce Walker": Ibid, pp. 52-53.
43. Footnote. "IWS boardshop": Ryan Sheckler Biography-Redbull USA, 2007.
44. "Barry Zaritsky": Ibid, pp. 54-55.
44. "demos at malls": *Rodney Mullen: From the Ground Up*, 2002.
45. "exercise regimen": Mullen, pp. 61-62.
45. "disco": Ibid, p. 66.

46. "Hawk took seventh": Ibid, p. 130.
46. "hated competing": *Thrasher Magazine*, July 9, 2010.
46. "his dad's thing": Mullen, p. 55.
46. "in a notebook": Ibid, p. 77.
47. "Clearwater Skatepark . . . Alva.": p. 57.
47. "had also moved": Mullen, pp. 44-45.
47. "Home movies": *From the Ground Up*, 2002.
48. "It's hard to emphasize": Ibid.
48. "There was me and there was cows": Speech, UCLA, January 18, 2008.
48. "ten thousand people": Mullen, pp. 65-66.
48. "where athletes really compete": Ibid, p. 69.
48-49. "military school . . . The Nutcracker": Ibid, pp. 75-76.
49. "sell his furniture": Ibid, p. 81.
49. "Peralta called": Ibid, pp. 82-83.
50. "Roller Boogie": Ibid, p. 78.
50. "one of the strangest": Ibid, p. 82.

# 7. Gunite, Snake Runs, and the Late Great '70s Skateparks

51. "40 million": Clement and Reinier, p. 616.
51. "investment by Larry Stevenson": Cassorla, p. 13.
52. "demo around Hermosa Beach": Ibid.
52. "reappeared around 1973": Brooke, p. 13.
52-53. "Pentagon Bowl": Cassorla, p. 100.
53. "hundreds of privately owned parks": Brooke, pp. 188-189.
53. "Tony Alva remembers": *Dogtown and Z-Boys*, 2001.
54. "Skateboard Heaven": Cassorla, pp. 99-101.
55. "The first skatepark": Brooke, p. 64.
55. "John O'Malley . . . Skatepark Constructors": Ibid, pp. 64-67.
55. Footnote: www.carlsbadskatepark.org.
56. "first vert contest": Brooke, p. 185.
56. "ran at a boil": Ibid, p. 66.
57. "one young pro": Ryan Sheckler Biography-Redbull USA, 2007.
57. "the premier issue": *The Quarterly Skateboarder*, Winter, 1964.
58. "2,000 miles of concrete tunnels": Weyland, pp. 41-42.
58. "real pioneer of wallrides": Weypland, pp. 76 and 103.
59. "Imagine what it's like": Brooke, p. 70.
59. "Matt Hensley": *Juice Magazine*, issue #65.
59. "Operation Ivy": *Not the New H-Street Video*, 1991.
59. "Patrick Melcher": GQ interview, April 16, 2010.
59. "early footage of Sheckler:" *Ryan Sheckler 13 Years Old*. July 12, 2008.

# 8. Technical Reinvention of the 1970s, or How Mitch Hedberg Did Not Give Urethane Wheels to Emil Hersh in Heath Ledger's Skate Shop

60. "beginning around 1950": Motil, p. 196.

60. "polyurethane": www.wordnet.princeton.edu, *Webster's New World College Dictionary*, p. 1048.
61. "Nasworthy": Brooke, pp. 46-47 and Weyland, pp. 34-35.
63. "first mega-ramp": Cassorla, pp. 14-15.
63. "G&S": Brooke, pp. 34-36.
64. Footnote: "Willi Winkels": Brooke, pp. 60-63.
65. "Precision bearings": www.skateboardballbearings.com.
66. "NHS was also": Brooke, pp. 48-50.
66. "Bones Bearings": *History of Bones Bearings*, 2011.
66. "Shake Junt": *Shake Junt Bearings*, October 11, 2009.
67. "Per Wilender": *Shop-Eat-Surf*, May 12, 2009
67. "Trucks were also reinvented": Brooke, pp. 52-53.
69. "Independent Truck Company": Brooke, pp. 54-55.
70. "recently for $1,300": *Skate and Annoy*, April 2006.

## 9. Dogtown, Stecyk, and the Business of Skate Media

72. "stands for Zephyr": Brooke, pp. 56-57.
72. "twelve-person skate team": Weyland, p. 48.
72. "Bahne-Cadillac Ocean Festival": Brooke, p. 184.
72. "We're here to win": *Dogtown and Z-Boyz*, 2001.
73. "Aspects of the Downhill Slide": *SkateBoarder Magazine*, Vol. 2, Issue 2. 1975.
76. "We weren't having as much fun": *Dogtown and Z-Boyz*, 2001.
76. "Peggy Oki": *Peggy Oki-Interview, Juice Magazine*, Issue 54, 2002
76. "It's like Hunter Thompson": *Dogtown and Z-Boyz*, 2001.
76-77. Lowboy quotes: Weyland, p. 90.
78. "last time he was out of jail": *The New York Times*, July 30, 2008.
78. "None of the": Weyland, pp. 88-95.
79. "Fausto Vitello . . . Larry Balma": *San Francisco Bay Guardian*, May 1994.

## 10. Ollieburgers, a World Championship, and the Skinniest Person I Have Ever Seen

80. "Rodney flew alone": Mullen, p. 82.
80. "Peralta's support": Ibid, pp. 83-84.
81. "watched a vert pro": Dissent TV, December 30, 2009.
81. Footnote: "Alan's nickname": Alan Gelfand interview.
81. Footnote: "Olliver 'Ollie' Gleichenhaus": *New York Times*, January 14, 1991.
81. "Precursor to the trick": Alan Gelfand interview, September 15, 2010.
82. "The birth of modern street skating": *Huck Magazine*, April 15, 2010.
82. "Street skateboarding exists": *Rodney Mullen: From the Ground Up*, 2002.
82. "'Every time you ollie'": Hawk, p. 83.
83. "V. C. Johnson": Brooke, p. 105.
84. "coveted T-shirt": Mullen, p. 86.
84. "Oasis Skatepark": Hawk, p. 26.
85. "Steve Rocco": Mullen, p. 87.
85. Footnote: "74.5 miles per hour": *New York Times*, July 29, 2009.

85. "Footage of the contest": *Rodney Mullen: From the Ground Up*, 2002.
85-87. Contest details: Mullen, p. 88-91.
87. "I was really surprised": *Rodney Mullen: From the Ground Up*, 2002.
87. "sprinted around in circles . . . rabid": Mullen, p. 91.
88. "skinniest person I have ever seen": Ibid.
88. "a gun that would turn the ocean waves": Hawk, p. 43.
89. "new corduroys and polo": Mullen, p. 82.
89. "watch him drive away": Mullen, pp. 93-94.

## 11. Unable to Do Anything, Magic Mountain, V. C. Johnson, and the Chess King

90. "time capsule": Mullen, p. 95.
90. "unable to do anything": Ibid, p. 96.
90. "*Skateboard News*": Ibid, p. 97.
90-91. Conversation: Ibid, pp. 97-98.
91. "very temporary": Speech, UCLA, January 18, 2008.
91. "footage of morning-show people": *That's Incredible*, circa 1982.
92. "if I ever needed anything": Mullen, p. 101.
93. Rocco details. Ibid, pp. 102-104.
93. "Coca-Cola factory": Ibid, p. 105.
93. "insurance costs": Borden, p. 174 and Weyland p. 72 and Wixon p. 114.
94. "*Action Now*": Brooke, p. 71.
94. "Del Mar Skate Ranch": Weyland, pp. 266-269.
94. "crowded as the moon . . . Barry": Mullen, p. 98.
94. "under $10": Ibid, p. 108.
94. "No one's going to beat you": Ibid, pp. 110-111.

## 12. The Golden Age of Skateboarding, or Tony Hawk was Sixteen in 1984

95. "500 decks a month": Brooke, p. 101.
95. "after six issues": Ibid, p. 71.
95. "extreme equestrian culture": *Action Now*, October 1980.
95. "Skateboard City": Brooke, pp. 188-189.
95. "Thirteen parks shut down": Weyland, p. 171.
95. "Sensation Basin": Mullen, p. 113.
95. "first *Thrasher* magazine": *Thrasher*, January 1981.
95. "sheaf of newsprint": Brooke, pp. 93-95.
96. "Ramps provide the same": Weyland, p. 178.
96. Ramp names: Weyland, p. 236.
97. Footnote: *Webster's New World College Dictionary*, p. 306.
98. "Neil Blender and Eddie Elguera": Weyland, p. 172.
99. "135 pounds": Hawk, p. 103.
100. "and the word TECHNICIAN": *Thrasher*, July 9, 2010.
100. "The Mutt Air": Mullen, p. 129.
100. "the fingerflip": Dissent TV, December 30, 2009.

100. "Steve Caballero": *Skate TV*, 1990.

101. "Hawk's one close competitor": Borden, p. 149.

102. "He shook the ramp": *Rising Son: the Legend of Christian Hosoi*. 2006

102. "W. C. Fields estate": *McSweeney's*, July 29, 2009.

103. "$250,000": *History of Hosoi Skates*, Hosoiskates.com.

103. "Nine months after": Weyland, p. 175.

103. "*TransWorld Skateboarding*": Brooke, pp. 96-97 and Weyland, p. 255.

103. "top-selling freestyle deck": Mullen, p. 183.

103. "hawk-skull graphic": Hawk, p. 79.

103. "Battle at the Berrics": *Battle of the Berrics 3*, October 2010.

103. "most-visited skate site": *Wall Street Journal*. February 27, 2009.

104. "*The Bones Brigade Video Show*": *The Bones Brigade Video Show*, 1984.

105. "the video cost $15,000": Brooke, p. 101.

105. "*Future Primitive*": *Future Primitive*, 1985.

105. "over 7,000 decks a month": Hawk, p. 82.

105. Footnote: "*The Search for Animal Chin*": *The Search for Animal Chin*, 1987.

106. "A young Hoosier": *Circus Magazine* circa 1987, posted by theworldsbestever.com, December 29, 2009.

106. "Swatch watch company": Mullen, p. 149.

106. "*Police Academy 4*": *Police Academy 4*, 1987.

106. "*Gleaming the Cube*": *Gleaming the Cube*, 1989.

106. "*Thrashin'*": *Thrashin'*, 1986.

106. "Downtown Julie Brown": *Stoked*, 2002.

106. "*SK8 TV*": *SK8 TV*, 1990.

107. "$89 million": articlebase.com.

107. "$2 billion": Reuters, August 6, 2010.

107. "Caballero hit 11 feet": Weyland, p. 238.

107. "185,000-square-foot facility": Brooke, p. 102.

108. "$20,000 a month": *The New Yorker*. July 26, 1999.

108. "Jonestown for skaters": Hawk, p. 117.

108. "The house had four acres": Ibid, pp. 138-139.

108. "one day get a 900": Ibid, p. 227.

## 13. Rodney Invents and Wins Everything, and His Dad Makes Him Quit, Again

109. "flew three times": Ibid, p. 117.

109. "stopped his Casio": Ibid, p. 76.

109. "20 miles away": Ibid, p. 44.

109. "strict routine": Ibid, p. 77.

110. "number theory and advanced mathematics": Ibid, pp. 137 and 125.

110. "premiered the ollie": Ibid, p. 115.

110. "late skate photographer": Brooke, p. 186.

110. "arrangement with Independent": Mullen, pp. 116-117.

110. "October cover of *Thrasher*": *Thrasher*, October 1982.

110. "Then came Mutt . . . What did he do wrong": Mullen, pp. 119-120.

110. "the kickflip": Ibid, p. 127-129.
111. "he could do four": *The Search for Animal Chin*, 1987.
111. Footnote: "so he'd double them": Dissent TV, December 30, 2009.
112. "where he placed second": Mullen, p. 129.
112. "Birdhouse Projects": Hawk, p. 170.
112. "placed seventh": Hawk, p. 130.
112-13. Vancouver/Impossible details: Mullen, pp. 143-146.
113. Footnote: "Chris Haslam": *United by Fate II*, 2007.
113. "nearly every month": Weyland, p. 245.
114. "made him quit again": Mullen, pp. 1-4.
115. "Mutt Air": Ibid, p. 134.

## 14. Natas, Gonz, and the Birth of Street Skating

116. "First called streetstyle": Ibid, p. 116.
116. "in a hang-ten": *SkateBoarder*, 1978.
116. "first street contest": Weyland, pp. 242-244.
116. "The New Etiquette": *Thrasher*, 1983.
116. "early lip tricks": Weyland, pp. 213, 242, 297.
117. "Engblom, you'll remember": Brooke, p. 111.
117. "Natas showed up one day": *Natas Kaupas: Street Skating 101*, 2006.
118. "September '84 cover": *Thrasher*, 1984.
119. "His name was Mark Gonzales": Weyland, p. 178.
119. "Half Gallery in New York City": *SkateBoarder*, 2005.
119. "November '84 cover": *Thrasher*, 1984.
119. "not street's only pioneers": *Street Skating 101*, 2006.
120. "Natas Pro Model": Ibid.
120. Footnote: "Lee Romero": *Thrasher*, September 2010.
121. "*Streets on Fire*": *Streets on Fire*, 1989.
121. "*Hocus Pocus*": *Hocus Pocus*, 1989.
121. "I don't know": *Natas Kaupas: Street Skating 101*, 2006.

## 15. The 1980s End, and Skaters Die and Go to Jail

122. "made $150,000": Hawk, p. 157.
122. "$75,000 in 1990": Ibid, p. 163.
122. "less than his wife, Cindy": Ibid, p. 169.
122. "The crash happened": Brooke, p. 90.
122. "Swindell was jailed": *Los Angeles Times*, May 3, 1993.
122. "second-degree murder": *Los Angeles Times*, October 11, 1995.
122. "Teammate Danny Way": *Los Angeles Times*, March 6, 1994.
122. "Jeff Phillips": *TransWorld Skateboarding*, March 6, 2003 and *Rolling Stone*, September 8, 1994.
122-23. "Hawk borrowed $8,000 . . . $300." Hawk, p. 178 and 180.
123. "arrested at Honolulu": *Honolulu-Star Bulletin*, September 11, 2001.
123. "*Transpottingly* huge": *Juice Magazine*, July 2004.
123. "bankruptcy": Christian Hosoi Facebook page.

123. "$150 million": *San Francisco Bay Guardian*, May 1994.
123. "$200,000": *The Me Magazine*, February/March 2008.
124. "P-Rod's flow shops": *LA Weekly*, June 16, 2005.
125. "Hawk's legacy": Hawk, p. 225.
125. Footnote: *CBS News/AP*, June 17, 2006.
125. "treated like actors": *San Francisco Bay Guardian*, May 1994.
126. "Department of Labor": Ibid.
126. "Kevin Ross graduates": *ESPN*. March 17, 2002.
126. "overused rookie pitchers": *Boston Globe*, April 13, 2009.

## 16. Rodney Nearly Dies in Sweden, and the Beginning of the 1990s

127. "feel the decay": Mullen, pp. 137-193.
128. "ran away from home": Ibid, pp. 160-161.
128. "long-lost uncle": Ibid, pp. 164-166.
128. "become a doctor": *Thrasher Magazine*, July 9, 2010.
128. "worthy recruit": Mullen p. 168.
128. "in a housing project": Ibid, p. 167.
129. "$10,000 and $20,000": Ibid, pp. 164 and 149.
129. "$800 a week . . . thirty copies": Ibid, p. 188.
129. "meltdowns at signings": Ibid, pp. 161 and 172-174.
129. "to jump off of": Ibid, p. 189 and p. 203.
129. "It completely destroys you": Ibid, p. 189.
130. "from secret advice": Havoc TV, July 2010.
130. "That is the coolest thing": Mullen interview.
131. "off this path": Mullen, p. 191.
131. "Rocco and Vallely:" Ibid, p. 183.
131. "won by doing . . . winning's not what you think": Mullen interview.
131. "2.6 million": Board Trac. Shared data.
131. "team manager . . . I've never seen anyone": *Rodney Mullen: From the Ground Up*, 2002.
132. "the ultimate skateboarding video" Mullen, p. 223.
132. "Rodney is a mule": *Rodney Mullen: From the Ground Up*, 2002.
132. "It was 1990 . . . Progress was slow": Mullen, p. 221-225.
133. "World's first video": *Paste Magazine*, 2009.
133. "BMX zines": *New York Magazine*.
133. "rides a freestylish board": *Rubbish Heap*, 1989.
133. "But it was the next video": *Questionable*, 1992.
133. "This . . . is the beginning": *Thrasher*, July 9, 2010.

## 17. Ryan Sheckler Can Kickflip and He's Six Years Old

134. "Ryan Allen Sheckler was born": *Los Angeles Times*, July 20, 2004.
134. "Magdalena Ecke Family YMCA": *TransWorld Business*, March 7, 2000.
134. "Tony Hawk had been": Hawk, p. 236.
134. "Shaun White": *San Diego Magazine*, June, 2007.

134. "Walk at seven months": *Examiner*, November 25, 2008.
134. "old Powell board": Sheckler interview.
134. "roof of their house": *Jimmy Kimmel Live!*, July 29, 2009.
135. "diagnosed with ADD": *ESPN Magazine*, July 16, 2008.
135. "Woody Woodpecker . . . Tony Hawk": Ryan Sheckler Biography-Redbull USA, 2007.
135. "he could kickflip": *ESPN Magazine*, July 16, 2008.
135. "'keep practicing'": Ryan Sheckler Biography-Redbull USA, 2007.
135. "clear a picnic table": *ESPN Magazine*, July 16, 2008.
135. "entered his first contest": Ryan Sheckler Biography-Redbull USA, 2007.
135. "Tony Hawk attended.": *Jimmy Kimmel Live!*, July 29, 2009.
135. "IWS Boardshop": About.com/skateboarding. Ryan Sheckler interview.
135. "Etnies . . . Volcom": *ESPN Magazine*, July 16, 2008.
136. "You start hearing stories": Mullen interview.
137. "banned from junior tournaments": Ryan Sheckler Biography-Redbull USA, 2007.
137. "small backyard park": *Los Angeles Times*, July 20, 2004.
137. "eighteen hours": *ESPN Magazine*, July 16, 2008.
138. "his dad hung up on him": Sheckler interview.
138. "American Sports Retailer trade show": Mullen interview.
138. "don't have the heart": Ibid.
139. "Sheckler's first . . . board": Ryan Sheckler Biography-Redbull USA, 2007.
139. "artist Marc McKee.": Brooke, p. 130.
139. "five months a year": *Los Angeles Times*, July 20, 2004.
139. "Slam City Jam": Mullen interview.
139. "forming Almost": Mullen, p. 268.
140. "Almost's premier video": *Almost Round 3*, 2004.

## 18. The 1990s Rebirth of Tech Skating, and Chris Haslam Makes P-Rod Crack Up

143. "Battle at the Berrics": *Battle at the Berrics 3*, October 2010.
143. "daughter, Heaven": *TransWorld Skateboarding*, January 29, 2009.
143. "*Skate Dreams*": *Skate Dreams*, 2009.
143. "including Sheckler": Sheckler interview.
143. "most-viewed skateboarding website": *Wall Street Journal*, February 27, 2009.
144-45. "*so* many tricks": Paul Rodriguez interview, October 14, 2010.
145-46. "Jason Lee." Video Days, 1991.
146. "young Brazilian named Bob": Weyland, p. 263.
147. "Toxic Skates": Borden, pp. 27-28.
148. "Everslick was released": Brooke, p. 49.
148. "it's what I liked to do": *The Man Who Souled the World*, 2007.
149. "The darkslide was born": *Carlsbad High School*, 1993.
149. "He was Frankie Hill": *TransWorld Skateboarding*, December 17, 2004.
149. "He rides off a cliff": *Propaganda*, 1990.
140. "appeared on MTV": MTV Sports, circa 1991.
150. "$5,000 a month": ESPN, October 14, 2010.
150. "a team called Legion:" Frankiehill.com, October 1, 2010.

## 19. Waist 66 Jeans and the Rise of World Industries

151. "$150 million": *San Francisco Bay Guardian*, May 1994.
152. "on the long back pocket": Borden, p. 147.
153. "on eBay for $760": Skate and Annoy, March 14, 2008,
153. "He's like eighty years old": *The Man Who Souled The World*, 2007.
154. "something that is truly evil": Ibid.
155. "$20 million": *Parenting Magazine*, May 27, 2009.
155. "spend Y2K": Mullen, p. 252.
155. "after being fired": Ibid, p. 155.
155. "$20,000": *The Man Who Souled The World*, 2007.
156. "$6,000": Mullen, p. 170.
156. "loan-shark loan": *The Man Who Souled The World*, 2007.
156. "$150 million": Mullen, p. 170.
156. "one was Mike Vallely": Sponsored, 2000.
157. "to start Birdhouse": Hawk, p. 170.
157. "Marc McKee": *The Man Who Souled The World*, 2007.
157. "huge freestyle board": Mullen, p. 187.
157. "Within a year . . .": *The Man Who Souled The World*, 2007.
158. "*Big Brother*": Brooke, pp. 162-165 and Ibid.
158. "Larry Flynt": Howe, p. 106 and *The Man Who Souled The World*, 2007.
159. "Devilman . . . sales tripled": Ibid.
159. "Simon Woodstock": Ibid.

## 20. The Insane Power of Television

160. "In late 1993": www.espneventwrapups.com.
160. "bungee jumping in kayaks": Hawk, p. 190.
160. "*Ban This*": Hawk, pp. 156-157.
160. "it was halved": Ibid, p. 162.
160. "touring that year": Ibid, p. 163.
161. "thirty people watched them compete": Ibid.
161. "tenth straight year": Ibid, p. 171.
161. "only competition of the year": Ibid, p. 176.
161. "bought a Civic": Ibid, p. 170.
161. "food allowance": *The New Yorker*, July 26, 1999.
161. "opened their warehouse": Hawk, p. 168.
161. "$40,000 from a refinance": Hawk, p. 170.
161. "mattress/boxspring split": Ibid, p. 175.
161. "YMCA most nights": Ibid, p. 183.
161-62. "newly single . . . roommate": Ibid, p. 176.
162. "Hudson Riley Hawk": Ibid, p. 176.
162. "The Games . . .": Ibid, pp. 188-89.
163. "200,000 people attended": *Time Magazine*, January 22, 2009.
163. "met with ESPN": Hawk, p. 223.
164. "His business card": *The New Yorker*, July 26, 1999.

165. "$38,000": Hawk, p. 193.
165. "Donald Trump": Ibid, p. 198.
165. "called The X Games": espneventmedia.com.
165. "in 21 different languages": Ibid.
165. "vert pro Andy Macdonald": Hawk, pp. 201-202.
165. "Slim Jim and the Marines": Ibid, p. 205.
165. "made a consultant": Ibid, p. 223.
166. "Pat . . . Sarah Hall": Ibid, p. 205.
166. "Peter Hess": Ibid, p. 225.
166. "reached $15 million": *The New Yorker*. July 26, 1999.
166. "Got Milk": Hawk, p. 222.
166. "$1 billion in revenue": *Encyclopedia Brittanica,* April 12, 2011.
167. "seventy-nine gaming platforms": *McSweeney's,* October 29, 2010.
167. "hired by Disney": Hawk, p. 229.
167. "the Loop": Ibid, pp. 217-19.
167. "The 900": Ibid, pp. 1-3, and pp. 236-237, and YouTube footage.

## 21. Mike V's Greatest Hits, or How Skating's Newfound Success Was Not So Successful

172. "Glory Bound Skatepark Tour": mikevallely.com, May 19, 2005.
174. "Vans Triple Crown tour": *Skateboarding Magazine,* December 24, 2010.
174. "outside at Universal Studios...": *Mike V's Greatest Hits,* 2003.
175. "*Sick Boys*": Sick Boys, 1988.
176. Footnote. "entire *My War* album": *Skateboarding Magazine,* June 16, 2006.
177. "*CKY*": CKY 3, 2001.
177. "sued for $10 million": *The News Tribune,* September 29, 2006.
177. "sponsored by his local": *Fairman's Skate Shop Video,* 1993.
178. "Jeff Tremaine": Brooke, p. 163; jefftremaine.com.
179. "discussed the incident": *The Tom Green Show,* February 21, 2007.
179. "similar footage of Vallely": *Mike V Vs. Security Guard,* YouTube, 2008 [recently retitled "Mike V Vs. Security Guard (skit)].
179. "*Paul Blart: Mall Cop*": Paul Blart: Mall Cop, 2009.
180. Footnote. *Good Morning America,* February 13, 2008; *Baltimore Sun,* August 25, 2010; *Washington Post,* March 1, 2011.

## 22. The Best Skateboarder in the World is a Seventh Grader

181. "youngest pro skater in history": *New York Times,* July 17, 2006.
181. "won the four big contests": Profile, MPORA-Pure Action Sports. www.mpora.com; Profile, Alli Sports, www.allisports.com; biography, Ryansheckler.com.
181. "5-foot-1 and ninety-seven pounds": *Los Angeles Times,* July 20, 2004.
181. "no one's done before": NBC coverage, YouTube, uploaded October 19, 2009.
182. "What are we seeing": ESPN, June 11, 2009.
183. "Being pro is awesome": ASA Entertainment, YouTube, uploaded August 31, 2008.
186. "on the plane": Mullen interview.
186. "took Ryan aside": Ibid.

186. "Shecklers' for dinner": Ibid.
187. "making life difficult": *54321* Episode, YouTube, uploaded April 2, 2007.
188. "probably by non-skaters": various YouTube postings.
188. *"LA Times"*: *Los Angeles Times*, July 20, 2004.
188. *"Cribs"*: *MTV Cribs*, March 15, 2005.
189. "Fuel TV:" *First Hand*, September 4, 2005.
190: "flew to Germany": Ibid.
191. "I'm a competitive person": *GQ* interview. August 6, 2010.
191. "I woke up": *First Hand*, September 4, 2005.
192. "took third": Ibid.
192. "flew home to heal": Ibid.
192. "the gold and $75,000": Volcom, September 12, 2005.
192. *"Seventeen"*: *Seventeen Magazine*, February 2008.
192. "due to travel": *54321* Episode, YouTube, Uploaded April 2, 2007.
193. "go to high school": *Los Angeles Times*, July 20, 2004.

## 23. Rodney Rids His Body of Scar Tissue, and the First Stanceless Skater

194. "Almost's *Round 3*": *Round 3*, 2004.
194. "premiered in London": Almost, 2004.
194. "window seat of the plane": Dissent TV, December 30, 2009.
194. "Tony Hawk's sports medicine doctor": Mullen interview.
194-95. Prying details, quotes: Ibid.
195-197. Details, quotes: Ibid.
197. "switch one-foot nose": *United By Fate*, Episode 3, 2008.
197-98. "If my body . . . behind the curtain": Ibid.

## 24. Life of Ryan

199. "August 27, 2007": *Pittsburg-Post Gazette*, August 27, 2007 and The TV IV, www.tviv.org.
199. *"The Hills"*: *Variety*, June 13, 2007.
199. "highest-rated . . . 2.3 million": LAT32.com, September 27, 2008,
199. "twelve- to twenty-four-year-old": *Media Life Magazine*, March 28, 2008.
200. Footnote: "first TV appearance": *20/20*, December 25, 2000. "direct-to-video movie": *MVP II: Most Vertical Primate*, 2001.
200. Footnote: "with Johnny Knoxville": Jackassworld, Feburary 12, 2001.
200. "wrestling team": *ESPN Magazine*, July 16, 2008.
200. "transfers to Futures": *USA Today*, July 9, 2006.
200. "$10,000": www.halstromhs.org.
200. "Sasha Cohen": *USA Today*, July 9, 2006.
200. "on the cover": *Dub Magazine*, August-October 2008.
200. *"Sports Illustrated Kids"*: *Sports Illustrated Kids*, July, 2008.
200. *"Rolling Stone* package": *Rolling Stone*, August 9, 2007.
201. "join Plan B": Caughtinthecrossfire.com, January 3, 2007.
202. "told Ryan so": Mullen interview.

203. "the day he turns eighteen": *ESPN Magazine*, July 16, 2008.
203. "with the Jonas Brothers": *The Tonight Show with Jay Leno*, January 18, 2008.
203. "went on *Ellen*": *The Ellen DeGeneres Show*, February 4, 2008.
203. "the mega-ramp": *Slap Magazine*, March 31, 2008.
203. "But not. Like that." *Ryan Sheckler vs. Mega Ramp*. Plan B. 2008.
203. Footnote: "tibia in three places": *Scarred*, April 24, 2007.
203. "cover of *TransWorld*": *TransWorld Skateboarding*, April 2008.
204. "cover of *Skateboard Mag*": *The Skateboard Mag*, June 2008.
204. "cover of *ESPN*": *ESPN Magazine*, July 16, 2008.
204. "four days later": *Los Angles Times*, July 9, 2008.
204. "fourth that day": Socalskateparks.com, July 14, 2008.
204. "the crowds grew": *Deseret News*, September 23, 2007.
204. "won the X Games": *USA Today*, August 4, 2008.
205. "Bust or Bail": *Thrasher*, August 30, 2008.
205. 'best day of my life": *Thrasher*, January 22, 2010.
205. "Nothing's too much": *GQ* interview. August 6, 2010.
206. "Oakley commercial": *Oakley Our Life*, January 6, 2008.
206. "super-agent Steve Astephen": *Sports Business Journal*, November 7, 2006.
206. "celebrity tournament": *Transworld Skateboarding*, July 22, 2008 and press release from Sheckler Foundation, July 29, 2008.
207. "Megan Fox and Zac Efron": *New York Daily News*, November 19, 2008.
207. "Sk8r Boi": *ESPN Magazine*, July 16, 2008.
207. "backside-flipped El Toro": *Thrasher*, January 22, 2010.
207. "achieved the superhuman": YouTube video. Uploaded September 25, 2007.

## 25. "I Hate Sheckler," and the Exploding of Ryan's Right Foot

209. "campaign was his idea": ESPN, June 21, 2010.
209. "*lot* of hate": Mullen interview.
210. "GETTIN' A CONCUSSION": YouTube video, uploaded February 8, 2009.
210. "filled a newsstand": *Thrasher,* March 9, 2010.
211. "Let's just leave it at that.": *Rolling Stone*, August 9, 2007.
211. "Got Milk": *OK Magazine*, July 30, 2009.
211. "Axe Body Spray": ESPN, July 20, 2009.
211. "The commercial": Double Pits to Chesty, *Transition Productions*, 2009.
212. Footnote: "the ad world": Power Balance-Double Take. 2010.
212. "Nike's 2010": *Debacle*, Nike Skateboarding, 2009.
213. "'Douchebag!'": *ESPN Magazine*, July 16, 2008.
213. "Mia Hamm": *Seventeen Magazine*, December 18, 2008.
213. "capitalize on everything I can . . . Every time": *ESPN Magazine*, July 16, 2008.
213. "hitting a kid": Skateparkperceptions.com, November 3, 2008.
214. "traveling up to 240 days a year": *MTV Cribs*, January 17, 2009.
215. "three-story": *ESPN Magazine*, July 16, 2008.
215. "take a tour": *MTV Cribs*, January 17, 2009.
215. "third season appeared": *Life of Ryan*: Season 3, 2009.
216. "100 percent mine": ESPN, June 21, 2010.

216. *"Tooth Fairy"*: *Tooth Fairy*, 2010.
216. "upcoming Plan B video": *Ryan Sheckler Super Future Promo*, Plan B Skateboards, 2010.
216. "200,000 people had attended": *Sports Business Daily*, August 3, 2009.
216. "44 million": espneventwrapups.com, August 2009.
216-18. Event details: *Los Angeles Times*-Outpost blog, August 1, 2009.

## 26. Healing at the Berrics
219. "new short parts": *United*, Plan B, April 30, 2010
220. "due to back pain": Sheckler interview.
221. "how it felt": Sheckler interview.
221. "hibachi grill": *ESPN Magazine*, July 16, 2008.
221. "horrible": *GQ* interview. August 6, 2010.
221. "South Coast Spine Center": Ethika, 2009.
221. "Dr. David Sales": Ibid.
222. "I made it smaller": Shecker interview.
222. "the new park": www.californiaskateparks.com, January 30, 2010.
222. "Dodgers game": ESPN, August 31, 2010.
224. "Chris Cole": Plan B, September 23, 2010.

## 27. To Try and Talk to Shaun White and Ryan Sheckler
225. "8 million skaters. . . .": Board-trak.
225. "12 to 18 million": New York Encyclopedia. Skateboarding. www.newworld encyclopedia.org/entry/skateboarding.
225. "Major League Baseball": Sports Industry Overview, Plunkett Research, Ltd. 2010.
226-28. "Interpolation": White interview.
229. "Steve Astephen": *Outside Magazine*, February 2008.
230. "$25,000": Press Release. Alli Sports: Dew Tour 2010.
230-32. Sheckler details. Sheckler interview, 2010.
232-33. "Greg Lutzka's standing": Ibid.
234. "never emotional": Mullen interview.
234. "Just go.": *Ryan Sheckler vs. Mega Ramp*. Plan B, 2008.
234. "awesome...so in-depth": Sheckler interview.

## 28. Dew Tour Finals 2010
236. "the last stop": Press release. All Sports: Dew Tour 2010.
236. "$3.5 million": *Complete Marketing Concepts*. Press release, May 26, 2009.
236. "NBC and MTV":
236. "Sheckler's won at least once:" Etnies, September 16, 2003; Volcom, September 29, 2003; *GQ* interview, August 6, 2010; *TransWorld Skateboarding*, July 28, 2009.
236. "October 16 and 17": Press release. All Sports Dew Tour 2010.
236. "Danny Way dropped from": *ABC News*, April 5, 2006.
238. Footnote: Chris Haslam Crazy Trick. YouTube, uploaded February 7, 2010.
241. "He's ahead the whole time": ESPN, October 17, 2010.
242. "the 1080": *Mirror*, November 25, 2009.

242. "White grew up": Shuanwhite.com/bio/about.

243. "to attempt the 1080": *Outside Magazine*, May 2011.

243. "Giorgio Zattoni, Sandro Dias, Alex Perelson": *Los Angeles Times*, July 13, 2009.

243. "Bob Burnquist (on the mega-ramp)": ESPN, September 9, 2010.

## 29. Watching Sheckler Skate

246. "Santos . . . Salabanzi . . . Saenz . . . Dyet . . . Majerus": Press Release, Alli Sports, Dew Tour 2010.

248. "$15,000 . . . Baltic Birch": Wilkins Interview, October 16, 2010.

252-53. "Chaz Ortiz" details: Press release, Alli Sports, Dew Tour 2010.

## 30. Watching Rodney Skate, or Switch Nollie Laserflip at Midnight

254-260. Mullen interview.

255. "Ronnie Creager": www.caughtinthe crossfire.com, August 15, 2006.

255. "Chris Haslam": Switch Laser Flip in Big Four, YouTube, uploaded May 4, 2007.

255. "Prince Gilchrist": Berrics.com/trickipedia.

259. "came back and won": ESPN, August 3, 2010.

# SOURCES

## Books

Borden, Iain. *Skateboarding, Space and the City: Architecture and the Body*. New York: Berg, 2001.

Brooke, Michael. *The Concrete Wave: The History of Skateboarding*. Toronto, Ontario: Warwick Publishing Inc., 1999.

Cassorla, Albert. *The Skateboarder's Bible*. Philadelphia: Running Press, 1976.

Guttman, Allen. *Sports: The First Five Millennia*. York, PA: The Maple-Vail, 2004.

Hawk, Tony (with Sean Mortimer). *Hawk: Occupation: Skateboarder*. New York: HarperCollins, 2004.

Howe, Susanna. (Sick) *A Cultural History of Snowboarding*. St. Martin's Griffin, 1998.

Latchman, Michael, ed. *Music of the Past—Instruments and Imagination*. Berne, Switzerland: Peter Lang, 2006.

McCarthy, Cormac. *Blood Meridian: Or the Evening Redness in the West*. New York: Random House, 1985.

Motil, Guy. *Surfboards*. Guilford, CT: Globe Pequot Press, 2007.

Mullen, Rodney (with Sean Mortimer). *The Mutt: How to Skateboard and Not Kill Yourself*. New York: HarperCollins, 2004.

Warsaw, Matt. *The Encyclopedia of Surfing*. Orlando: Harcourt Books, 2003.

Weyland, Jacko. *The Answer Is Never: A Skateboarder's History of the World*. New York: Grove Press, 2002.

Wixon, Ben. *Skateboarding: Instruction, Programming, and Park Design*. United States of America: Versa Press, 2009.

## Print Articles

Barayuga, Debra. "Noted Skateboarder Nets Jail Time for Drug Charges." *Honolulu Star-Bulletin*, September 11, 2001.

Branch, John. "From Violin to Skateboard." *New York Times*, November 20, 2010.

Carrera, Katie. "A City Charmed and Stoked." *Washington Post*, June 22, 2007.

Da Silva, Alexandre. "Thrill Ride." *Honolulu Star-Bulletin*, July 24, 2005.

Dean, Josh. "Cool Millions." *Outside*, February 2006.

Devon, McReynolds. "Q and A with Skateboarder Rodney Mullen." *The Daily Bruin*, January 15, 2008.

Dougherty, Conor. "Skateboarding Tourney Stirs Its Own Midnight Madness." *Wall Street Journal*, February 27, 2009.

Eborn, Jared. "Sheckler Skating Way to Stardom." *Deseret News*, September 23, 2007.

Eppridge, Bill. "The Craze and Menace of Skateboards." Life, May 14, 1965.

Ferrell, David. "Skateboard Pros: Life on the Edge." *Los Angeles Times*, March 6, 1994.

Finn, Chad. "Fidrych Killed in Accident." *Boston Globe*, April 13, 2009.

Fry, John. "Snowboarding Is Older Than You Think." *Ski Magazine*, April 2010.

Glock, Allison. "Just Another Lonely Teenage Millionaire." *ESPN Magazine*, July 28, 2008.

Hamm, Keith. "Hosoi: Christian Hosoi Interview." *Juice Magazine* Issue 57, July 2004.

Hermann, Peter. "City Police Officer Who Berated Skateboarder Fired." *The Baltimore Sun*, August 25, 2010.

Higgins, Matt. "A Lord of Dogtown Re-emerges." *New York Times*, July 30, 2008.

————. "Navigating a Pro Career and the Preteen Scene." *New York Times*, July 17, 2006.

————. "Stepping Aside as His Creation Soars." *New York Times*, July 29, 2009.

Hucks, Karen. "Viva la Resolution: Bam Settles Fight Lawsuit." *The News Tribune*. September 29, 2006.

Johnston, Bret Anthony. "Danny Way and the Gift of Fear." *Men's Journal*, July 2010.

Lee, John. "Christian Hosoi Reborn." *The Me Magazine* Issue 13, Feb/Mar 2008.

Levin, Gary. "Who Had the Best Debut?" *USA Today*, October 24, 2007.

Levin, Mark. "The Birdman." *The New Yorker*, July 26, 1999.

*Los Angeles Times*, "Pro Skateboarder Sentenced to 15 Years in Beating Death." October 11, 1995.

MacArthur, Paul J. "It's Older Than You Think." *Skiing Heritage 21, no. 1(2009): 30*.

Meyer, Josh. "Families Left in the Dark After Tragedies in Mexican Jails." *Los Angeles Times*, May 3, 1993.

Moore, Michael Scott. "100 Years of Hanging Ten." *Los Angeles Times*. July 21, 2007.

*New York Times*, obituary. "Oliver Gleichenhaus, Burger Maker, 79." January 14, 1991.

Olson, Steve. "Dogtown Chronicles: Jay Adams Interview." *Juice Magazine* Issue 54, 2002.

————. "Matt Hensley Interview." Juice Magazine. Issue 65.

Owen, Rob. MTV's *Life of Ryan*. *Pittsburg-Post Gazette*, August 27, 2007.

Powlison, Justin. "Sandboarding: Takes Sand to the Extreme." *Brass Magazine*, Fall 2005.

Quiñones, Ben. "Chicanos and the Man." *LA Weekly*, June 26, 2005.

Quirk, Mary Beth. "Ryan Sheckler's Got Milk?" *OK!*, July 30, 2009.

*Rolling Stone* #690. "Jeff Phillips: King of Texas Skateboarding." September 8, 1994.

*Rolling Stone* #1032. "Lifestyles of the Extreme and Famous." August 9, 2007.

*San Francisco Bay Guardian*, "Hell on Wheels." May 1994.

*San Diego Magazine*, "Skatepark." June 2007, p. 118.

Stecyk, Craig. "New Etiquette for a Street Society." *Thrasher*, June 1983.

Steeg, Jill. "Sheckler Rewriting the Rules of Pro Skateboarding." *USA Today*, July 9, 2006.

Smith, Ethan. "Spike Jonze Unmasked." *New York Magazine*, October 18, 1999.

Sun, Victoria. "Teen Skateboarder Sheckler Doesn't Disappoint at X-Games." *USA Today*, August 4, 2008.

Thomas, Pete. "A Young Head of Skate." *Los Angeles Times*, July 20, 2004.

————. "Sheckler Has a Broken Arm." *Los Angeles Times*, July 9, 2008.

## Blogs and Web Articles

Abrams, Micah. "Ryan Sheckler Wins Third X Games Gold." *ESPN*, August 3, 2010. http://sports.espn.go.com/action/xgames/summer/2010/news/story?id=5426817.

Aguirre, Mario. "Rodriguez wins Skateboard Street Title as Sheckler Leaves with Injury." *Los Angeles Times* online, August 1, 2009. http://latimesblogs.latimes.com/outposts/2009/08/rodriguez-wins-skateboard-street-title-as-sheckler-leaves-with-injury.html.

Alley, Blair. "Paul Rodriguez Web Interview Exclusive." Transworld Skateboarding website, January 29, 2009. http://skateboarding.transworld.net/1000079881/features/paul-rodriguez-web-exclusive-interview/.

Araiza, Karen. "Bam Margera's Mom: My Jackass Son Didn't Overdose." NBC Philadelphia website, July 20, 2009. www.nbcphiladelphia.com/news/local/Bam-Margeras-Mom-No-He-Didnt-Overdose.html.

"Back to Sand." *Sandboard* magazine, June 2000. http://www.sandboard.com/drdune/pr/index2.htm.

"Baltimore Officer Rivieri's Firing Upheld." *Washington Post*-The Crime Scene Blog, March 1, 2011. http://voices.washingtonpost.com/crime-scene/baltimore/baltimore-officer-rivieris-fir.html.

Bane, Colin. "Father Figure: Celebrity Skate Dad Randy Sheckler on His Sons Ryan, Shane, Kane." November 25, 2008. www.examiner.com/fatherhood-in-denver/father-figure-celebrity-skate-dad-randy-sheckler-on-his-sons-ryan-shane-kane.

Britton, Veronica. "Surfing: The Sport of Kings." Interactive Media Lab, University of Florida, 2004. http://iml.jou.ufl.edu/projects/Spring04/Britton/history.htm.

Carlsbad Skatepark Memorial, last post May 20, 2005. www.carlsbadskatepark.org

Cave, Steve. Ryan Sheckler Interview. About.com. http://skateboard.about.com/od/proskaters/a/RyanShecklerMin.htm.

Christian Hosoi History. Christian Hosoi's official website. www.hosoiskates.com.

Craft, Kevin. "16 Things You Didn't Know about Mark Gonzales." *SkateBoarder* magazine website, October 12, 2005. http://www.skateboardermag.com/features/16thgsgnz/

Crupi, Anthony. "MTV Finds Life in Ryan." *Adweek*, August 30, 2007. www.adweek.com/?vnu_content_id=1003633631.

Curtis, Carleton. "AST PlayStation Pro Starts Today." TransWorld Skateboarding website, October 16, 2008. http://skateboarding.transworld.net/1000075436/news/ast-playstation-pro-starts-today/.

Downey, Kevin. "MTV, Network for the Forever Young." *Media Life Magazine*, March 28 2008. www.medialifemagazine.com/news2005/mar05/mar28/1_mon/news3monday.html.

"Ebay Watch." Post on Skate and Annoy online magazine, April 2006. http://skateandannoy.com/features/ebay/2006/ebay039/.

"Ebay Watch." Post on Skate and Annoy online magazine, March 14, 2008, http://skateandannoy.com/features/ebay/2008/ebay060/.

"The Fingerboard Controversy." Transworld Skateboarding website, accessed March 3, 2000. http://skateboarding.transworld.net/1000010680/news/the-fingerboard-controversy/.

"40 Winks—A Squinted Looks at Skateboarding's Greatest." Transworld Skateboarding website, posted March 6, 2003. http://skateboarding.transworld.net/1000012705/photos/40-winks/.

Gandert, Sean. "Salute Your Shorts: Spike Jonze Skate Videos." *Paste* magazine website weekly online column, March 26, 2009. www.pastemagazine.com/articles/2009/03/salute-your-shorts-spike-jonze-skate-videos.html.

Gavelda, Ben. "The Very First Snowboard?" Post on Transworld Snowboarding Blog, February 11, 2010. http://snowboarding.transworld.net/1000116837/featuresobf/the-very-first-snowboard/.

"Has MTV Hurt Ryan Sheckler?" September 27, 2008. LAT34.com. www.lat34.com/skate/has_mtv_hurt_ryan_sheckler.htm.

"Hawaiians Slide Into Dangerous Sport." Surfer Magazine Blog Post, August 22, 2005. http://forum.surfermag.com/forum/showflat.php?Cat=0&Number=799549&page =&fpart=&vc=1.

"How One Man Changed Skateboarding Forever." *Skateboarding Magazine*, April 10, 2010. www.stumbleupon.com/su/1VSQmg/skateboardingmagazine.com/blog/2010 /04/10/how-street-skateboarding-was-revolutionized-in-the-90s.

Huh, Chang, Byound Kwan Lee, Euidong Yoo. "The Commodification Process of Extreme Sports: The Diffusion of the X-Games." United States Department of Agriculture Forest Service: Northern Research Station website, 2002. www.nrs.fs.fed.us/pubs/ gtr/gtr_ne289/gtr_ne289_049.pdf.

Jim Goodrich Studio. "Skateboard History Timeline." www.jimgoodrich.net/skateboard timeline.htm.

Johnston, Bret Anthony. "Half of California: Notes For An Unwritten Review of the New Tony Hawk CEO Book." McSweeney's, July 29, 2009. www.mcsweeneys.net/links/ skateboard/flip13.html.

Latell, James M. "Dustin Diamond Can't Be Saved By the Bell." CBS News website, June 17, 2006. www.cbsnews.com/stories/2006/06/17/entertainment/main1726443.shtml.

Leyba, Ryan. "Sheckler's Got a New Move for the Ladies." ESPN Action Sports, July 20, 2009. http://espn.go.com/action/news/story?id=4339355.

Louison, Cole. "Why Every Professional Skateboarder Should Look Like Patrick Melcher." *Gentleman's Quarterly*, April 16, 2010. www.gq.com/blogs/the-q/2010/04/why -every-professional-skateboarder-should-look-like-patrick-melcher.html.

Louison, Cole. "X Games Champ Ryan Sheckler Gets the Last Laugh." *Gentleman's Quarterly*, August 6, 2010. www.gq.com/blogs/the-q/2010/08/x-games-champ-ryan-sheckler-gets-the-last-laugh.html.

Lovgren, Stefan. "Bone Ice Skates Invented by Ancient Finns, Study Says." National Geographic News, January 4, 2008. http://news.nationalgeographic.com/news/ 2008/01/080104-first-skates.html.

MacArthur, Paul J. "The Top Ten Important Moments in Snowboarding History." Post on Smithsonian website, February 5, 2010. www.smithsonianmag.com/history-archae ology/The-Top-Ten-Most-Important-Moments-in-Snowboarding-History.html.

MacClain, Alexia. Those Exhilarating Roller Skates. Smithsonian Institute Library web-page, September 27, 2010. http://smithsonianlibraries.si.edu/smithsonianlibraries/ 2010/09/those-exhilarating-roller-skates.html.

Merlin, John Joseph. Blog post on Engines of our Ingenuity, article #630, University of Houston, by John H. Leinhard. http://www.uh.edu/engines/epi630.htm.

———. Post on National Museum of Roller Skating, 2010. www.rollerskatingmuseum .com/homework.html.

Mickle, Tripp. Sheckler Leaving Octagon for Wasserman Media Group. *Sports Business Journal*, November 7, 2006. www.sportsbusinessdaily.com/Daily/Issues/2006/11/ Issue-40/Sports-Industrialists/Ryan-Sheckler-Leaving-Octagon-For-Wasserman-Media-Group.aspx.

Montgomery, Tiffany. "Talking With Per Wilender About Changes at Blitz and the Fu-ture." Shop-Eat-Surf.com, May 12, 2009. www.shop-eat-surf.com/news-item/912/ blitz-distribution-per-welinder-changes.

"Morning Dose of Awesome—Just Axl and McGill." Posted on The World's Best Ever art and culture website, December 10, 2008. www.theworldsbestever.com/2008/12/10/ morning-dose-of-awesome-17/.

Nieratko, Chris. "Checking In With Ryan Sheckler." ESPN Action Sports, June 21, 2010. http://espn.go.com/action/skateboarding/news/story?page=catching-up-with-ryan-sheckler.

"Nike Steps Up." Transworld Business website, posted March 7, 2000. http://business .transworld.net/4099/uncategorized/nike-steps-up/.

Ninan, George. "D.O.P.E. Premiers to Inmates." PR Web, November 27, 2007. www.prweb .com/releases/martinez/prison/prweb572233.htm.

"Officer Salvatore Rivieri's Firing Upheld." WBALTV, NBC News. February 28, 2008. www .wbaltv.com/r/27022220/detail.html.

"Officer Suspended After Skateboard Rant." Good Morning America, ABC News, February 13, 2008. http://abcnews.go.com/GMA/story?id=4282823&page=1.

"The Origin of Snowboarding Discovered." Post on Jones Snowboards Blog, September 13, 2008. http://blog.jonessnowboards.com/2008/09/the-origin-of-snowboarding-discovered/.

Pickert, Kate. "A Brief History of the X Games." Time, January 22, 2009. www.time.com/ time/nation/article/0,8599,1873166,00.html.

Plimpton, James L. Roller Skate Innovator. Post on Barrier Removers Section of the Sports—Breaking Records Page, Smithsonian National Musuem of History website, Smithsonian Institute. http://americanhistory.si.edu/sports/exhibit/removers/ plimpton/index.cfm.

"Professor Tom Pohaku Stone Revives Ancient Hawai'ian Sport: Lava Sledding." Article by K38rescue on Zimbio, May 25, 2008. www.zimbio.com/KANALU+K38/articles/54/ Professor+Tom+Pohaku+Stone+Revives+Ancient.

"Recreation, Racing, or Road-Runner—Fat Wheels Were Once Better Than Thin." Blog post on I Love Toys, British Broadcasting Corporation. www.bbc.co.uk/cult/ilove/ toys/rollerskates.shtml.

Rice, Joel. Interview with Christian Hosoi, July 29, 2009. McSweeney's www.mcsweeneys .net/links/skateboard/29Flip3.html.

"Ryan Sheckler Wins Bust or Bail." Thrasher, August 30, 2008. www.thrashermagazine .com/articles/events/thrasher-s-bust-or-bail/.

"Ryan Sheckler X-Games Golf Tournament." Transworld Skateboarding website, July 22, 2008. http://skateboarding.transworld.net/1000070064/news/ryan-sheckler-x -games-golf-tournament/.

"Ryan Sheckler: Pussy Magnet or Publishing Magnate?" Thrasher, March 9, 2010. www .thrashermagazine.com/articles/digital-dumpster/ryan-sheckler-pussy-magnet/.

Sage, Alexandria. "Nike Cites Ripple Effect in Action Sports." Reuters website, August 6, 2010. http://in.reuters.com/article/2010/08/06/idINIndia-50691420100806.

"Sheckler Gets Into Fight at Redbull Party." Skate Perception website, November 3, 2008. http://forums.skateperception.com/index.php?showtopic=200823.

"Sheckler, P-Rod to Open Dodgers Game." ESPN Action Sports, August 31, 2010. http:// sports.espn.go.com/action/skateboarding/news/story?id=5516631.

"Sheckler's Megaramp Adventure." Slap Magazine Post. March 31, 2008.

"Skaters Defend Themselves From Power-Tripping Rent-A-Cops." *Skateboarding Magazine*, December 24, 2010. http://skateboardingmagazine.com/blog/2010/12/24/skaters-defend-themselves-from-power-tripping-rent-a-cops/.

"Sporty Skin Care That's Good For Your Skin and the World." *Seventeen* website, December 18, 2008. www.seventeen.com/fashion/blog/mission-skincare-products.

Stricker, Eric. "Paycheck Frankie Hill." Transworld Skateboarding website, December 17, 2004.

Sullivan, Adam. "Sheckler Jumps the Mega Ramp." Transworld Business website. March 31, 2008. http://business.transworld.net/887/features/sheckler-jumps-the-mega-ramp/.

"This History of X Games." July 30, 2007. http://skateboard.about.com/cs/events/a/XGamesHistory.htm.

"Tony Hawk's Pro Skater." *Encyclopedia Britannica* website, April 12, 2011. www.britannica.com/EBchecked/topic/1428795/Tony-Hawks-Pro-Skater.

Trap, Jack. "History of Roller Skating." Google Docs. http://docs.google.com/viewer?a=v&q=cache:fhT-OpXufbkJ:www.driv-rollkunstlauf.de/driv-archiv/downloads/informationen/informationen_2004/geschichte/history_of_roller_skating pdf+Der+Maler+oder+die+WintervergnUgungen+roller+skating&hl=en&gl=us&pid=bl&srcid=ADGEESg9YwpCzcjfZ4FXBQB22nFofsYbNV0d2VY5RCtT0sZnd JvXEfyYb0BUUhEQkX4J0QEppz6fKMZMHUaRNR6qyhhW8hzYpu0NFvTM b5SmGnk73I38Uj1fuuNyeEZHoMcBBgLWt3n9&sig=AHIEtbS9yoCm-fP71O qJPUyxJ7K1GXlTig.

Warsaw, Matt. "Surfing: A History." Post on Times Topic Blog. *New York Times*. May 30, 2008. http://topics.blogs.nytimes.com/2008/05/30/surfing-a-history/.

"What is Femoral Anteversion?" John Hopkins Orthopedic Surgery website, www.hopkins ortho.org/femoral_anteversion.html.

Wilton, Pete. Yule Blog: Ancient Ice Skating. Post on Oxford Science Blog, Oxford University, December 16, 2008. www.ox.ac.uk/media/science_blog/081216.html.

"X Games Sees Slight Attendance Increase for Four Day Event." *Sports Business Journal*, August 3, 2009. http://www.sportsbusinessdaily.com/Daily/Issues/2009/08/Issue-219/Events-Attractions/Xgames-Sees-Slight-Attendance-Increase-For-Four-Day-Event.aspx.

"Your Trucks Have Them . . ." Post on Skate and Annoy online magazine, December 11, 2009. http://skateandannoy.com/2009/12/welcome-to-the/.

Zeitchik, Steven. "MTV Overhauls Programming Strategy." *Variety*, June 13, 2007. http://www.variety.com/article/VR1117966918?refCatId=14.

## Transcript

Ley, Bob. "Outside the Lines: Unable to Read." ESPN, March 17, 2002.

## Interviews

Gelfand, Alan. Phone interview, September 15, 2010. Hollywood, Florida.

Melcher, Patrick. Phone interview, April 16, 2010.

Mullen, Rodney. December 1, 2010. Hernando Beach, California.

Mullen, Rodney. February 26, 2008. Los Angeles.

Sheckler, Ryan. August 6, 2010. Las Vegas.
Sheckler, Ryan. October 15, 2010. Las Vegas.
Sheckler, Ryan. Phone interview, August 6, 2010.
Smith, Dale. Phone interview. September 2010.
Smith, Rodney. September 30, 2010. New York.
White, Shaun. October 14, 2010. Las Vegas.
Wilkins, Charlie. October 16, 2010. Las Vegas.

## Movies

*The Boy Who Could Fly*. Directed by Nick Castle. 20th Century Fox, 1986.
*Dogtown and Z-Boyz*. Directed by Stacy Peralta. Sony Picture Classics, 2001.
*Gleaming the Cube*. Directed by Graeme Clifford. Pioneer Studios, 1989.
*Man Who Souled The World*. Directed by Mike Hill. Whyte House Productions, 2007.
*MVP II: Most Vertical Primate*. Directed by Robert Vince. Keystone Family Pictures, 2001.
*Paul Blart: Mall Cop*. Directed by Steve Carr. Columbia Pictures, 2009.
*Point Break*. Directed by Kathryn Bigelow. 20th Century Fox, 1991.
*Police Academy 4: Citizens on Patrol*. Directed by Jim Drake. Warner Bros., 1987.
*Rising Son: The Legend of Skateboarder Christian Hosoi*. Directed by Cesario Montano. QD3 Entertainment and Quiksilver, 2006.
*Stoked: The Rise and Fall of Gator*. Directed by Helen Stickler. Lions Gate Studios, 2002.
*Street Dreams*. Directed by Chris Zamoscianyk. Berkela Motion Pictures, 2009.
*Thrashin'*. Directed by David Winters. Winters Hollywood Entertainment Corporation, 1986.
*Tooth Fairy*. Directed by Michael Lemback. 20th Century Fox, 2010.

## Skateboarding Videos and DVDs

*Almost Round 3*. Directed by Matt Hill. Almost Skateboards, 2004.
*Ban This*. Directed by Stacy Peralta and Craig Stecyk. Powell-Peralta, 1989.
*The Bones Brigade Video Show*. Powell-Peralta and Stacy Peralta and Craig Stecyk, 1984.
*CKY 3*. Directed and Produced by Bam Margera and Brandon Dicamillo, 2001.
*Future Primitive*. Powell-Peralta and Stacy Peralta and Craig Stecyk, 1985.
*Hocus Pocus*. H-Street Skateboards, 1989.
*Mike V's Greatest Hits*. Directed by Ryan Young. Redline Entertainment, 2003.
*Not the New H-Street Video*. H-Street Skateboards, 1991.
*Propaganda*. Directed by Stacy Peralta. Powell-Peralta, 1990.
*Questionable*. Directed by Mike Ternasky. Plan B Skateboards, 1992.
*Rubbish Heap*. Directed by Spike Jonze. World Industries, 1989.
*The Search for Animal Chin*. Directed by Stacy Peralta. Powell-Peralta, 1987.
*Skater Dater*. Directed by Noel Black. Produced by Noel Black and Marshall, 1965.
*Sick Boys*. Mack Dawg Productions, 1988.
*Streets on Fire*. Santa Cruz Skateboards, 1989.
*Video Days*. Blind Skateboards, 1991.
*Wish You Were Here*. Strange Notes, 2009.

## Online Short Films and Videos

*A Skateboarding Lesson with Ryan Sheckler.* February 12, 2001, uploaded June 16, 2008.

*Chris Haslam-Switch Laser Flip in Big Four.* Posted May 4, 2007. www.youtube.com/ watch?v=DcPSiqgj-pA.

*Debacle.* Directed by Jason Hernandez. Nike Skateboarding, 2009.

*Dixon: Who Is Antwuan Dixon.* Directed by Zack Warren. Havoc TV, July 2010. www.havoc .tv/page/antwuan-dixon.

*Double Pits to Chesty.* Directed by Kevin Harrison. Transition Productions, 2009.

*Double//Take-Ryan Sheckler.* Presented by Power Balance, 2010.

Interview with Jakes Phelps. "Ask the Phelper: Ryan Sheckler" video interview series. *Thrasher,* posted January 22, 2010.

Interview with Vallely and Weird Al Yankovic. *Tom Green Show,* February 21, 2007. www .youtube.com/watch?v=sDkBfYDwvGk.

Jackassworld.com. www.youtube.com/watch?v=6BqeYNyBbR4.

"Mike V vs Security Guard." Posted 2008. www.youtube.com/watch?v=5TL6okaSupo [Recently retitled "Mike V vs Security Guard (skit)"].

"Natas Kaupas: Street Skating 101." 2006. www.youtube.com/watch?v=SXRo4HbQLNk &feature=related.

*Oakley Our Life.* Presented by Oakley and 411 Studio, uploaded January 6, 2008.

*Rebuilding Ryan Sheckler's Warehouse.* Californiaskateparks.com, January 30, 2010. http://californiaskateparks.com/2010/01/ryan-sheckler-warehouse/.

Rodney Mullen & Tony Hawk Talk. Dissent TV Internet show on shredordie.com, December 30, 2009. www.youtube.com/watch?v=99VPnJ8-ol8.

Rodney Mullen First Darkslide Session: Carlsbad High School. Posted December 11, 2008. www.youtube.com/watch?v=JWsGjs8BGkA.

*Rodney Mullen: From the Ground Up.* Directed by Kirk Dianda. On Video Magazine. 2002. www.youtube.com/watch?v=p12CfR5ktzI.

Rodney Mullen Speaks at UCLA. Uploaded January 18, 2008. www.youtube.com/ watch?v=x_6MJJMvwO0.

Rodney Mullen Talks. Ninja Studioz, uploaded October 25, 2009. www.youtube.com/ watch?v=-cgJ0glrzw0.

"Ryan Sheckler Becomes Youngest To Win Gold." Memorable X-Games Moments on ESPN, June 11, 2009. www.youtube.com/watch?v=y8luOLHPoOg.

Ryan Sheckler biography. Produced by Red Bull, 2007.

"Ryan Sheckler: A Day in the Life." Fuel TV, 2004. www.youtube.com/watch?v=sayYimR Citg&feature=related.

Ryan Sheckler: From the Vault-Profile 2003. Video from the 2003 LG Action Sports Championships profile on Sheckler, uploaded August 31, 2008.

*Ryan Sheckler Super Future Promo.* Plan B Skateboards, 2010.

Ryan Sheckler 12 Years Old. NBC video profile of Sheckler, uploaded October 19, 2009. www.youtube.com/watch?v=BwsKBTf5ML4.

Ryan Sheckler 13 Years Old. Collected footage of Sheckler. Uploaded July 12, 2008. www .youtube.com/watch?v=jk3MPtJXyWc.

*Sheckler vs. Mega Ram.* Plan B Skateboards, April 11, 2008.

Short film produced by Ethikia, 2:48, 2009. www.youtube.com/watch?v=PzDqQpoWUT0.

Short film produced by Plan B. 1:25, uploaded September 23, 2010. www.youtube.com/watch?v=SE_y3hIglkM.

Short Film: Shake Junt Bearings. Uploaded by Shake Junt, October 11, 2009. www.youtube.com/watch?v=3ohFACXUj0Y.

*Sponsored*. Directed by Wing Ko. Produced by Etnes, 2000.

Tony Hawk 900. Posted July 23, 2008. www.youtube.com/watch?v=RstrPAUmtnA.

*United By Fate*. *Episode 2*. Produced by Globe, 2007. www.dailymotion.com/video/x4zwaf_united-by-fate-episode-2_sport.

*United by Fate*. Episode 3, 2008. www.youtube.com/watch?v=DcPSiqgj-pARyan.

*United*. The Berrics, April 30, 2010. www.theberrics.com/dailyopspost.php?postid=1905.

Video Interview. Rodney Mullen and Jake Phelps. *Thrasher*, July 9, 2010. www.thrashermagazine.com/component/option,com_hwdvideoshare/Itemid,93/task,viewvideo/video_id,682/.

Young Bam: Fairman's Skate Shop Video. 3:01. Filmed by Dan Wolfe, 1993.

## TV Shows

*Charlie's Angels*. "The Prince and the Angel." Directed by Cliff Boyle. Episode 77 of 110, aired November 14, 1979.

*The Ellen DeGeneres Show*. NBC, Warner Bros. Season 5, episode 96, aired February 4, 2008.

*Jimmy Kimmel Live!* Interview with Ryan Sheckler. Season 7, episode 105, aired July 29, 2009.

*MTV Cribs*. MTV. Season 11, episode 2, aired March 15, 2005.

*MTV Cribs*. MTV. Season 16, episode 5, aired January 17, 2009.

*MTV Sports*. Host Dan Cortese. MTV. Distributed by Paramount, circa 1991.

*The Simpsons*. "Lisa the Iconocolast." Aired February 18, 1996.

*Sk8 TV*. Directed by Troy Miller and Stacey Peralta. California: Nickelodeon Studios, 1990.

*That's Incredible!* Host John Davidson. California: Universal Studios, 1980-1984.

*The Tonight Show*. NBC, Warner Bros., aired January 18, 2008.

*20/20*. Downtown segment. Aired December 25, 2000.

"Talking Tampa Pro with Greg Lutzka." ESPN.com. http://espn.go.com/video/clip?id=4982732.

## Press Releases and General Information

"Adrenaline Marketing Recruited by the Alliance of Action Sports." Press Release. Complete Marketing Concepts, May 26, 2009.

"AST Announces Dew Tour Schedule." PR Newswire, February 19, 2008.

History of Hosoi Skates. www.hosoiskates.com.

"The Life of the Winter X Games." Press release. Europe: Winter X Games 2011. www.espneventmedia.com/History/Index.

"Malloof Money Cup 2008 Final Results." Press release. July 14, 2008. http://discussion.socalskateparks.com/showthread.php?t=6016

"Overview X Games." Press release, Los Angeles: X Games 15. www.espneventwrapups
.com/xgamesfifteen/About/Overview.aspx.
Powell, George. History of Bones Bearings. Posted 2011. www.bonesbearings.com.
Press Booklet from the 2010 Dew Tour. Distributed to media by Alli Sports.
Ryan Sheckler Bio. Ryan Sheckler Official Website. www.ryansheckler.com/bio.
"Ryan Sheckler." Press release. Alli Sports: Dew Tour Profile. www.allisports.com/
alli/athlete/ryan-sheckler?sort=latest&offset=0&limit=7&fromAjax=0&page_
num=3&athlete=ryan-sheckler.
"Ryan Sheckler." Press release/profile. MPORA-Pure Action Sports website. http://mpora
.com/pros/ryan-sheckler.html.
"Sheckler Charity Golf Tournament." Press release. Sheckler Foundation, July 29, 2008.
"Sheckler joins Plan B." Press release. January 3, 2007. www.caughtinthecrossfire.com/
skate/skate-news/sheckler-joins-plan-b/.
Tony Hawk Bio. Tony Hawk Official Website. www.tonyhawk.com/bio.html.

## Selected Magazines

*Dub Magazine.* Issue 56, July 2008.
*ESPN,* July 28, 2008.
*The Quarterly Skateboarder.* Vol. 1, Issue 1, Winter 1964.
*Seventeen,* February 2008.
*SkateBoarder,* Vol. 2, 1975.
*SkateBoarder,* Vol. 2, 1975.
*SkateBoarder,* Vol. 2, issue 6, August 1976.
*SkateBoarder,* Vol. 4, 1978.
*The Skateboard Mag,* June 2008.
*Sports Illustrated For Kids,* August 2008.
*Thrasher,* October 1982.
*Thrasher,* cover, September 1984.
*Thrasher,* cover, November 1984, cover.
*Thrasher,* July 1991.
*Thrasher,* September 2010.
*Transworld Skateboarding,* April 2008.

## Websites

Glen Friedman images: www.burningflags.com
www.jefftremain.com
www.tomgreen.com
www.berrics.com
www.freepatentsonline.com
www.patents.com
www.tviv.org
www.sidereel.com
www.wordnet.princeton.edu
www.ryansheckler.com

## Additional Sources

*Oxford English Dictionary.* University of Oxford Press, 1986.

*Webster's New World College Dictionary,* 3rd ed. New York: Macmillan General Reference, 1997.

# INDEX

Footnotes are indicated with "n" following the page number.

# ABOUT THE AUTHOR

Cole Louison grew up skateboarding in Rochester, New York, and has written about skateboarding and other topics for *Outside*, *McSweeney's*, the *New Yorker*, the *New York Times*, and *GQ*—where he works today.